The Political Logics of
Anticorruption Efforts in Asia

SUNY series in Comparative Politics

Gregory S. Mahler, editor

The Political Logics of
Anticorruption
Efforts in Asia

Edited by

Cheng Chen and Meredith L. Weiss

SUNY
PRESS

Cover art: Asian money in handcuffs from iStockphoto.

Published by State University of New York Press, Albany

© 2019 State University of New York Press

For information, contact State University of New York Press, Albany, NY
www.sunypress.edu

Library of Congress Cataloging-in-Publication Data

Names: Chen, Cheng, 1976– editor. | Weiss, Meredith L. (Meredith Leigh), 1972– editor.
Title: The political logics of anticorruption efforts in Asia / Cheng Chen and Meredith L. Weiss.
Description: Albany : State University of New York Press, [2019] | Series: SUNY series in comparative politics | Includes bibliographical references and index.
Identifiers: LCCN 2019000540 | ISBN 9781438477152 (hardcover : alk. paper) | ISBN 9781438477145 (pbk. : alk. paper) | ISBN 9781438477169 (ebook)
Subjects: LCSH: Political corruption—Asia—Prevention. | Asia—Politics and government—1945–
Classification: LCC JQ29.5 .P65 2019 | DDC 364.1/323095—dc23
LC record available at https://lccn.loc.gov/2019000540

10 9 8 7 6 5 4 3 2 1

Contents

Illustrations

Figures

Tables

Acknowledgments

The publication of this book benefited from the contributions and efforts of many people. This book started as an organized panel on anticorruption efforts in Asia at the 2016 annual meeting of the American Political Science Association (APSA) in Philadelphia. After the conference, our panelists and discussants committed to extending the project to develop this book, building upon the theoretical framework that we later put forth in the introduction. In 2017, we organized a one-day book workshop in conjunction with the APSA meeting in San Francisco. We are grateful to Lily Ann Villaraza and James Martel for helping us secure a workshop venue; to Barbara Mathews and Joan Nellhaus for their invaluable administrative support; and to the participants, who extended their conference travel or participated via Skype for an intense, productive day. Having clarified our overall framework and plans for refining individual chapters at that workshop, we then set to work on revisions. Our contributors' amazing work ethic and conscientious attention to detail were vital in helping us deliver a manuscript that we are all proud of in a timely fashion.

Intellectually, this book is the fruit of the collective labor of its contributors, who commented on each other's drafts, accepted critical feedback gracefully, and worked assiduously to build solid country cases around a cohesive central theme. We would like to thank Lily Ann Villaraza and Eva Hansson for their participation and helpful comments during our book workshop. SUNY Press's anonymous reviewers likewise engaged deeply with our manuscript to offer very detailed and constructive comments and suggestions, which greatly helped us in finalizing this collection.

Our department, the Political Science Department at the Rockefeller College of Public Affairs and Policy at the University at Albany, provided us with a supportive intellectual environment. We greatly appreciate the university's financial support as well: a subsidy for our book workshop from Rockefeller College's International Programs small-grants initiative and a Faculty Research Awards Program grant to support final revisions and editing. Two graduate students, Jiacheng Ren and Chelsea Foster, provided research assistance.

Of course, we offer, too, our heartfelt thanks to our wonderful editor at SUNY Press, Michael Rinella, whose enthusiasm for the project and steady guidance were both encouraging and constructive in the final publication of the book. Working with Michael has been a real pleasure. We would also like to express our gratitude to Dana Foote for copyediting and Kendra H. Millis for indexing.

Finally, teaching is an integral and especially rewarding part of our careers. With their enthusiasm for learning and their strong intellectual curiosity, including about the questions we engage in this volume, many of our students have offered ongoing inspiration. They consistently remind us that intellectual pursuit is not, and should never be, a lonely enterprise. We therefore dedicate this collaborative book to them.

Introduction

Theorizing Anticorruption as a Political Project

CHENG CHEN AND MEREDITH L. WEISS

Corruption plagues all countries, democratic or authoritarian. Just as endemic are efforts to eradicate and prosecute corruption. The first several months of 2017 alone witnessed the inauguration of a populist president in the United States whose major campaign slogan was to "drain the swamp"; the impeachment of a South Korean president on corruption charges; massive demonstrations in Romania, leading to a plan for an anticorruption referendum; and the continuation and even intensification of anticorruption politics in all BRICS countries.[1] It seems that anticorruption is now a sort of "cure-all" embraced by regime incumbents, opposition challengers, and the masses alike across a wide range of settings. People of disparate class, ethnic, educational, and even ideological backgrounds agree on the need to stop the "corrupt people in power." Yet, common outrage and indignation mask profound differences regarding the means by which corruption should be opposed, and the *political* ends that anticorruption efforts should serve. Instead of uniting different political forces under a common goal, anticorruption efforts have time and again proved especially versatile political weapons, useful for advancing divergent personal, partisan, ideological, or programmatic agendas (Gillespie and Okruhlik 1991).[2] While varieties of corruption and the tools to combat these have long interested political scientists, economists, and policymakers alike (among recent examples, Mungiu-Pippidi 2015; Rose-Ackerman

and Palifka 2016; You 2016; Rothstein and Varraich 2017), the distinct
political logics undergirding anticorruption efforts—when these campaigns
develop, who they target, with what framing or justification, and by what
impetus or under whose direction—have attracted less systematic study.

While corruption may be defined broadly as the misuse of public authority for private gain,[3] the phenomenon—conceptualized most
clearly via campaigns against it—spans a wide range. One dimension,
often the most visible and punishable aspect, is bribery, graft, and other
rent-seeking. Another is privilege: the extent to which the rich or well
connected achieve preferential treatment, which various reformist political movements contest in the name of combatting political inequality. In
addition, anticorruption efforts sometimes extend to wider issues of bad
behavior, such as sexual indiscretions. Such offenses may involve abuse
of office, but without the same intrinsic public costs.

Within the political science literature, some have argued that, in
the context of modernization, corruption could have beneficial economic
effects in developing settings by "substituting" for political institutionalization and potentially facilitating economic development (for example,
Nye 1967; Huntington 1968, 59–71; Leff 1964). Nevertheless, it is now
commonly recognized that rampant corruption is detrimental to economic
development and political governance. Economically, it drains resources,
distorts expenditure, and inhibits economic growth (Mauro 1995; Wei
1999). Politically, it weakens regime support by undermining public trust
in formal institutions (Seligson 2002) and exacerbating socioeconomic
inequality (Uslaner 2008), hence fueling social discontent. If left unchecked,
it may lead directly to political instability and, eventually, regime decay.[4]

Notwithstanding the widely recognized harmful effects of corruption,
combatting corruption is not necessarily a normal part of routine politics.
Whether led from the top or the ground, anticorruption efforts demand
significant energy and resources and can carry considerable political risks,
with no guarantee of long-term success, especially in contexts where
patronage ties feature prominently in politics. Although economically
damaging, corruption often serves an important informal political function of generating and maintaining elite support for the regime (Darden
2008). More importantly, by changing and even abolishing the existing
informal rules of the game, anticorruption efforts are likely to induce
uncertainty among elites, which could potentially lead to elite infighting
and weaken elite support for the regime, and hence risk political instability.
Meanwhile, efforts from the ground, whether spearheaded by or simply

engaging civil society activists or the masses, may foster disillusionment with, and alienation from, political elites and institutions.[5] In addition, those targeted by such anticorruption efforts, should they retain authority, might exact retribution later.

Given these inherent difficulties and potential pitfalls, the political will and capability to carry out anticorruption efforts cannot be assumed. Even so, a wide variety of political regimes in differently capacitated states, over polities with divergent historical backgrounds, and at disparate levels of economic development, have attempted such efforts in recent decades, with varying results. What are the political motivations behind anticorruption efforts, across regime types? Whose interests do they advance or threaten? And what ramifications do these efforts have for government legitimacy, standards of accountability, popular engagement or cynicism, the nature of linkages between politicians and citizens, and regime durability? These are the questions this volume sets out to address. They are theoretically and empirically important, not only because combatting corruption presents a nearly universal challenge in both developed and developing settings and across regime types, but also because anticorruption efforts' political, rather than economic and policy, aspects remain understudied and undertheorized.

Why Asia?

This volume focuses on the geographical area of Asia, particularly, Northeast and Southeast Asia. This analytic choice was made for several reasons. First of all, both corruption and anticorruption efforts are pervasive in Northeast and Southeast Asia. To be sure, these phenomena are not unique to the region, but previous scholarship has identified culture as an important contextual factor accounting for corruption (Bardhan 1997). Political culture in the region, although far from uniform, traditionally emphasizes interpersonal relationships, norms of reciprocity, and patronage ties. Many countries in the region share historical and cultural affinities, especially those that are still under the influence of Confucian values,[6] which provide moral justifications for maintaining political hierarchy and social harmony. Some therefore argue that the collectivist emphasis on group obligation in many Asian cultures creates a breeding ground for corruption (for example, Lipset and Lenz 2000). Indeed, this political-cultural background constitutes a common and maybe even unique challenge for the region's anticorruption efforts, as corrupt politicians are frequently elected and reelected in Asian democracies (Chang and Chu 2006, 262). Repeated anticorruption efforts, even in stable and developed democracies such as Japan, South Korea, and Taiwan, have been compromised by their governments' own involvement in corruption, as politicians have continued to adapt to new regulations and find new loopholes, giving rise to new forms of corruption (Chang and Chu 2006, 269–270). What this pattern means, in effect, is that political rather than economic or policy concerns often assume prominent roles in shaping anticorruption efforts in the region.

Second, across Northeast and Southeast Asia, we find a wide array of political regimes that have engaged in large-scale anticorruption efforts. This volume covers several types of regime, including relatively stable democracies, as represented by South Korea and Taiwan; low-quality democracies, as represented by Indonesia and the Philippines; a "hybrid" regime as represented by Thailand, which oscillates between military authoritarianism and democracy; and "closed" authoritarian regimes as represented by China and Vietnam. Moreover, these countries are at different levels of development, following disparate developmental trajectories with diverse historical legacies ranging from colonialism to communism. South Korea and Taiwan are usually considered developed economies. China is now the world's second largest economy after nearly three decades of high-speed growth, though those gains have been distributed over a massive population and growth has slowed down recently. Indonesia, the Philippines, Thailand, and Vietnam are all developing economies with varying rates of growth. It is worth noting that high growth rates in parts of the region have traditionally been associated with high levels of corruption—what Andrew Wedeman (2002) calls the "East Asian paradox." Despite all this regime heterogeneity, anticorruption efforts have been undertaken, often repeatedly, across these diverse political and economic settings. These efforts in turn have led to varying outcomes. Such empirical variations, not just in the efficacy of anticorruption efforts but, specifically, in their political repercussions offer important analytical leverage when it comes to examining the politics of anticorruption in the region.

Finally, the regional focus of this volume takes into account the possibility of cross-national diffusion[7] or political-learning effects within a closely knit geographical area. Geographical proximity as well as long-term economic and cultural ties make it possible for countries in the region to borrow from each other's experiences, both positive and negative, or learn from each other's mistakes, including in the area of anticorruption efforts.[8] In particular, Indonesia, the Philippines, Thailand, and Vietnam are all members of the Association of Southeast Asian Nations (ASEAN), the largest regional bloc in Asia. China, South Korea, and Taiwan also have close political or trade ties with ASEAN. In addition, Asia is the only non-Western region where a few governments, such as Singapore and Hong Kong, have been highly successful in curbing, if not eliminating, previously rampant corruption, leading to improved governance. This variation indicates that corruption is not culturally deterministic: it is entirely possible to achieve anticorruption successes in the Asian context.

Therefore, this volume focuses on Asia for its political and economic diversity, its challenging environment for fighting corruption, and the variations it offers in anticorruption outcomes. Our case study approach allows an in-depth and holistic understanding of political dynamics driving anticorruption efforts across a wide range of comparable contexts within a broadly similar time frame of the past several decades. Its sensitivity to spatially and temporally bounded contexts helps reveal the multidimensionality of anticorruption efforts often obscured by large-N quantitative analyses. The regional focus is analytically useful, but it does not mean the theoretical insights generated by this volume are only limited to the region. As the following discussion shows, the theoretical framework this volume presents is potentially generalizable to any developmental setting where regime legitimacy remains contested among the state, political parties, and private interests.

Anticorruption Efforts and Contested Regime Legitimacy

Regime legitimacy refers to the belief of citizens that the nature and functioning of national state institutions conform to their own basic political and moral values (Muller and Jukam 1977, 1566). In other words, a regime is legitimate to the extent that its citizens believe that it provides a satisfactory order and that there is no available alternative that is vastly superior (Fish 2001, 27). Democracy can be an important source of regime legitimacy as it provides procedural justifications for the regime's right to hold power and exercise its authority. But regime legitimacy is conceptually different from democracy. Legitimacy often crucially depends on the substantive values that are realized, including expectations regarding the provision of such valued public goods as social order, economic stability, and distributive justice (Sil and Chen 2004).[9] Therefore, beyond electoral competition, these substantive areas also become important arenas of political contestation. Among these issue areas, the need to combat corruption is often the least controversial, as almost all actors, regardless of ideological background, agree that unchecked corruption is detrimental and perhaps even fatal to the society and the economy. This sentiment, coupled with persistent problems of corruption in both developed and developing settings, marks anticorruption as a most prominent and convenient site for contestation over regime legitimacy.

Although few would refute the desirability of curbing corruption, different political actors, motivated by different objectives, disagree over what constitutes corruption, what enables corruption, and how to combat corruption. These disagreements often form the basis for these actors to attack or challenge their opponents, as well as shape the trajectories of anticorruption efforts. The source of these disagreements, we argue, is contention over the basis of regime legitimacy driven by three often-competing yet sometimes overlapping motivations: private interests, party loyalty, and political institutionalization. The heterogeneity of anticorruption efforts stems from a fundamental question: Should regime legitimacy be based on private networks and interests, partisan (including military) allegiance, or formal and impersonal institutions? Any given effort may span these categories to some extent, especially over time or subnational regions. However, we find that the brunt of campaigns in a given regime tends to reflect a prevailing logic from among these types.

Anticorruption Driven by Private Interests

Patronage ties and clientelism, as informal and hierarchical forms of traditional politics, have been prevalent in human societies throughout history.[10] Their existence far predated the emergence of the modern state, which is supposed to be nonpatrimonial, or "impersonal" (Fukuyama 2014, 10). Indeed, it was with the emergence of the modern state that a distinction between private and public interests made identification of "corruption" possible. Nevertheless, across a wide range of settings, including in Asia, forms of "neopatrimonialism" have often repurposed a legacy of patrimonialism beneath the veneer of a modern state, enabling widespread corruption and nepotism (Fukuyama 2014, 26). Pervasive and entrenched patron-client relations undermine the legal-rational approach to political and economic organization, "personalizing" politics (Compton 2000, 43–45). In this sense, patronage ties and clientelism are often "default" positions for political elites to fall back on when formal and impersonal institutions, across regime types, are unable effectively to check elite behavior. Therefore, it is no surprise that private rather than public interests constitute a highly common motivation driving anticorruption efforts in many countries. This type of anticorruption effort often targets oppositional individuals or patronal networks, but it could also be a defensive reaction to attempts at party or state institutionalization; it may render anticorruption efforts mundane "politics," in the sense of contests for power and spoils, rather than steps toward a normative conception of "the political."

Antoinette Raquiza's chapter, "Anticorruption Campaigns and the Proprietary Polity: The Philippine Case," for example, offers a vivid analysis of this type of anticorruption effort. Raquiza presents the Philippines as a case in which private interests, especially in the form of political families, have captured formal party and state institutions, including by using anti-corruption campaigns as mobilizing vehicles to fight for political offices. In this case, anticorruption campaigns undermine rather than strengthen party and state institutions, as these campaigns are instrumental in reinforcing and perpetuating the clan-based political ecosystem in the Philippines.

Private interests are also often present in, and sometimes even obstruct and hijack, other types of anticorruption efforts. The case of Indonesia, as analyzed by Edward Aspinall in "Fighting Corruption When Corruption Is Pervasive: The Case of Indonesia," offers such an example, even though its post-Suharto anticorruption efforts were broadly motivated by political institutionalization. Private and patronal interests also played significant roles in largely ineffective anticorruption efforts in Vietnam, as presented in the chapter by Edmund Malesky and Ngoc Phan, "Rust Removal: Why Vietnam's Historical Anticorruption Efforts Failed to Deliver Results, and What That Implies for the Current Campaign."

As these case studies show, anticorruption efforts driven by private interests share a number of similarities. First, these efforts tend to target specific individuals and patronal networks rather than focusing on policy changes or institutional reforms that could address long-term structural sources of corruption. The focus is on punishment rather than prevention. As a result, these anticorruption efforts are usually highly inconsistent, as different standards are applied to different networks and individuals. Those calling for anticorruption crackdowns, whether they are incumbents or in opposition, are often corrupt themselves. For example, the sequence of

anticorruption campaigns in the Philippines since the anti-Marcos mobilization of 1986, particularly against Joseph Estrada and his successor, Gloria
Macapagal Arroyo, were led by representatives of the oligarchy. Marcos,
Estrada, and Macapagal Arroyo were extremely corrupt, but so were many
of the elites behind these and other "people power" campaigns, some
of whom have used anticorruption efforts to propel their own political
careers—though they then face the challenge of demobilization. Anticorruption efforts driven by private interests also tend to be stop-and-go, as
their objectives are to take down specific individuals or networks.

Second, and relatedly, this type of anticorruption effort is unlikely
to curb corruption effectively. These campaigns could yield short-term
results following a few high-profile cases, but they usually do not produce
long-term effects on overall levels of corruption, as structural sources of
corruption stay in place and are even reinforced by these selective anticorruption efforts. Both the Philippines and Indonesia, for example, continue
to be plagued by rampant corruption and rank consistently poorly on
Transparency International's Corruption Perceptions Index, despite their
formal democratic trappings. Over time, the populace tends to develop
feelings of cynicism and apathy toward such anticorruption efforts and to
perceive most politicians as inherently and hopelessly corrupted.

Finally, repeated corruption/anticorruption cycles involving feuding
individuals and patronal networks are usually indicative of the persistence
of parallel or "shadow" informal institutions that undermine the party
system as well as formal state institutions. The Corruption Eradication
Commission (KPK) in Indonesia, for instance, continues to be threatened
and attacked by forces in the political and law-enforcement establishments.
In other words, the issue of regime legitimacy remains unsettled as informal
rather than formal institutions still constitute the basis of political authority.

Anticorruption Driven by Party Loyalty

Political parties are an intrinsic part of modern politics and an essential
institution of modern democracy. It is true that some parties are highly
personalistic, lack any coherent platform, and are little more than vehicles
of patronal networks. Anticorruption programs initiated by such parties
would therefore fall into the previous category. But most political parties
do claim to represent certain identities or positions and hence demand
a degree of impersonal allegiance from their members, however salient
patronal networks also often remain, such as in many Asian countries.

In democratic and semi-democratic settings, political parties regularly engage in electoral politics to compete for political offices. During electoral competitions, they frequently use corruption charges as powerful political weapons against political opponents. From the United States to France to Brazil, corruption allegations dog political parties during every electoral season. But even in many nondemocratic settings, ruling political parties regularly face the challenge of disciplining political elites in order to protect their organizational integrity and cohesion as well as to fend off potential political challengers.

In his chapter, "(Anti-)Corruption and Partisan Bias in Taiwan's Newspapers," Christian Goebel analyzes the crucial role of politically aligned newspapers in Taiwan in acting as the two major political parties' mouthpieces in negatively reporting anticorruption efforts initiated by their political opponents. Such partisan reporting is instrumental in creating and maintaining the public perception of pervasive corruption even though decades of anticorruption efforts have led to long-term institutional changes, moderate setbacks notwithstanding. In other words, the media-manufactured and largely negative public perception ironically obscures a far more complicated reality, in which initially partisan motivations, especially in the case of the Democratic Progressive Party (DPP), result in far-reaching systematic anticorruption efforts.

On the authoritarian side, the Maoist era in China was marked by anticorruption efforts driven by ideological demands for party loyalty, as Andrew Wedeman describes here in "The Evolution of China's Anticorruption Strategy." Beyond an element of private interest in holding on to power, Mao's anticorruption mass campaigns were very much motivated by ideology and the need to mobilize "revolutionary classes" to find and eliminate "hidden counterrevolutionaries" and "reactionary elements." And in Thailand, too, as Michael Connors's chapter, "Anticorruption Politics in Thailand: From Regime Institutionalization to Sovereignty Wars," details, recurrent stints of military rule, justified largely in terms of getting the country back on track after the foibles of democratically elected but self-serving or insufficiently competent leaders, require that the military (and its ultimate patron, the monarchy) itself sustain "ersatz virtue." Crafting and sustaining distinctive "ideologies of accountability" not only discredits potential opponents but also justifies authoritarian leadership that meets these (self-promulgated) standards. That said, these efforts in Thailand may be more productively seen as representing efforts by different regime framers—military or party-based—to institutionalize a particular vision of the regime (as further detailed later). Vietnam offers a similarly ambiguous picture, as Edmund Malesky and Ngoc Phan describe. Here, we see efforts styled as highly normative but, at best, really more about bolstering the legitimacy and position of the Vietnamese Communist Party (VCP). Intermittent high-profile anticorruption efforts largely sidestep serious systemic reform, targeting instead specific government and business leaders, and largely lacking thus far in long-term efficacy or wide impact.

Anticorruption efforts driven by party loyalty also share similarities across regime types. First of all, such efforts tend to pay much more attention to corruption outside the party than within the party. This is not to say within-party corruption is necessarily overlooked or condoned, but anticorruption campaigners usually put much greater emphasis on cracking down on corruption committed by perceived political opponents, such as opposing political parties or Mao's "Rightists" and "counterrevolutionaries"; if the emphasis is intraparty corruption, the intent is more likely a purge, still for the purpose of advancing the party as a corporate body under particular leadership, than to uphold a "neutral" normative standard. The partisan media in Taiwan, for example, tend to extensively and sensationally expose the opposing party's corruption scandals while staying relatively mute about those committed by their "own" politicians. In China, too, Mao went so far as to link corruption inherently with political and ideological opposition, and actually used anticorruption mass campaigns to identify and crush critics of the Chinese Communist Party (CCP). A prominent example was Mao's Anti-Rightist Campaign following the Hundred Flowers Movement of 1956, which ironically was supposed to help the CCP rid itself of corruption. Anticorruption efforts driven by party loyalty are thus characterized by an "us versus them" mentality rather than seeking to eradicate corruption per se.

Second, anticorruption efforts driven by party loyalty may or may not lead to long-term institutional changes; either way, they tend to generate negative public perceptions due to the unequal treatment of corruption cases within and outside of the party. In the long run, the public rightly comes to perceive anticorruption efforts as instruments of power struggle or repression by political parties. As the case of Taiwan demonstrates, even real progress made may hence be obscured by the excessive focus on political competition. In Vietnam, meanwhile, citizens' experience of corruption has not measurably changed, despite dramatic campaigns; not surprisingly, positive impacts on perceptions of corruption and regime legitimacy have proved ephemeral. And in Thailand, too, such efforts have contributed to a prevalent "antipolitics" sentiment within society, which a self-proclaimed "honest" military has, in turn, mobilized against elected governments.

Finally, anticorruption efforts driven by party loyalty tend to lose steam once electoral victory is secured or campaigners perceive political "enemies" as vanquished. But compared to anticorruption efforts driven by private interests, there is more chance for anticorruption efforts driven by party loyalty to lead to long-term institutional changes, especially under democratic settings. This difference is because under democracy, parties, once in power, are less likely to be able to change anticorruption policies arbitrarily, even if those policies were enacted to target these parties in the first place. This pattern is illustrated by the case of Taiwan, where anticorruption efforts enacted alternately by the Kuomintang (KMT) and DPP governments, but especially the latter, have led to cumulative positive long-term changes. The DPP, for example, did not single out the KMT specifically in its anticorruption programs. In order to remain credible, it had to turn also against its own people. In other words, anticorruption policies and institutions could create their own momentum and take on lives of their own, despite their origins in electoral competition.

ANTICORRUPTION DRIVEN BY POLITICAL INSTITUTIONALIZATION

Other than serving private or partisan interests, anticorruption efforts can also be for the purpose of political institutionalization—the creation and maintenance of a set of formal institutions that effectively guide and regulate elite behavior across party lines. As Samuel Huntington once argued, "a society with weak political institutions lacks the ability to curb the excesses of personal and parochial desires," and the "capacity to create political institutions is the capacity to create public interests" (Huntington 1968, 24). In this sense, rampant corruption itself could be seen as one key indication of the combination of "weak political institutions" and "strong social forces" found in many developing societies, including in Asia (Huntington 1968, 11). Regardless of regime type, political institutionalization plays a crucial role in contributing to regime stability and durability.

It is important to note that pursuing a core objective of political institutionalization does not necessarily exclude an element of private or partisan interests in anticorruption efforts. But the essential difference is that, unlike the two other aforementioned types, this type of anticorruption effort aims at long-term, enduring institutional reforms that transcend short-term power struggles. These campaigns' intent is an enduring, politically neutral norm; these are more programmatic than targeted reforms. Such efforts may be the result of public demands from below, pushing for political and legal equality, but they may also be initiated from the top in order to shore up regime popularity and legitimacy as well as to improve economy and governance. The case of Thailand, as presented by Michael Connors in his chapter, best demonstrates this fungibility: military and civilian party leaders alike have sought to promulgate moral messages, centered on anticorruption claims and priorities, to their own advantage. Clearly, there is an element of party/military-based legitimation here. Yet both camps' objectives run deeper and longer-term: to institutionalize a new regime, premised on a particular set of norms. Connors thus suggests that while the conventional view of oscillations in Thailand's anticorruption politics is that all are for partisan advantage, we should instead understand these as being "about higher order questions of sovereignty, state form, and hegemony." In addition, as the case of Vietnam shows, international factors could well play a role, as institutional reforms for the purpose of curbing corruption, attached as "conditions" to foreign investment and aid, create external, politically disinterested arbiters and lasting effects (Jensen and Malesky 2018). Their usually sustained and systematic trajectory does not mean that anticorruption efforts driven by political institutionalization will always succeed, but these efforts are usually designed in a way that focuses on preventing corruption over time rather than simply punishing corrupted individuals and groups.

In his chapter on Indonesia, Edward Aspinall argues that, even though the official post-Suharto anticorruption agenda has been embodied in formal institutions, such as the establishment of the powerful Corruption Eradication Commission (Komisi Pemberantasan Korupsi, KPK) and a specialist anticorruption court, these efforts have often been obstructed and even penetrated by private and patronal interests seeking personal gains. Despite the establishment of a new enforcement regime, corruption remains nevertheless central to Indonesia's political economy. On the one hand, these formal institutions enable nongovernmental organizations and other social groups to campaign against corrupt political leaders. On the other hand, at the local level, political actors often form temporary alliances with social groups to bring down political enemies in the name of battling still-endemic corruption. The result is a sort of stalemate: despite some victories by the institution-builders, corruption remains persistent and pervasive, with few signs of decisive improvement.

Nevertheless, anticorruption efforts motivated by political institutionalization have achieved sustainable results in some cases. In his chapter, "Korea's Anticorruption Struggles: Fighting against Networks," Ray Dongryul Kim demonstrates the difficulty of achieving success. Kim traces South Korea's long-term efforts to combat corruption, which evolved from actor-based individual corruption to more bureaucratic, network-based collective corruption following the country's neoliberal reforms. Sweeping new efforts shifted the focus from punishing corrupt individuals to institutional reforms intended to break down entrenched, corruption-enabling bureaucratic networks. This chapter shows that even serious anticorruption efforts that attempt to address structural sources of corruption are usually protracted struggles, as new forms of corruption emerge and adapt.

Meanwhile, Andrew Wedeman presents a much more mixed picture of post-Mao anticorruption efforts in China, which moved away from Mao's "politics in command" approach and relied on party and state institutions rather than the "mass line" to combat corruption crimes. Intermittent efforts in anticorruption institutionalization have still been periodically punctuated by politically motivated, high-profile crackdowns, such as the sensational Bo Xilai case, indicating an element of power struggle. But in general, the overall trend seems to be shifting from a combination of routine policing and short-term bursts of hyper-enforcement to systematic and sustained enhanced enforcement, especially under the current president, Xi Jinping, who has primarily focused on expanding institutional capacity for enduring corruption prevention and punishment in addition to tightening his political grip.

Clearly, and as the cases of Thailand, South Korea, and China illustrate to dramatic effect, anticorruption efforts driven by political institutionalization not only can be observed across regime types but may also coexist with other types of anticorruption efforts. Compared to anticorruption efforts driven by private interests or party loyalty, anticorruption efforts driven by political institutionalization are usually more consistent and last longer. This approach does not mean individuals or groups will not be specifically targeted or that there will not be any selective enforcement or treatment, but these anticorruption efforts tend to stay in place even after their original "targets" are gone. In the case of China, for example,

Xi's anticorruption campaign has continued unabated at all levels of the government and has led to the routinization of many anticorruption measures, beyond the point at which he firmly consolidated his political power. In South Korea, a groundbreaking new anticorruption law, the Improper Solicitation and Graft Act, took effect in 2016 with the goal of eradicating bureaucratic corruption in the long run by dissolving the institutional roots of corruption. In Thailand, each new regime establishes itself with a new constitution, often entailing substantial institutional changes, to formalize a new order.

Moreover, anticorruption efforts driven by political institutionalization are characterized by attempts to change the "rules of the game" instead of simply meting out punishment to individuals and groups. In both contemporary South Korea and China, these efforts center on breaking up the informal patronal or bureaucratic networks that gave rise to rampant corruption in the first place. The underlying message is that formal institutions and rules, rather than informal networks and norms, should form the basis of regime legitimacy and hence the ultimate guideline for elite behavior.

Finally, compared to the previous two types, anticorruption efforts driven by political institutionalization are more likely to generate positive public responses over time once they are perceived as "serious." In other words, anticorruption efforts are only likely to provide a long-term boost to regime legitimacy when people perceive such efforts as persistently and consistently applied and see that no group is exempt from such efforts. The recent corruption scandal surrounding South Korea's ex-president Park Geun-hye led to massive political turmoil, but Park's orderly impeachment and subsequent prosecution also indicate the country's determination to combat corruption systematically by following institutional due process. Of course, not all such efforts result in sustained success, as "backsliding" can take place whenever anticorruption policies are reversed or undermined by new forms of corruption. But at least these campaigns are less likely to be viewed with the kind of cynicism that the other two types of anticorruption efforts tend to induce.

Rudra Sil's concluding chapter, "The Comparative Study of Anticorruption: Where Do We Go from Here?," reviews the distinctive logics and pathways of anticorruption efforts as laid out in the three parts of the volume. It considers what might happen if the cases that come closest to blurring the boundaries among the three motivations were employed to explore a more eclectic perspective on the emergence and execution of anticorruption efforts. The chapter suggests a more nuanced approach to assessing just how close each of the cases examined in this volume gets to an ideal-typical scheme for using anticorruption efforts to bolster the official capacity and autonomy of the state, with those efforts that are most dominated by conflicts over private interests doing the least in this regard.

In sum, this volume proposes a framework for understanding the diversity of anticorruption efforts, arguing that these variations be taken seriously: they reflect different political dynamics in different institutional settings, and carry distinct implications. Rather than focus on policy-making and policy-implementation, then, we shed light on the diverging political logics behind, and political ramifications of, anticorruption efforts. The cases on which the chapters here elaborate suggest that anticorruption efforts serve a wide range of political purposes, characterized most importantly by whether they are driven by private interests, party loyalty, or a goal of political institutionalization. Significantly, this three-ideal-type analytic lens should not be understood as implying a kind of hierarchy, in which any one type is inherently more beneficial or more enduring. Not only may strategies be mercurial or opportunistic, as the chapters here demonstrate well, but also further political institutionalization of authoritarianism (as in the cases of China or Vietnam) or military dictatorship (as in the case of Thailand) would hardly be desirable, even if the level of corruption decreases over time. At the same time, having democratic institutions alone does not entail political will on the part of elites or incentives on the part of citizens to make corruption an issue. Likewise, lack of democracy in and of itself does not necessarily preclude serious and systematic attempts to deal with corruption. Instead, this volume reveals that to fully understand the political dynamics underlying anticorruption efforts, we need to go beyond a simple democracy-versus-authoritarianism dichotomy, and that anticorruption strategy may be associated more closely with shifting bases of regime legitimacy than with regime type itself. What is more, anticorruption strategies can and do evolve within regimes. In cases such as South Korea and China, anticorruption strategy has gone through significant changes over time, after repeated failures, even as the regime type per se has remained relatively constant.

This is not to say, however, that regime types do not matter, especially the distinction between democracies and nondemocracies, when it comes to facilitating positive anticorruption outcomes. Although democracy alone, as demonstrated in cases such as the Philippines and Indonesia, does not guarantee any particular anticorruption strategy or outcome, it may be conducive to anticorruption efforts motivated either by party loyalty as a sign of healthy competition embedded in a wider system of checks and balances or goals of political institutionalization. As the cases of South Korea and Taiwan show, too, democratic settings could help in institutionalizing anticorruption efforts that originate in party competition, leading to long-term positive effects.

As anticorruption demands sweep the globe today, it is all the more important for us to heed the diverging logics of and motivations behind anticorruption efforts. The challenges might appear common; the responses vary greatly. Ultimately, as this volume shows, anticorruption efforts tend to create unintended momentum or externalities, making it all the more critical that we understand what their intent and expected scope actually was. These campaigns may strengthen regime legitimacy or boost parties' or leaders' popularity, but they may also undermine a regime or specific leaders in the long run, including opening the door to legal reforms and democratization. At a time when calls to combat corruption have become almost reflexive, we cannot afford to ignore the potential of anticorruption efforts to be double-edged swords.

Organization of the Volume

This volume comprises three parts, reflecting our tripartite framework for conceptualizing anticorruption efforts: whether the basis of regime legitimacy at issue is personal, partisan, or institutional. It should be emphasized that these three ideal-typical categories are not separated by clear-cut boundaries. As multiple cases demonstrate, one type of anti-corruption effort over time could intentionally or unintentionally evolve into another, and differing, even countervailing, strategies may coexist, sometimes prominently, or succeed one another within a regime. For example, anticorruption efforts driven by party loyalty may lead to insti-tutionalized anticorruption mechanisms as illustrated by the Taiwanese case. Thus anticorruption efforts driven by party loyalty could be a sign of systemic health or decline, depending on the context. We classify cases per the *dominant* or most defining type of anticorruption effort we see there, albeit acknowledging the diversity of campaigns we may find even within a given case, particularly over time.

The first part contains those cases reflecting primarily private networks and interests, including the Philippines and Indonesia. In both these states, weakly institutionalized parties and engrained clientelist, including clan-based, networks shape the use of anticorruption efforts and undermine even promising efforts at more systematic reform—although Indonesia has made significant progress in shifting toward institutionalization of its anticorruption efforts. The second part focuses on those cases reflecting largely a partisan basis for allegiance: Taiwan and Vietnam. In Taiwan, institutionalization has taken place over time, despite the strong public perception of the partisan nature of anticorruption efforts, but such public perception remains highlighted and even exaggerated by partisan-leaning media. In Vietnam, although a recent anticorruption campaign seemed more far-reaching, the VCP's largely politically driven anticorruption efforts have been instrumental and inconsistent. The third part examines those cases in which anticorruption efforts have strived significantly to propound political legitimacy based on formal and impersonal institutions, including Thailand, South Korea, and China. In all these cases, we may find earlier or overlapping anticorruption efforts reflecting private or partisan interests, but the drive for institutionalization more substantially characterizes present-day efforts. Finally, we tie these cases together, considering, too, the awkwardness of some cases' fit within their "dominant" category—foreshadowed already in this introduction—in the conclusion.

Notes

1. This volume discusses the case of China in detail. In Brazil, corruption charges had brought down Dilma Rousseff, and ex-president Lula was soon to be convicted for corruption. In Russia, both the Putin regime and the opposition led by Alexei Navalny then claimed to pursue anticorruption agendas. In India, nonelite individuals such as Arvind Kejriwal and Anna Hazare were able to capture media attention and mobilize grassroots pressure on elites to expand anticorruption activities, including the withdrawal of large-denomination rupee notes often used for black market transactions. In South Africa, Zuma was embroiled in corruption charges and would eventually be removed as head of the African National Congress.

2. While Gillespie and Okruhlik focus on conceptual development and a typology mostly based on authoritarian examples from the Middle East and North Africa, however, we highlight political motivations cutting across regime types.

3. Scholars have offered a wide range of definitions of corruption. For some prominent examples, see Nye (1967), Rose-Ackerman (1999), and Manion (2004).

4. It is important to point out that high corruption does not necessarily lead to state breakdown. Keith Darden (2008), for example, finds many illiberal states in which high "informally institutionalized" corruption actually contributes to elite compliance and therefore high state capacity.

5. It has been argued that heightened publicity of official corruption could lead to social unrest. See, for example, Lorentzen (2014).

6. These countries include China, Japan, Singapore, South Korea, Taiwan, and Vietnam.

7. Koesel and Bunce (2013, 753) define cross-national diffusion as "the transfer among countries of an innovative idea, product, policy, institution, or repertoire of behavior."

8. For example, ASEAN held an anticorruption workshop in Jakarta in 2016. Later in the year, China hosted a China–ASEAN anticorruption workshop, and it has sought help from ASEAN to set up a regional mechanism to help it hunt down fugitives from its anticorruption campaigns.

9. Bo Rothstein (2011) uses a similar concept of "quality of government."

10. The very words "patron" and "client" trace their origins back to ancient Rome. James Scott (1972, 92) defines the patron-client relationship as "a special case of dyadic ties involving a largely instrumental friendship in which an individual of higher socioeconomic status (patron) uses his own influence and resources to provide protection or benefits, or both, for a person of lower status (client) who, for his part, reciprocates by offering general support and assistance, including personal services, to the patron."

Bibliography

Bardhan, Pranab. "Corruption and Development: A Review of Issues." *Journal of Economic Literature* 35, no. 3 (1997): 1320–1346.

Chang, Eric C. C., and Yun-han Chu. "Corruption and Trust: Exceptionalism in Asian Democracies?" *Journal of Politics* 68, no. 2 (2006): 259–271.

Compton, Robert W. *East Asian Democratization: Impact of Globalization, Culture, and Economy.* Westport: Praeger, 2000.

Darden, Keith. "The Integrity of Corrupt States: Graft as an Informal State Institution." *Politics and Society* 36, no. 1 (2008): 35–60.

Fish, M. Steven. "When More Is Less: Superexecutive Power and Political Underdevelopment in Russia." In *Russia in the New Century: Stability or Disorder?*, edited by Victoria E. Bonnell and George W. Breslauer, 15–34. Boulder: Westview Press, 2001.

Fukuyama, Francis. *Political Order and Political Decay: From the Industrial Revolution to the Globalization of Democracy*. New York: Farrar, Straus and Giroux, 2014.

Gillespie, Kate, and Gwenn Okruhlik. "The Political Dimensions of Corruption Cleanups: A Framework for Analysis." *Comparative Politics* 24, no. 1 (1991): 77–95.

Huntington, Samuel. *Political Order in Changing Societies*. New Haven: Yale University Press, 1968.

Jensen, Nathan M., and Edmund J. Malesky. "Nonstate Actors and Compliance with International Agreements: An Empirical Analysis of the OECD Anti-Bribery Convention." *International Organization* 72, no. 1 (2018): 1–37.

Koesel, Karrie J., and Valerie Bunce. "Diffusion-Proofing: Russian and Chinese Responses to Waves of Popular Mobilizations against Authoritarian Rule." *Perspectives on Politics* 11, no. 3 (2013): 753–768.

Leff, Nathaniel H. "Economic Development through Bureaucratic Corruption." *American Behavioral Scientist* 8, no. 3 (1964): 8–14.

Lipset, Seymour, and Babriel Lenz. "Corruption, Culture and Markets." In *Culture Matters*, edited by Lawrence Harrison and Samuel Huntington, 112–124. New York: Basic Books, 2000.

Lorentzen, Peter. "China's Strategic Censorship." *American Journal of Political Science* 58, no. 2 (2014): 402–414.

Manion, Melanie. *Corruption by Design: Building Clean Government in Mainland China and Hong Kong*. Cambridge: Harvard University Press, 2004.

Mauro, Paolo. "Corruption and Growth." *Quarterly Journal of Economics* 110, no. 3 (1995): 681–712.

Muller, Edward N., and Thomas O. Jukam. "On the Meaning of Political Support." *American Political Science Review* 71, no. 4 (1977): 1561–1595.

Mungiu-Pippidi, Alina. *The Quest for Good Governance: How Societies Develop Control of Corruption*. New York: Cambridge University Press, 2015.

Nye, Joseph S. "Corruption and Political Development: A Cost-Benefit Analysis." *American Political Science Review* 61, no. 2 (1967): 417–427.

Rose-Ackerman, Susan. *Corruption and Government: Causes, Consequences, and Reform*. New York: Cambridge University Press, 1999.

Rose-Ackerman, Susan, and Bonnie J. Palifka. *Corruption and Government: Causes, Consequences, and Reform*, 2nd ed. New York: Cambridge University Press, 2016.

Rothstein, Bo. *The Quality of Government: Corruption, Social Trust, and Inequality in International Perspective*. Chicago: University of Chicago Press, 2011.

Rothstein, Bo, and Aiysha Varraich. *Making Sense of Corruption*. New York: Cambridge University Press, 2017.

Scott, James C. "Patron-Client Politics and Political Change in Southeast Asia." *American Political Science Review* 66, no. 1 (1972): 91–113.

Seligson, Mitchell A. "The Impact of Corruption on Regime Legitimacy: A Comparative Study of Four Latin American Countries." *Journal of Politics* 64, no. 2 (2002): 408–433.

Sil, Rudra, and Cheng Chen. "State Legitimacy and the (In)significance of Democracy in Post-Communist Russia." *Europe-Asia Studies* 56, no. 3 (2004): 347–368.

Uslaner, Eric M. *Corruption, Inequality, and the Rule of Law: The Bulging Pocket Makes the Easy Life*. New York: Cambridge University Press, 2008.

Wedeman, Andrew. "Development and Corruption: The East Asian Paradox." In *Political Business in East Asia*, edited by Edmund Terence Gomez, 34–61. London: Routledge, 2002.

Wei, Shang-Jin. "Corruption in Economic Development: Beneficial Grease, Minor Annoyance, or Major Obstacles?" World Bank Policy Research Working Paper No. 2048, February 1999. Retrieved from http://papers.ssrn.com/sol3/papers.cfm?abstract_id=604923.

You, Jong-sung. *Democracy, Inequality and Corruption: Korea, Taiwan and the Philippines Compared*. New York: Cambridge University Press, 2016.

Part I

Anticorruption Driven by Private Interests

1

Anticorruption Campaigns, Regime Change, and the Proprietary Polity

The Philippine Case

Antoinette R. Raquiza

Anticorruption campaigns have been a staple of Philippine politics. Such campaigns produced street protests that ousted two presidents and led to the defeat of a frontrunner in the 2016 presidential elections. Yet, anticorruption campaigns have remained largely in the realm of politics, with very little follow-through in the realm of prosecution. The Supreme Court's dismissal of the plunder case against former president Gloria Macapagal Arroyo on July 16, 2016, due to a lack of evidence exemplifies this puzzle. Macapagal Arroyo's detention since 2011 had been used by her successor, President Benigno Aquino III, to stress his administration's supposed hardnosed approach toward corruption. However, not only did the Aquino administration fail to make its case against Macapagal Arroyo during its six-year term, Macapagal Arroyo, who won three congressional elections in her district after she stepped down from the presidency in 2010, became the 17th Congress's House Speaker in July 2018. She thus became the fourth highest official in the land. This sudden turnaround is illustrative of the seasonal nature of anticorruption campaigns in the country.

The author wishes to thank Noel Padalhin for his valuable assistance in data collection and Cheng Chen and Meredith Weiss for their feedback and suggestions.

This study examines anticorruption campaigns in the Philippines, specifically those that led to plunder cases against President Joseph Estrada and his successor, Macapagal Arroyo. Notably, the anticorruption campaigns that confronted the two presidents took off from the so-called People Power revolution (i.e., the convergence of multisectoral street protests, an aggressive media campaign, legal and parliamentary actions, and military rebellion) that ended authoritarian rule in 1986, though only one led to regime change. A close and comparative analysis of the anticorruption campaigns against the two former presidents raises the question of why a mobilized citizenry that forcibly removed Estrada from office was unable to prevent the abuse of power by his successor. Equally puzzling: What would account for the differences in outcomes of the two movements?

This chapter argues that the configuration of state power delimits the effectiveness of anticorruption measures and campaigns targeting national political figures. In the Philippines, political power is organized around and regarded as an entitlement by individual politicians whose rise to national prominence is a function of their families' social status and wealth instead of their membership in state institutions or political parties—an institutional setting that I have called the proprietary polity in earlier studies (Raquiza 2012). In such a setting, anticorruption campaigns themselves assume a personalistic character. Instead of contributing to the establishment of institutional reforms, such campaigns become vulnerable to co-optation by political elites who are likely to use them to further their own personal and political agendas. In this light, the chapter presents the proprietary polity as a specific institutional configuration of neopatrimonial rule, discussed by Cheng Chen and Meredith Weiss in their introduction to this volume.

Toward gaining a deeper understanding of the nature, constraints, and prospects of national anticorruption campaigns under a proprietary polity, this chapter undertakes a comparative analysis of those waged against Estrada and Macapagal Arroyo. The present study makes use of national media coverage and secondary sources to identify scandals that were instrumental in building a case against Estrada and, later, Macapagal Arroyo and traces the protest actions broad anticorruption forces under-took in response. The comparative study aims to draw out similarities and differences between the two cases toward identifying factors that would account for their different outcomes.

The next section provides an overview of the institutional setting of the country's anticorruption campaigns and the different analytical frameworks scholars have used to study such initiatives. Next, the chapter situates the nature of anticorruption measures and campaigns in a specific state configuration and then provides a detailed account of the anticorruption campaigns against the two heads of state. The concluding section discusses the emerging pattern of interaction between political contestation and anticorruption campaigns in a proprietary polity.

History of Anticorruption Initiatives

The fight against graft and corruption has been front and center in Philippine politics since the country gained its independence from the US in 1946 (Gonzales and Mendoza 2004). From the short-lived Integrity Board set up by President Elipio Quirino in 1950 to President Benigno Aquino III's ill-fated Presidential Truth Commission in 2010,[1] the country has seen the march of high-level anticorruption bodies and one presidential fiat after another with each change in administration (Batalla 2000; Balboa and Medalla 2010). The country also has several anticorruption laws, including the 1930 Revising the Penal Code Act, imposing penalties and fines on corrupt government officials; the Anti-Graft and Corruption Act of 1960, which specifies corrupt government practices such as receiving gifts, commissions, or favors in relation to the performance of official duties or decisions made in government transactions, bars relatives of officials from engaging in business with government, and requires public officials to submit annual sworn statements of assets and liabilities (amended in 1989 to include net worth); and, more recently, the Plunder Law passed in 1991, imposing stiffer penalties, including the death penalty, on public and private individuals found guilty of graft and corruption involving at least PHP50 million.

The country also has an extensive legal system designed to keep corruption in check. The 1987 Constitution provides for the establishment of constitutional bodies, notably, the Commission on Audit that monitors revenues and expenditures of government offices (Art. IX-D), and the Civil Service Commission, responsible for enforcing the merit system among government personnel (Art. IX-B). It also called for the retention of the anti-graft court, the Sandiganbayan (Art. XI, Section 4), and the reconfiguration of the Office of the Ombudsman that investigates and prosecutes government officials and employees accused of performing acts that are "illegal, unjust, improper, or inefficient" (Art. XI, Section 13-1).

In this sense, therefore, anticorruption initiatives have not been wanting throughout the country's history. In the main, presidential initiatives were done in the wake of political turnovers, usually undertaken by the incumbent to go after erring officials of the previous government—a move that, if we go by public choice theory, should provide a check against any attempt by the president and vice president, who are constitutionally prohibited from running for reelection, to get the most of their term in office. This tradition of presidential house-cleaning can be traced all the way back to the postwar era and was restored after the downfall of President Ferdinand Marcos's authoritarian rule in 1986, with President Corazon Aquino overhauling the bureaucracy ostensibly to rid government of corrupt officials identified with the previous regime and establishing the Presidential Commission on Good Governance to recover the Marcoses' ill-gotten wealth.

In fact, policy-oriented studies tend to treat anticorruption measures as mirror images of corruption practices (Quah 1999; Nawaz 2008). In this connection, the structural-functional approach has been useful in explaining anticorruption and administrative reform initiatives, both in and out of government, as responses to apparent rising levels of bureaucratic corruption. For instance, much of the Philippine legal system set up today to fight corruption is based on the 1987 Constitution—itself a product of a fourteen-year anti-dictatorship struggle and thus informed by the country's experience with crony capitalism.

Unfortunately, such an approach is less helpful when it comes to explaining the tenacity of corruption that is partly due to the failure of institutional reforms to keep pace with changing political contexts. One study of corrupt practices in government procurement transactions, for instance, argues that greater globalization, privatization, and decentralization starting in the 1990s have created new opportunities and greater space for corruption (Mendoza 2001). There is also the long-standing critique that anticorruption measures do not take into account the country's relatively weak state that is, by most accounts, captured by vested interests (Simbulan 2005; Batalla 2000).

Thus, despite an extensive system of anticorruption measures, the country's pursuit of clean and accountable government remains elusive. Implementation of the laws and the resolution of graft and corruption cases filed in the different legal bodies have been slow. Since the enactment of the Plunder Law more than twenty-six years ago, only thirteen plunder cases have been filed with the Sandiganbayan, and only two of these cases—against a Bureau of Internal Review official and Estrada—have led to convictions (Bueza 2017). More significantly, as with Estrada and Macapagal Arroyo, those under investigation for graft and corruption are not barred from seeking public office. Comparing the May 2013 list of candidates and the Sandiganbayan records from 1979 to 2013, the Philippine Center for Investigative Journalism (PCIJ 2013) found that seventeen of those elected had prior convictions. A total of 504 candidates were at one time or another respondents in graft and corruption cases; of these, 169 ran under President Benigno Aquino III's Liberal Party and its anticorruption (Daang Matuwid or Straight Path) platform.

Other studies have focused on the role played by civil society in pushing forward the anticorruption agenda in the face of weak state institutions. This approach, which first gained traction in the aftermath of the People Power or EDSA revolution (named after the major thoroughfare, Epifanio de los Santos Avenue, where street protesters joined cause with military rebels to oust President Ferdinand Marcos on February 22–25, 1986), has likewise been applied to the study of EDSA 2, the mobilization on January 17–20, 2001, that led to the ouster of Estrada. Only the second time in the country's history that massive street protests combined with military action to effect regime change, EDSA 2 has been hailed as a clear sign of the growing political maturity of the Filipino people and, more notably, the middle class (Doronila 2001; Rivera 2011).

Focusing on civil society mobilization, scholars have also used social movement theory to explain the success of the anticorruption campaign against Estrada. For instance, one such study, using contentious politics theory, attributes EDSA 2 to the combination of the following ingredients: the existence of civil society and movement organizations that led and sustained mobilizations; the use of the "resignation, impeachment, or ouster" call to frame political negotiations, mobilizations, and contestation; engagement in different forms of struggles (i.e., media, legal and parliamentary, and street protests); and the opening up of political opportunities to advance the movement in and out of government, including splits within the ruling coalition (Arugay 2004, 76–80). Such studies also stress the important role the middle and upper classes played in the success of EDSA 2 mobilizations, thus raising the specter of elite cooptation (Davis and Zald 2005; Hedman 2006). As with EDSA 1, the civil society narrative and social movement literature provide an analysis of the outcomes of contentious politics as the coming together of organized forces, a mass phenomenon, and an enabling political environment.

Yet, the approach falls short in explaining more recent events. Only a few years after Estrada's ouster, many civil society and political actors who saw action in EDSA 2 would again find themselves waging an anti-corruption campaign, but this time, against a former movement ally whom they helped put into office, Macapagal Arroyo. Echoing EDSA 2's battle cry and playbook of a four-pronged attack (media, parliamentary and legal, street protests, and networking with reformist elements in the military), the movement peaked in 2005–2007, to no avail. What would account for the different outcomes of the two anticorruption campaigns, one waged almost immediately after the other, and in relation to each other? Why did EDSA 2 fail to ensure a more accountable political leadership and instead produce a regime that would itself be charged with grave abuse of power (Mangahas 2009)?

Current trends, in fact, suggest that anticorruption campaigns in the Philippines seem more effective in removing top-ranking government officials than setting up institutional measures to promote accountability and transparency—conditions that might help constrain abuse of power in the long run. It is also curious that anticorruption campaigns have become more salient with every presidential election, a trend that suggests a growing constituency for clean government but also, paradoxically, the failure of all previous campaigns to check the problem they had sought to address.

The structural-functionalist approach and social movement theory have been helpful in understanding the specific contours and ebb and flow of anticorruption campaigns. Nevertheless, unless they are accompanied by a theory of the state that takes into account the fractiousness and thus pattern of competition among state actors, they cannot fully anticipate the direction such campaigns take.

Institutional Setting

To better understand the potency and limitations of high-stakes anticor-ruption campaigns in the country, it helps to examine the institutional setting from which they arise. As studies have suggested, while forms and sources of corruption vary little from state to state at different levels of development, the contours and success of anticorruption efforts depend on the political context (Rose-Ackerman 1999). Perhaps nowhere is this more true than in the Philippines, where political leaders gain national power based on their personal or family wealth and social networks, rather than from their membership in robust political parties or state institutions. Solidifying the political leadership's hold on power is the common practice of appointing as heads of national government agencies people who come not from the state bureaucracy but from the incumbent's social network in academe, business, and civil society. Since the heads of bureaucratic offices start out as outsiders, they are more vulnerable to the dictates of the appointing authority (who is often the incumbent) than those who rose from the ranks and thus possess the institutional memory and bureaucratic resources to assert more independence in decision-making (Raquiza 2012).

I call this organization of elite rule the proprietary polity to stress the merging of class and political power, usually at the level of the family, whose members branch out into business and politics (McCoy 1993). As such, the basic unit of rent generation in Philippine politics has been the political family (Raquiza 2012, 88). Moreover, in a proprietary polity, neither the political leadership nor heads of agencies (technocrats) are based in strong state institutions.

This state configuration has implications for anticorruption campaigns. First, where state institutions are weak and political power often centers around individuals, anticorruption campaigns will focus almost exclusively on individual politicians and will work to reinforce personalistic politics. Second, the bureaucracy's lack of critical distance from the political leadership makes it vulnerable to partisan politics. This arrangement, for instance, has been cited as a factor in the tendency of the Supreme Court and the Sandiganbayan to rule in favor of the incumbent on highly political issues.[2]

The proprietary polity framework takes off from an appreciation that, in the Philippines, political elites are wont to use the issue of corruption against each other to win political points (see, for instance, Bello et al. 2005). As the history of anticorruption measures in the country suggests, corruption has been the issue of choice among political elites who have benefited from rules and practices that permit them to amass wealth and power through corrupt means but must promise reform during the election season. In order to meet this demand for change, a contender can isolate and then target the abhorrent behavior of a corrupt incumbent or political rival—in other words, change the players but not the rules. The proprietary polity model, however, examines how elite anticorruption struggles play out in a specific state configuration, distinguishing between the political leadership and heads of the bureaucracy and examining the relationship of each to the state and to each other. In effect, the proprietary polity model contributes to cross-country comparative analyses of neopatrimonial systems along the dimensions cited, thereby accounting for variations in outcomes.

The framework also draws out implications for multiclass campaigns, especially those leading to extra-parliamentary regime change. From a proprietary polity perspective, anticorruption campaigns that focus mainly on specific individuals may be a double-edged sword. On the one hand, because of their episodic nature, anticorruption campaigns can easily form part of the repertoire, so to speak, of partisan, electoral politics, led by challengers who themselves have checkered family histories. On the other hand, cleavages among the ruling elites also allow for more targeted competition so that anticorruption campaigns are able to generate multiclass alliances, bringing together mass movement activists and the traditional opposition and business. The proprietary polity framework draws out patterns of interaction among political forces in and out of government that pave the way for regime change.

The Case of Two Anticorruption Campaigns and Their Aftermath

To illustrate the proprietary polity framework, I will examine the rise of the anticorruption campaigns against Estrada and Macapagal Arroyo and their aftermath. The Estrada case study focuses on the period starting in 1999, when scandals first hit the news, and ending in 2001, with the ouster, arrest, and detention of Estrada, while the Macapagal Arroyo case study centers on the period beginning almost as soon as she took over from Estrada in 2001 until 2005–2007, when the anticorruption movement exploded, then immediately lost steam. The comparative study will seek to identify trends in anticorruption struggles that have emerged from these two cases and the precedents they have set for future political contestations.

The two anticorruption campaigns were more or less similar in terms of mobilizing issues and the political figures and forces at the forefront of the struggles. The successful campaign against Estrada took three years, from the time the news of an anomalous PHP200 million textbook deal linked to a cousin and a cabinet member broke on January 19, 1999 (EIU 1999), to when people massed at the EDSA site, joined by the top police and military officers, on January 18–20, 2001, for what has since been called EDSA 2. During this period, national media ran one exposé after another on topics ranging from Estrada's drinking and mistresses to the undeclared wealth in his Statement of Assets, Liabilities, and Net Worth or SALN (Møller and Jackson 2002; Coronel 2001). It was not until September 14, 2000, however, when a provincial governor broke ranks and publicly accused his former patron of having received a cut of revenues from *jueteng* (an illegal numbers game) and tobacco excise taxes that the anticorruption campaign came to a head. On September 21, the anniversary of Marcos's declaration of martial law, the protest movement, led by left-wing political organizations, staged rallies in Metro Manila and other urban centers. In October, EDSA 1 figures, notably former president Corazon Aquino and Manila Archbishop Jaime Cardinal Sin, as well as the Bishops-Business Conference, lent their voices to the movement; business conglomerates associated with the Makati Business Club, concerned over the harm a long drawn-out "class war" would bring to the economy and the impasse's impact on foreign investments, followed suit (Reyes and Luz 2000). By year-end, mass mobilizations shifted to high gear, fueled by contributions from well-heeled anti-Estrada participants.[3]

During this time, the parliamentary and legal processes also kicked in. An impeachment complaint was filed at the House of Representatives on October 12, and on November 3, the House voted to endorse the Articles of Impeachment against Estrada. The case then moved to the Senate, which the 1987 Constitution gives sole responsibility for trying impeachment cases. On October 23, graft, corruption, and bribery cases were also filed at the Office of the Ombudsman; another case was filed on November 24. None of these cases, however, were resolved through the legal process before EDSA 2 broke out. Just a month into the Senate impeachment trial, which began on December 7, the anti-Estrada movement accused the Senate—then dominated by Estrada's allies—of withholding vital evidence. On January 18, 2001, the broad opposition called on the public to go to EDSA and demand Estrada's resignation. The next day, Armed Forces of the Philippines Chief of Staff General Angelo Reyes and Philippine National Police Director General Panfilo Lacson withdrew their support from the president and joined the demonstration. At noon on January 20, Gloria Macapagal Arroyo was sworn into office by Supreme Court Chief Justice Hilario Davide, who earlier had presided over the Senate impeachment trial; Estrada left the presidential palace two hours after.[4] Estrada was arrested in April 2001 and found guilty of plunder by the Sandiganbayan,[5] then pardoned by Macapagal Arroyo in 2007.

The anticorruption campaign against Macapagal Arroyo took almost six years to gain momentum and present a credible challenge to her rule, even as her term had been marred by a string of scandals. These included, in 2001, the reported misuse of Philippine Charity Sweepstakes Office (PCSO) funds for the ruling People Power coalition party's campaign for the midterm general elections in May and an alleged PHP50 million bribe to the president's husband for the president to recall her veto of franchise bills favoring two telecommunication corporations (GMA 2009); in 2002, overpricing and other anomalies related to the construction of President Diosdado Macapagal Boulevard, allegedly approved by Macapagal Arroyo (Go 2002) and the awarding of Poverty Eradication and Alleviation Certificates (or PEACe Bonds) to the Caucus of Development NGO Networks (CODE-NGO), which was at the frontline of the EDSA 2 protests (Añonuevo et al. 2002; FDC 2011); and, from 2003 onward, multibillion peso infrastructure contracts allegedly involving foreign corporations and the first family (PCIJ 2005; GMA 2009).[6] Nevertheless, neither these scandals nor the coup attempt on July 26–27, 2003, by a faction of the military calling itself the Bagong Katipuneros (or more popularly known as the Magdalo soldiers)[7] led to a crisis of legitimacy for the administration that EDSA 2 forces put into office. In fact, Macapagal Arroyo and the ruling coalition went on to win the 2004 national elections.

The elections, however, were hotly contested and the dominant opposition, led by movie star and Estrada ally Fernando Poe Jr., accused Macapagal Arroyo of committing massive electoral fraud—charges that the administration and its allies in Congress and civil society dismissed as partisan politicking. Only after June 10, 2005, when the opposition got hold of and released a wiretapped phone conversation believed to be between Macapagal Arroyo and Commission on Elections official Virgilio Garcillano discussing the May 2004 elections and a one-million-vote margin did the anticorruption movement see its ranks swell and gather momentum toward an EDSA scenario.[8]

The period 2005–2007 saw a flurry of protest activities, punctuated by key events. First, in 2005, ten department secretaries, including EDSA 2 figures, resigned from the cabinet. Subsequently, Makati Business Club and other business leaders called for Macapagal Arroyo's resignation and a broad, multisectoral coalition, the Bukluran para sa Katotohanan, formed to unite EDSA 2 forces and the opposition identified with Estrada and Poe. During this period, the House of Representatives received and summarily rejected eleven impeachment complaints against Macapagal Arroyo. Equally significant were two failed military coup attempts, on February 24, 2006, and November 29, 2007, by the Magdalo soldiers (who resurfaced after their 2003 aborted power grab).

By 2008, Macapagal Arroyo had weathered the political storm, allowing her to complete her term. Notably, the key issues that triggered EDSA 2 were also present in the anti-Macapagal Arroyo campaign, but these did not provoke the same level of public outcry. For instance, the revelation in 2003 of a "Jose Pidal" bank account into which allegedly illegally procured campaign funds were funneled did not have the same impact as the "Jose Velarde" exposé had against Estrada. Evidently, by 2008, the anticorruption movement had run its course and EDSA 2 forces had shifted their sights to the 2010 presidential elections.[9] For this election, key EDSA 2 forces threw their lot behind the presidential candidacy of Liberal Party standard-bearer Senator Benigno Aquino III, who ran with the battle cry, "kung walang kurap, walang mahirap" (roughly, if no one is corrupt, no one will be poor) and ordered the arrest of Macapagal Arroyo as one of his first acts in office.

Why did graft and corruption issues work to unseat Estrada and not Macapagal Arroyo? A close comparison of the two anticorruption campaigns reveals that, despite an aggressive media campaign, growing street mobilizations, active support of the Catholic Church and big business, and potentially game-changing military action, it was the parliamentary and legal arena that set the pace and direction of the anticorruption campaigns. In this regard, two variables mattered: one, whether there was a clear line of succession and thus an undisputed challenger to the incumbent; and, two, which party dominated in the House of Representatives, the body that has the sole power to initiate impeachment proceedings, and the Senate, which tries and decides impeachment cases.

With regard to the first variable, the anticorruption struggles against Estrada and Macapagal Arroyo had put into sharp focus the political significance of the vice presidency. In the Philippines, the president and vice president are directly elected and thus may belong to different political parties. Nevertheless, prior to the anti-Estrada campaign, this institutional arrangement had not led to any power struggle between the country's two top officials. For the most part, the vice presidency had largely been ceremonial and those elected to the office waited their turn to vie for the top spot, while accepting any cabinet post offered to them to stay relevant (Cruz 2016). With EDSA 2, Vice President Macapagal Arroyo became the de facto rallying figure of the broad anticorruption movement. In contrast, the broad anticorruption movement against Macapagal Arroyo lacked a rallying figure, mainly because the two vice presidents under her extended term belonged to the ruling coalition. In this context, the broad anticorruption movement divided on alternatives: big business opted for the constitutional process of succession,[10] opposition political parties called for snap elections (Tubeza 2006), and the different left political movements agitated for more militant extra-parliamentary actions.

The different outcomes of the two anticorruption campaigns suggest the importance of having an undisputed successor to the incumbent. Macapagal Arroyo as vice president to Estrada also led the dominant opposition and, thus, worked to minimize competition among the disparate groups in the anticorruption movement. Having a clear path to succession also removed the uncertainty of an extra-parliamentary political transition, making the "resign, impeach, or oust" call more palatable to risk-averse groups, especially the military establishment. Finally, being the clear beneficiary of an anticorruption campaign, a successor could be expected to invest in its success. As early as April 2000, Macapagal Arroyo began holding public consultations on the political situation around the country, and, in October, after resigning as Estrada's social welfare and development secretary, publicly took up the cudgels for the parliamentary opposition and began forming a shadow cabinet (Rodell 2002). In November, a National Day of Protests saw opposition party figures led by Macapagal Arroyo and left political groups at the frontlines.

The second factor that distinguished the anti-Estrada campaign from that against Macapagal Arroyo was the role that partisan politics played in the impeachment case. The speed with which the House of Representatives dispensed with the impeachment complaints was revealing. The Lower House arrived at its decision to endorse Estrada's impeachment on November 14, 2000, just a little over a month after the October 12 filing of the complaint. Each of the eleven complaints social movement activists and opposition figures filed against Macapagal Arroyo were dealt with just as quickly. It took merely a month or so for the Lakas-dominated House of Representatives to approve the impeachment complaint against Estrada and reject those against Macapagal Arroyo. The haste with which complaints against a sitting president was decided suggests that politics rather than justice drove the trials.

To better understand the speed with which the House resolved these complaints, one needs to also take into account the balance of power in Congress during those periods: in the 1998 elections, Estrada's popularity

with the masses helped win the day for him but not his party, the fledg-
ling Partido ng Masang Pilipino, while Macapagal Arroyo, who ran under
the outgoing President Fidel Ramos's political party, Lakas, inherited the
established campaign machinery that had dominated the 1998 congressional elections. Significantly, the exposé on the textbook scam linked to
the Estrada administration broke when it was investigating the overpriced
Centennial Expo Pilipino Project in Clark Airbase, allegedly linked to the
Ramos administration and the Lakas fundraising efforts for the 1998 elections (Florentino-Hofilena and Sayson 1999; Mendoza 2001). After EDSA
2, when the Estrada-aligned opposition took its turn to file impeachment
cases against Macapagal Arroyo, based on the alleged illegal use of public
funds to ensure the administration party's victory in the 2001 and 2004
elections, it had to contend with Congress being dominated by those
who likely benefited from such illegal fundraising activities. Eventually,
however, the main bases of the Aquino III administration's plunder case
against Macapagal Arroyo laid mainly on the 2004 incident.

In fact, the pursuit of corrupt government officials closely followed
party lines that also hewed to patronal networks of national politicians,
especially those linked to the administration. For instance, in investigating a series of pork barrel scams starting in 2013, in which government
officials had channeled millions of pesos of public funds to bogus nongovernmental organizations, the Ombudsman focused on three leading
opposition figures.[11] That emphasis raised questions regarding the office's
impartiality, in light of allegations that members of the ruling Liberal Party
were culpable as well (Go 2013; Placido 2014). Regardless, in his last State
of the Nation Address in 2015, Aquino cited the plunder cases against
and detention of Macapagal Arroyo and the three opposition senators as
proof of his administration's pursuit of justice (Cayabyab 2015).

Nevertheless, trends since 2000 have shown that justice has been
selective, reinforcing the personalistic nature of anticorruption campaigns.
Specifically, impeachment has provided a way to replace high-ranking
individuals without having to wait for the end of their constitutionally
prescribed term of office. Since EDSA 2, ruling political elites have sought
to impeach or remove through other legal processes Supreme Court justices and the Ombudsman in charge of the prosecution of anticorruption
cases at the Sandiganbayan. While corrupt practices or poor performance
have been cited as the bases for the removal of prosecutors or judges,
their identification with the previous administration also weighed heavily against them. Analyses of the outcome of plunder cases usually take

into account who appointed the presiding judge (Mangahas and Ilagan 2011; Rufo 2014; Santos 2014). This widely held impression of partisan bias has caused the Supreme Court and anticorruption special bodies to come under fire. Under Aquino III, impeachment cases were filed against Macapagal Arroyo appointees Ombudsman Merceditas Gutierrez and Supreme Court Chief Justice Renato Corona. Gutierrez resigned after the Lower House endorsed her case to the Senate for the trial; Corona chose to fight it out and thus became the first official to be actually convicted by the Senate.[12]

Since Corona's case set a precedent, it deserves a closer reading. In this case, the deliberation and decision-making in the Lower House took only one day: on December 12, 2011, the House endorsed the Articles of Impeachment against the chief justice. A poorly crafted eight-point Articles of Impeachment revolving around the Supreme Court's alleged track record of pro-Macapagal Arroyo decisions and the chief justice's failure to declare a reported PhP200 million worth of property in his Statement of Assets, Liabilities, and Net Worth (SALN) reflected the House's haste (Chua 2012; Meruenas 2016). In the end, after three months of deliberation, twenty senator-judges voted in May 2012 to convict Corona largely on the basis of the SALN misdeclaration (Rappler 2012). That said, two points need to be factored into what the Aquino administration hailed as a win against corruption. First, the main protagonists were a president whose 6,453-hectare family estate was about to be distributed to its tenant farmers under the Comprehensive Agrarian Reform Program, as approved by the Supreme Court, and a chief justice who shepherded this landmark ruling through just two weeks before impeachment proceedings began;[13] and, second, PhP6.5 billion from the president's discretionary funds were reportedly released to lawmakers for their pet projects before and after the impeachment proceedings.[14]

As these trends imply, recent anticorruption campaigns' focus on going after erring individuals through impeachment could very easily play into longstanding rivalries among political elites, the families of whom came into wealth by gaming the system (some earlier than others) and who are thus equally vested in money politics. As anticorruption activists channel campaigns more and more toward the parliamentary arena, these campaigns are more easily co-opted by the ruling elites. As such, while the militant political movements, especially from the left, led the street protests against Estrada and Macapagal Arroyo, by the time the

campaigns peaked, the loudest voices came from those occupying the highest positions in the land.

The Politics of Anticorruption Campaigns

It has been argued that the ouster of Estrada in 2001 is a testament to the critical role anticorruption campaigns can play in bringing about more accountable leadership in the Philippines. That the 2001 anti-Estrada mobilization actually produced an EDSA 2 scenario only adds to popular views of the potency of the corruption issue to effect regime change.

In this sense, the successful anticorruption campaign in 2001 has been likened to the 1986 People Power revolution, today more commonly known as EDSA 1. Like EDSA 1, the anti-Estrada campaign was able to successfully mobilize a wide section of the political spectrum for protest activities, using the mass media, legal and parliamentary processes, street rallies and marches, and agitation among the security forces. Establishing the link, too, between these two historic events was the participation of key EDSA 1 figures—former presidents Corazon Aquino and Fidel Ramos and Archbishop Jaime Cardinal Sin—as leading members of the EDSA 2 coalition. Moreover, both movements' success was facilitated by their narrow target to unseat the incumbent. That the 2001 anticorruption campaign took less than three years to effect a transfer of power may be attributed to the 1986 movement experience having become part of the country's collective action repertoire (Davis and Zald 2005). All told, the 2001 experience solidified what has become an EDSA blueprint for regime change.

Yet, latter-day EDSA-inspired movements, including the anticorruption campaign against Macapagal Arroyo, have differed from the prototype in a fundamental way. While EDSAs 1 and 2 were both largely anchored in charges of grave abuse of power and corruption and greatly benefited from the participation of the upper classes (Davis and Zald 2005; Hedman 2006), EDSA 1 led to a change in form of rule, while EDSA 2's main accomplishment was Estrada's replacement. This difference may be partly explained by the fact that the anticorruption campaign that contributed to Marcos's ouster was grafted on a fourteen-year struggle to end authoritarian rule. Moreover, because power is highly centralized in a dictatorship, even a personalistic campaign focused on unseating the incumbent can shake the foundation of this form of rule. In contrast, an anticorruption campaign aimed at ousting the incumbent can work within the logic of a well-established elite democracy. Such campaigns are akin to surgical strikes aimed at neutralizing political figures while deflecting attention to the need to reform the political system in which corruption operates. This would explain why anticorruption campaigns are relatively easy to transform into likely electoral vehicles for oligarchs.

Having failed to link the problem of corruption to deeper issues that ail the system, EDSA-patterned campaigns that went after the highest officials of the land seem to have mainly worked to strengthen the executive power of those who have risen to take their place. As such, in a country that has experienced two so-called EDSA revolutions aimed at making the government more accountable and that has an extensive anticorruption legal system, corruption remains high.

The anticorruption literature has yet to fully address the disconnect between anticorruption initiatives or campaigns and their outcomes. For instance, a World Bank study that argues for the need to situate anticorruption measures in the specific country's "governance environment" nevertheless gives textbook recommendations that can be summed up in three points: increase public involvement in governance, strengthen anticorruption bodies, and reduce government size (Bhargava and Bolongaita 2004, 34–35). In fact, it would seem that much of the "good governance" agenda is influenced by the structural functionalist approach, which focuses on drawing up ways to make formal organizations and administrative processes more accountable and transparent; where this approach fails— say, in cases of state capture—the default setting has been to recommend government downsizing to minimize opportunities for corruption (35).

Such an approach, however, cannot explain how EDSA 2 could produce an administration that would come to be accused of being more corrupt than the last. In keeping with how she came to power, Macapagal Arroyo set up various anticorruption bodies, notably, the Presidential Anti-Graft Commission (PAGC), aimed at monitoring and investigating presidential appointees, and the government–civil society Governance Advisory Council. It was during her term that Congress passed the Anti-Money Laundering Act and Government Procurement Reform Act. Her track record, however, was no different from that of those who came before and would come after her. A close study of executive decrees since the 1950s reveals that among the first acts of each incoming president has been to replace the anticorruption mechanisms set up by the previous administration with their own, partly to trumpet their anticorruption credentials. These anticorruption mechanisms have also been used to go after the previous regime and their economic allies, even when doing so has proved damaging to the economy as a whole (Raquiza 2012, 83).

On the other hand, while the social movement literature provides us with the analytical tools to understand the ebbs and flows of anticorruption protests, it does not fully explain the divergent outcomes of similarly inspired protests. Here, comparing the anticorruption campaigns against Estrada and Macapagal Arroyo proves instructive. Both campaigns were patterned after EDSA 1, but a comparative analysis of the two movements reveals that traditional politics rather than social movement dynamics prevailed. The present study, thus, suggests that Estrada proved a much easier target because he was an "outsider," that is, he did not command established lines of patronage. Even as the anti-Estrada campaign culminated with a massive demonstration at the EDSA shrine, it was the wheeling and dealing in Congress that proved critical to the final act.

The proprietary polity model also calls attention to additional factors that structural-functional and social movement theories leave out: the social bases and politics of two sets of state elites who get involved in anticorruption campaigns, whether as the accusers or the accused. These sets of elites are the political leadership and the heads of bureaucratic offices, whom the proprietary polity model disaggregates as a heuristic device, in order to more fully discern the different interests that drive state elites' participation in anticorruption campaigns. As discussed earlier, both the political leadership and heads of bureaucratic offices (including the technocracy) originate from outside state institutions. Under a proprietary polity, the political leadership rises to power by virtue of their personal or family wealth and social networks, while those who head technocratic or legal bodies are recruited from the incumbent's social network and are appointed based on their professional record and, at least equally as much, their political connections.

By stressing the social foundations of political power, the concept of proprietary polity shares a view of elite rule with Benedict Anderson's (1988) framework of "cacique democracy" or Paul Hutchcroft's (1998) "oligarchic patrimonialism": the country's political leadership merges class and political power. The proprietary polity concept, however, also takes into account the deep cleavages or splits among state elites that explain the persistence of personalistic rule. On the one hand, since most of the country's top politicians come from second- and third-generation political families (Mendoza et al. 2012), many have been raised to regard public office as an entitlement or a birthright and source of personal and family wealth—a situation that makes political contestations extremely personal. At the same time, many of those occupying top posts in the state apparatus have been known to engage in partisan politicking. Lacking strong political parties or any other institutional mechanisms to mediate among competing political elites, political contestations easily cross over to the state bureaucracy, with presidential appointees' being mobilized or affected in the process.

This institutional setting explains why anticorruption campaigns in the country are most potent when they focus on erring individuals rather than push for institutional reforms. In fact, since 1987, individual lawmakers, working with prodemocracy activists, have filed different versions of the freedom of information, election-campaign financing, and (needless to say) anti-dynasty bills but have had little success in sustaining a national conversation around them. Partly, this is due to the lack of interest of the executive branch to mobilize resources to get these bills passed. In contrast, anticorruption campaigns, targeting high-profile political figures, play into partisan politics that translates into career-making headlines.

Unfortunately, narrow anticorruption campaigns that are not linked to a comprehensive critique of the system will only further strengthen personalistic rule, especially of those whom the campaign stands to benefit. As EDSA 2 and its aftermath show, in their haste to remove erring individuals, Congress took shortcuts in legal procedures—all of which weakened institutions previously established to promote rule of law and check abuse of power. This sloppiness is true as well of cases against top officials in constitutional commissions and the judiciary, including the Supreme Court. The implications of these could be seen in the rise of President Rodrigo Duterte: being from the southern island of Mindanao, he lost no time in securing his hold on national power by going after top Aquino III appointees, notably then Supreme Court Chief Justice Maria Lourdes Sereno, as well as known EDSA 2 business and media critics who, for one reason or another, are vulnerable legally.

All in all, since EDSA 2, the Philippines has witnessed discretionary executive power grow under the guise of ridding the government of corruption. Current trends suggest that not only is the proprietary polity thriving, but also that without correcting personalistic rule, anticorruption campaigns may strengthen arbitrary and authoritarian tendencies in elite politics.

What does this pattern say to movement activists? Just as the proprietary polity model raises distinct analytical puzzles for researchers, it also suggests implications for anticorruption activists' consideration. The anticorruption campaigns targeting individuals—using means ranging from impeachment to an EDSA-patterned ouster—reinforce the impression that in a country that continues to be wracked by communist and Islamic insurgencies and where poverty leads to corruption (perhaps more so than the reverse), regime change is possible, with minimal costs to oligarchic rule. Targeting erring officials, especially those located at the pinnacle of power, has been effective in building broad coalitions between the left and the right, and between progressive movements and conservative forces. Nevertheless, such coalitions also tend to minimize more structural issues that contribute to poverty *and* corruption.

In this connection, the impeachment of Supreme Court Chief Justice Corona in 2011 stands out as the quintessential case of an anticorruption campaign that sends mixed signals. It serves as a cautionary tale for justices who—like perhaps almost everyone else in the system—have unexplained wealth but who also, for whatever reason, would rule in favor of landless farmers against landed politicians. In this light, movement activists with a broad reform agenda need to be aware of the trade-offs of carrying out narrowly conceived single-issue campaigns. Anticorruption campaigns have natural constituencies among members of the middle and upper classes worried about waste, inefficiencies, and extra-economic burdens on business activities. For this reason, they easily provide opportunities for broad and multiclass alliances that can put movement actors in alliances with big business and traditional politicians (both groups of which control significant mobilization resources). This very broadness, however, is anchored on activists accepting partners with essentially conservative outlooks and interests. As such, working in such coalitions to be more effective can pull activists away from progressive politics and from supporting members of their base who depend on movement work to change the material conditions of their lives.

Indeed, from a proprietary polity perspective, what would need to happen to curb corruption in high places is to establish institutional constraints on executive power at different levels of governance, rather than to contribute to strengthening the hands of those whom such campaigns have catapulted to power. In this light, there is a need to set up enduring alliances that would push for institutional reforms, including the building of strong political parties.

Notes

1. A 2010 study identified fourteen anticorruption flagship committees established by past presidents from Quirino to Macapagal Arroyo (Balboa and Medalla 2010). Aquino's Presidential Truth Commission followed this tradition, although it was struck down as unconstitutional by a Supreme Court decision because, unlike other presidential bodies, it was set up solely to investigate Macapagal Arroyo. Significantly, in 2010, Aquino also appointed as head of the Truth Commission former chief justice Davide, who swore in Macapagal Arroyo as president at the EDSA shrine in 2001, replacing Estrada. At the same time, the media noted that Macapagal Arroyo appointees dominated the High Court.

2. To illustrate, one news report drew attention to the "one-year syndrome" among appointees in the Supreme Court and Sandiganbayan and noted that, of the Sandiganbayan justices in 2014, one had been appointed by Joseph Estrada, ten by Macapagal Arroyo, and four by Aquino III (Rufo 2014). Regarding political factors for the Office of the Ombudsman's low conviction rate since 1989, see Mangahas and Ilagan (2011).

3. One study on social movements and the convergence of domestic and global corporate interests in times of political transitions said of Philippine business in the months leading up to EDSA 2: "Directors of the five largest Philippine business groups met in October . . . and generated a plan to induce Estrada's resignation. . . . Actions included mass walkouts from the stock exchange by traders wearing black armbands, and a free catered 'People Power Lunch' to bring laborers and the rural poor into Manila's business district and thus increase the perceived inclusiveness of the anti-Estrada coalition" (Davis and Zald 2005, 341).

4. For the impeachment complaint, see Supreme Court (2001).

5. See Supreme Court (2001) for details on how EDSA 2 played out in relation to the impeachment process, and on the constitutionality of Macapagal Arroyo's assumption of the presidency.

6. Anomalous deals that were linked to the first family and cabinet members included, in 2003, the rehabilitation of the Caliraya-Botocan-Kalayaan hydroelectric plant in Laguna, involving an Argentinian firm, the construction of the Ninoy Aquino International Airport 3, and a deal involving a Philippine private corporation and a German firm (Coronel 2005); and in 2007, a deal between the National Broadband Network and a Chinese firm (GMA 2007).

7. Some of the leaders of the Magdalo participated in EDSA 1. See PCIJ (2006).

8. For more details on the "Hello Garci Tape" scandal, see de Guzman (2011).

9. See, for instance, a statement by business associations and economic think tanks that criticized the passage of the House Resolution No. 1109, which would set up the process for charter change; the signatories called instead for the holding of clean elections in 2010 (Makati Business Club et al. 2009).

10. In calling for Macapagal Arroyo's resignation, the heads of Makati Business Club and Financial Executives Institute of the Philippines wrote: "A transition must now take place following our Constitutional processes of succession. We reiterate our view that all moves for change must take place firmly within the context of our Constitution" (Romulo and Salazar 2005).

11. The three senators are Macapagal Arroyo's party mate Ramon "Bong" Revilla Jr. and Estrada's political ally, Juan Ponce Enrile, and son, Jose "Jinggoy" Estrada.

12. Contrary to the popular narrative, Estrada and Gutierrez were impeached but not convicted. The impeachment trial against Estrada at the Senate was cut short by EDSA 2, while Gutierrez simply resigned after the House of Representatives ruled in favor of the impeachment complaint.

13. On November 22, 2011, just before the impeachment complaint was filed in the lower house, the Supreme Court, led by Corona, ruled in favor of distributing land to the tenants of Hacienda Luisita, the sugar estate of the family of Aquino III's mother, former president Corazon Cojuangco Aquino (Meruenas 2012). For a history of Hacienda Luisita, see Dychiu (2010).

Corona's impeachment allowed Aquino to appoint the chief justice. He did so by elevating to the post one of his appointees to the high bench, Maria Lourdes Sereno. While Sereno's appointment was celebrated as she became the country's first woman chief justice, not a few noted that she also was among those who dissented from the Supreme Court majority ruling of giving the Cojuangcos a lower land-valuation compensation package (see Meruenas and Geronimo 2012). Fast forward to May 2018 under the term of President Rodrigo Duterte: Sereno herself was ousted as chief magistrate when her colleagues in the Supreme Court ruled in favor of a quo warranto plea from the solicitor general and declared her appointment as associate justice in 2010 invalid on account of gaps in her SALN filings (see Supreme Court 2018).

14. As reported, the Aquino administration distributed the funds from its Disbursement Acceleration Program (DAP), giving members of the Lower House P5 billion and senators about P1.5 billion (Cabacungan 2014).

Bibliography

Anderson, Benedict. *The Spectre of Comparisons: Nationalism, Southeast Asia, and the World*. London: Verso, 1998.

Añonuevo, Carlito, Jenina Joy Chavez, Prospero J. De Vera, Alvin Firmeza, Jose Ernesto Ledesma, Nepomuceno Malaluan, Ma. Cristina Morales, Rene Ofreneo, Rene Raya, Jessica Reyes-Cantos, and Filomeno Sta. Ana III Action for Economic Reforms and Friends. "The CODE-NGO PEACE Bonds: A Case of Impermissible Rent-Seeking." Action for Economic Reforms,

January 2002. Retrieved from http://aer.ph/the-code-ngo-peace-bonds-a-case-of-impermissible-rent-seeking/.

Arugay, Aries. "Mobilizing for Accountability: Contentious Politics in the Anti-Estrada Campaign." *Philippine Sociological Review* 52 (2004): 75–96.

Balboa, Jenny, and Erlinda M. Medalla. "Anticorruption and Good Governance: the Philippine Experience." *Development Research News* 28, no. 6 (2010): 1–9.

Batalla, Eric. "De-institutionalizing Corruption in the Philippines: Identifying Strategic Requirements for Reinventing Institutions," 2000. Retrieved from http://unpan1.un.org/intradoc/groups/public/documents/APCITY/UNPAN 013117.pdf.

Bello, Walden, with Herbert Docena, Marissa de Guzman, and Marylou Malig. *The Development State: The Political Economy of Permanent Crisis in the Philippines.* London: Zed Books, 2005.

Bhargava, Vinay, and Emil Bolongaita, eds. *Challenging Corruption in Asia: Case Studies and a Framework for Action.* Washington, DC: The International Bank for Reconstruction and Development / The World Bank, 2004.

Bueza, Michael. "Plunder Cases in the Philippines: Was Anyone Punished?" *Rappler,* February 18, 2017. Retrieved from https://www.rappler.com/move-ph/issues/corruption/161476-plunder-cases-philippines-status-convictions.

Cabacungan, Gil C. "Solons Got P5B in DAP during Impeachment Trial of Corona." *Philippine Daily Inquirer,* February 24, 2014.

Carino, Ledivina V. *Bureaucracy for Democracy: The Dynamics of Executive-Bureaucracy Interaction during Governmental Transitions.* Quezon City: College of Public Administration, University of the Philippines, 1992.

Cayabyab, Marc Jayson. "Sona: Aquino Touts Detention of Arroyo, Enrile, Revilla, Estrada." *Philippine Daily Inquirer,* July 27, 2015.

Chavez, Lei. "Scandals." *ABS-CBN News,* July 18, 2009, and January 18, 2010. Retrieved from http://news.abs-cbn.com/special-report/07/17/09/scandals.

Chua, Ryan. "The Corona Trial: A Summary." *ABS-CBN News,* January 15–16, 2012. Retrieved from http://news.abs-cbn.com/-depth/01/15/12/corona-trial-summary.

Coronel, Sheila S. "The Unmaking of a President." 2001. Retrieved from http://pcij.org/blog/wp-docs/The_Unmaking_of_a_President2.pdf.

Coronel, Sheila S. "The unmaking of the President." *i Report,* July 1, 2005. Retrieved from http://pcij.org/stories/the-unmaking-of-the-president/.

Cruz, Elfren S. "The Vice Presidency: Looking Back." *Philippine Star,* May 29, 2016, 29.

Davis, Gerald F., and Mayer N. Zald. "Social Change, Social Theory, and the Convergence of Movements and Organizations." In *Social Movements and Organization Theory,* edited by Gerald F. Davis, Doug McAdam, W. Richard Scott, and Mayer N. Zald, 335–350. Cambridge: Cambridge University Press, 2005.

de Guzman, Laurence. "What Went Before: 'Hello Garci Scandal' Investigation." *Philippine Daily Inquirer*, July 22, 2011.

Doronila, Amando, ed. *Between Fires: Fifteen Perspectives on the Estrada Crisis.* Pasig City: Anvil, 2001.

Dychiu, Stephanie. "Hacienda Luisita's Past Haunts Noynoy's Future." *GMA News Online*, January 18, 2010. Retrieved from http://www.gmanetwork.com/news/news/specialreports/181877/hacienda-luisita-s-past-haunts-noynoy-s-future/story/.

Economist Intelligence Unit (EIU). *Country Report: The Philippines.* 1st quarter. London: Economist Intelligence Unit, 1999.

Florentino-Hofilena, Chay, and Ian Sayson. "Centennial Expo: Convenient Cover for Election Fundraising." Philippine Center for Investigative Journalism, June 14–16, 1999. Retrieved from http://archive.is/iiU1#selection-53.0-458.2.

Freedom from Debt Coalition (FDC). "Position Paper: On the PEACe Bonds." December 7, 2011. Retrieved from http://fdc.ph/news/12-features/91-position-paper-on-the-peace-bonds.

GMA News Online. "ZTE Controversy Timeline." September 18, 2007. Retrieved from http://www.gmanetwork.com/news/news/content/61035/zte-controversy-timeline/story/.

GMA News Online. "Controversies Involving First Gentleman Jose Miguel Arroyo." February 8, 2009. Retrieved from http://www.gmanetwork.com/news/news/content/147857/controversies-involving-first-gentleman-jose-miguel-arroyo/story/.

Go, Miriam Grace A. "Macapagal Boulevard: Who's Accountable?" News Break Archives, November 11, 2002. Retrieved from http://archives.newsbreak-knowledge.ph/2002/11/11/macapagal-boulevard-whos-accountable/.

Gonzalez, Eduardo T., and Magdalena L. Mendoza. "Anticorruption Initiatives in the Philippines: Breakthroughs, Limits, and Challenges." In *Challenging Corruption in Asia: Case Studies and a Framework for Action*, edited by Vinay Bhargava and Emil Bolongaita, 77–133. Washington, DC: The International Bank for Reconstruction and Development / The World Bank, 2004.

Hedman, Eva-Lotta. *In the Name of Civil Society: From Free Election Movements to People Power in the Philippines.* Honolulu: University of Hawai'i Press, 2006.

Hutchcroft, Paul D. *Booty Capitalism: The Politics of Banking in the Philippines.* Ithaca: Cornell University Press, 1998.

Makati Business Club, Management Association of the Philippines, Financial Executives Institute of the Philippines, Action for Economic Reforms, and the Foundation for Economic Freedom. "Joint Statement on House Resolution No. 1109." June 9, 2009. Retrieved from http://aer.ph/joint-statement-on-house-resolution-no-1109-2/.

Mangahas, Malou. "Can President Arroyo Explain Her Wealth? Gloria Gets Richer Fastest, Beats Cory, Ramos, Erap." August 9, 2009. Retrieved from http://pcij.org/stories/gloria-gets-richer-fastest-beats-cory-ramos-erap/.

Mangahas, Malou, and Karol Anne M. Ilagan. "4 Ombudsman, 4 Failed Crusades vs. Corruption." Philippine Center for Investigative Journalism, 2011a. Retrieved from https://pcij.org/stories/4-ombudsmen-4-failed-crusades-vs-corruption/.

Mangahas, Malou, and Karol Anne M. Ilagan. "After 22 Years, Who's afraid of the Ombudsman?" *GMA News Online*, March 1, 2011b. Retrieved from http://www.gmanetwork.com/news/news/specialreports/214165/after-22-years-who-s-afraid-of-the-ombudsman/story/.

McCoy, Alfred, ed. *An Anarchy of Families: State and Family in the Philippines.* Madison: University of Wisconsin Center for Southeast Asian Studies, 1993.

Mendoza, Amado M., Jr. "The Industrial Anatomy of Corruption: Government Procurement, Bidding, and Award of Contracts." *Public Policy* 5, no. 1 (2001): 43–71.

Mendoza, Ronald U., Edsel L. Beja Jr., Victor S. Venida, and David B. Yap. "Inequality in Democracy: Insights from an Empirical Analysis of Political Dynasties in the 15th Philippine Congress." *Philippine Political Science Journal* 33, no. 2 (2012): 132–145.

Meruenas, Mark. "Corona: They Want My Head over P10-B Stake in Luisita." *GMA News Online*, March 7, 2012. Retrieved from http://www.gmanetwork.com/news/news/nation/250580/corona-they-want-my-head-over-p10-b-stake-in-luisita/story/.

Meruenas, Mark. "Ex-CJ Corona Championed Agrarian Reform." *GMA News Online*, April 29, 2016. Retrieved from http://www.gmanetwork.com/news/news/nation/564435/ex-cj-corona-championed-agrarian-reform/story/.

Meruenas, Mark, and Gian Geronimo. "PNoy Names Sereno New Chief Justice." *GMA News Online*, August 24, 2012. Retrieved from http://www.gmanetwork.com/news/news/nation/271066/pnoy-names-sereno-new-chief-justice/story/.

Møller, Lars, and Jack Jackson. "Journalistic Legwork That Tumbled a President: A Case Study and Guide for Investigative Journalists." World Bank Institute, 2002.

Nawaz, Farzana. "Overview of Corruption and Anti-Corruption in the Philippines." 2008.

Philippine Center for Investigative Journalism (PCIJ). "The First Family Shame and Scandal in the Family." *i Report*, 2005. Retrieved from http://pcij.org/stories/shame-and-scandal-in-the-family/.

Philippine Center for Investigative Journalism (PCIJ). "Three Generations of Military Rebels." *PCIJ Blog*, February 24, 2006. Retrieved from http://pcij.org/blog/2006/02/24/three-generations-of-military-rebels.

Philippine Center for Investigative Journalism (PCIJ). "Sandiganbayan Files: 256 Poll Winners Have Graft, Crime Cases; 17 Convicted." June 10, 2013.

Retrieved from http://pcij.org/stories/sandiganbayan-files-256-poll-winners-have-graft-crime-cases-17-convicted/.

Placido, Dharel. "Drilon Included in Sandra Cam's 'Pork Scam' List." *ABS-CBNnews. com*, May 16, 2014. Retrieved from http://news.abs-cbn.com/nation/05/16/14/drilon-included-sandra-cams-pork-scam-list.

Quah, Jon S. T. "Corruption in Asian Countries: Can It Be Minimized?" *Public Administration Review* 59, no. 6 (1999): 483–494.

Quimpo, Nathan. "The Philippines: Political Parties and Corruption." *Southeast Asian Affairs* (2007): 277–294.

Rappler. "Corona Found Guilty, Removed from Office." *Rappler*, May 29 and July 2, 2012. Retrieved from https://www.rappler.com/nation/special-coverage/corona-trial/6099-corona-found-guilty.

Raquiza, Antoinette. *State Structure, Policy Formation, and Economic Development in Southeast Asia: The Political Economy of Thailand and the Philippines.* London: Routledge, 2012.

Reyes, Alejandro, and Kristina Luz. "The Elites vs. Estrada." *Asiaweek.com*, November 11, 2000. Retrieved from https://edition.cnn.com/ASIANOW/asiaweek/magazine/2000/1117/nat.philippines.html.

Rivera, Temario C. "The Middle Class and Democratization in the Philippines: From the Asian Crisis to the Ouster of Estrada." In *Southeast Asian Middle Classes: Prospects for Social Change and Democratisation*, edited by Abdul Rahman Embong, 230–261. Bangi: Penerbit Universiti Kebangsaan Malaysia, 2011.

Rodell, Paul A. "The Philippines: Gloria in Excelsis." In *Southeast Asian Affairs 2002*, edited by Daljit Singh and Anthony L. Smith, 215–236. Singapore: Institute of Southeast Asian Studies, 2002.

Romulo, Ricardo J., and Melito S. Salazar Jr. "Time for Change." July 8, 2005. Retrieved from http://pcij.org/blog/wp-docs/MBCFinex.pdf.

Rose-Ackerman, Susan. *Corruption and Government: Causes, Consequences, and Reform.* Cambridge, UK: Cambridge University Press, 1999.

Rufo, Aries. "How Will Sandigan Justices Handle Plunder Cases?" *Rappler*, August 16, 2014. Retrieved from https://www.rappler.com/newsbreak/66392-sandiganbayan-justices-plunder-cases.

Santos, Reynaldo Jr. "Get to Know the Anti-Graft Court Sandiganbayan." *Rappler*, June 14, 2014. Retrieved from https://www.rappler.com/newsbreak/iq/60572-know-sandiganbayan-graft-plunder.

Simbulan, Dante. *The Modern Principalia: The Historical Evolution of the Philippine Ruling Oligarchy.* Quezon City: University of the Philippines Press, 2005.

Supreme Court, Philippines. G. R. Nos. 146710-15. March 2, 2001. Retrieved from http://www.chanrobles.com/cralawscdecisionestradavsarroyo2001.htm#.WlqhIVWYOL0.

Supreme Court, Philippines. G. R. No. 237428. May 11, 2018. Retrieved from sc.judiciary.gov.ph/jurisprudence/2018/may2018/237428_jardeleza.pdf.

Tubeza, Philip. "5 Senators Launch 'Gloria Resign Movement.'" *Philippine Daily Inquirer*, April 5, 2006.

2

Fighting Corruption When Corruption Is Pervasive

The Case of Indonesia

Edward Aspinall

How do anticorruption movements operate in conditions in which corruption is not simply pervasive but where it is critical to the personal and organizational relationships that structure political and economic life? This chapter addresses this question by discussing the case of Indonesia, a country where it has long been recognized that corruption is endemic and deeply embedded within the political system and in wider political, social, and economic relationships. As we shall see, opposition to corruption in Indonesia has also been widespread, having become a more or less permanent feature of Indonesian politics over several decades. At times, it has galvanized mass movements, including several waves of student protest in the 1970s, as well as the massive *reformasi* protests of 1998 that actually succeeded in ending the rule of President Suharto, up to that point one of the world's most successful and resilient authoritarian leaders. In post-Suharto Indonesia, despite numerous institutional reforms aimed at rooting it out, corruption has remained pervasive. So too has collective action aimed at fighting it, though street mobilizations aiming at regime change have been replaced by a myriad of forms of action that are arguably both more piecemeal, insofar as they tend to focus on particular sites or sources of corruption, and more systematic, insofar as they aim to address root causes of corruption, not merely symptoms. Despite the great visibility of anticorruption activism, the ubiquity of anticorruption discourse, the new anticorruption institutions, and the many successes they have recorded, it is questionable whether the overall quantum of corruption in Indonesia has significantly declined.

The problem for anticorruption activists in a country like Indonesia, put simply, is the enormity of the task that confronts them. The centrality of corrupt exchanges and personal favors to so many political relationships, including those connecting the political class to both the state and private economy, makes it hard to pick targets: How to prioritize when almost everyone in a position of authority is involved in corruption of one form or another? When corrupt relationships also pervade the law enforcement agencies upon which the eradication of corruption must ultimately depend, it can be equally hard to confidently propose remedies in the form of investigations and punishment of corrupt actors, precisely because legal processes themselves can become vulnerable to political intervention or corruption. The (at least partially) hidden nature of corruption also makes social movement alliance building problematic. Rather than targeting a particular policy change, or aiming to bring down a particular government or leader, corruption eradication ultimately requires a thorough remaking of the entire pattern of state behavior. In conditions in which much of the population also participates in, or at least accedes to, corrupt exchanges, it also requires changes in social norms. In such circumstances, corruption is so intractable because "it is frequently more convenient for individuals to try to accede to the privileged group or to become clients of influential patrons than to engage in a long-term battle to change the rule of the game to ethical universalism" (Mungiu-Pippidi 2015, 184). A suboptimal equilibrium where particularism feeds on itself is reached, and "attempts to change this are bound to have high costs with few immediate returns" (Mungiu-Pippidi 2015, 184; see also Persson, Rothstein, and Teorell 2013). Such circumstances have perverse consequences for anticorruption movements. The pervasiveness *and* the hidden nature of corruption mean that social movement actors find it difficult to discern between allies and opponents, such that fighting corruption through conventional social movement modes is sometimes akin to progressing through a hall of mirrors.

In order to explore this broader phenomenon, this chapters zeroes in on variation across time and form in anticorruption movements in Indonesia. During the Suharto period (1966–1998), public opposition to corruption was typically bound up with opposition to the ruling establishment. Accordingly, anticorruption protests were episodic, mobilizational in style, and anti-regime. Most notably, the anti-Suharto movement of 1998 made condemnation of "corruption, collusion and nepotism" a central plank of its appeal. Since that time, though corruption has remained central to Indonesia's political economy, the anticorruption agenda has also been embodied in formal institutions, most obviously through the establishment of a powerful Corruption Eradication Commission (Komisi Pemberantasan Korupsi, KPK) and a specialist anticorruption court. The changed institutional setting and the new enforcement regime have dramatically affected the space available for, and the shape of, anticorruption activism in civil society.

Overall, therefore, the broad arc of the struggle to control corruption in Indonesia fits into what is described in this volume as an anticorruption effort driven by political institutionalization. Both during and since the transition to the post-Suharto era, reformers have sought both to reshape the basic structures of the regime so as to reduce opportunities for abuse of office for private gain and to construct new agencies and procedures designed to punish corruption. One of their chief goals has been to make the punishment of corruption rule-based rather than a matter of personal discretion. However, we shall also see that these efforts are frequently obstructed, or hijacked, by private interests seeking to either impede or advance particular cases for personal gain. Though the institution builders have achieved many important victories, it is by no means clear that the balance of forces has tipped decisively in their favor in the post-Suharto period.

Accordingly, the chapter identifies three modes of anticorruption campaigning in the post-Suharto period. The first mode is an investigatory style in which NGOs campaign against corrupt political leaders and public officials, with one major goal being to uncover evidence of malfeasance and feed it to formal enforcement agencies, notably the KPK. The second is a social movement style, involving street protests and social media and conventional media campaigns, through which NGOs, students, and other groups have endeavored to defend the KPK at times when it has been threatened by backlash by forces in the political and law enforcement establishments. As we shall see, private interests have repeatedly tried to obstruct and sabotage the KPK and the broader effort at political institutionalization of an anticorruption ethos it represents. The third manifests as local protest campaigns in which temporary alliances are formed between social movement and formal political actors to bring down corrupt local political leaders. Though an element of institution-alization is visible in these efforts, they also provide considerable scope for penetration by private interests. Before analyzing these varieties of anticorruption activism, however, it is necessary to first set the stage by explaining the broad historic context from which the contemporary anticorruption social movement scene has evolved.

Anticorruption Campaigning
in the Suharto Era and Beyond

Corruption is not an exception but the rule in contemporary Indonesia. Though this situation has deep roots in Indonesia's colonial and even precolonial history, the pervasiveness of corruption is generally dated to the authoritarian "New Order" regime of President Suharto (1966–1998). During this period, officeholders treated their bureaucratic or military positions as being akin to appanages, or grants of land or positions given to junior nobles in a feudal order (Crouch 1979), or to the franchises offered by large corporations (McLeod 2011), using them to extract personal benefits—by skimming money directly from the budgets they controlled or using the political power they possessed to extract informal fees or kickbacks from businesses, bureaucratic subordinates, ordinary citizens, lawbreakers, or others who fell under their ambit—but ensuring that part of the benefit was transferred upward to their bureaucratic and political superiors. The system was highly centralized, with power concentrated on the presidential palace and the major beneficiaries—such as the children and other family members of the president—located near the apex of the pyramid. However, state functionaries and their allies at all levels could access patronage rewards, contributing greatly to the stability of the sys-tem. Ultimately, too, this system facilitated tremendous accumulation of private wealth, helping not only mid-ranking bureaucrats, military officers, and their business partners but, above all, facilitating the emergence of an enormously wealthy oligarchy, who owed their family and individual riches to their links to the state, at the very topmost levels of Indonesian society (Robison and Hadiz 2004.) By the end of the 1990s one obvious result was the great wealth of Suharto's children, other family members, and their business cronies, but in fact similar patterns of accumulation had occurred at all levels of government administration.

It should be noted, however, that this situation was to some of Suharto's early supporters a betrayal of the promises upon which his "New Order" regime had been established in 1966. Suharto's military regime had been legitimated during its early years by a movement of students, middle-class intellectuals, and others who had condemned the "feudal" nature of the predecessor Sukarno regime and hoped for a more rational and rule-based order (Raillon 1989). As time passed, and evidence mounted that corruption had not been eradicated but was in fact growing—including in Suharto's personal circle—corruption became a major issue driving disillusionment with Suharto and his government in middle-class intellectual circles. Early on, in the late 1960s, much of this disillusionment was expressed through the New Order press and by student groups. In response, Suharto formed a "Commission of Four" to look into the corruption problem and report on possible solutions (Mackie 1970). However, the entire logic and stability of the regime depended upon the informal distribution of patronage, ensuring that such efforts were never going to be more than cosmetic.

As students and others began to express their disillusionment more forcibly, the regime responded by becoming more repressive and gradually closing off avenues for lawful expression of dissent. The vanguard of regime critics—students at Jakarta's Universitas Indonesia and other major campuses—became increasingly convinced that corruption was an integral part of how the regime functioned and not merely an aberration. Thus, while, critics of the regime at first adopted a moralizing tone, calling on the rulers to reform their behavior and on Suharto, in particular, to provide proper guidance, by the late 1970s, many student activists, intellectuals, and their allies could see that eradicating or even reducing corruption would require root-and-branch change of the regime. Some began to turn against Suharto himself. Changing attitudes were measured by the changing sobriquets given to Suharto's wife, Tien, nicknamed first "Mrs. Ten Percent," for the cut she allegedly required from major projects, which was later changed to "Madame Fifty-Fifty" (Reeve 2005). A more dramatic sign of the hardening mood among critics was an upsurge of mass student protests in 1973–1974 and 1977–1978, with students during the second period openly calling for Suharto to step down. However, on both occasions the government responded with repression, arresting large numbers of critics and introducing harsh new regulations to prevent a return to protests. By the end of the 1970s, it became all but impossible to frankly discuss the nature and extent of corruption in the public domain.

However, the government's increasing reliance on repression did not prevent subterranean dissemination of anticorruption discourse. Stories about the depredations of high officials, and even the president's family, seeped widely among bureaucrats, intellectuals, and business people, into the wider urban middle classes, and further afield. By the regime's later years, they had become pervasive. The extreme wealth of Indonesia's ruling elite was visible in media depictions of their parties, homes, and hobbies in the popular press or through reports on their latest mega-projects and monopolies in the business pages. Most people saw their gains as ill-gotten. Journalists, intellectuals, and other public figures sometimes expressed muted criticisms of official corruption by using euphemistic language, or by talking about corruption in general terms. In student discussion groups, campus seminars or NGO meetings, it was possible to be much more explicit. From time to time, the government would provide minor concessions to public opinion, prosecuting a minor official for abuse or launching a campaign to promote "simple living" among civil servants.

But precisely because corruption involved the most senior actors in the regime, including the president, his family, and the armed forces leadership, it became impossible to speak frankly and in public about high-level corruption. Doing so would require talking about the political circumstances that caused corruption and so invite repression. As a result, the struggle against corruption became inextricably linked to the putative struggle against the authoritarian regime itself; in the eyes of the government's critics, the goal of eliminating corruption became inextricably linked to the goal of introducing a new kind of political order, one based on popular accountability rather than personal rule. Accordingly, from the late 1980s, there was a shift in the nature of the demands made by the government's most forthright critics: in the 1970s, student protestors had focused on corruption and abuse of power and called for moral rectification; by the 1990s, students and NGOs called for protection of human rights and democratization. This did not mean that they no longer believed corruption was important; rather, it implied that they now realized that a change of regime was necessary (Aspinall 2005).

The Fall of Suharto and the Transition to Democracy

When the Asian financial crisis of 1997–1998 hit Indonesia, the subtext finally became text and opposition to corruption—along with calls for democratization—became *the* rallying cry of the student protests and other mass movements that erupted in early 1998, eventually forcing Suharto out of office in May of that year (McRae 2001). Opposition to corruption was so central to the demands of the 1998 *reformasi* movement in part simply as an expression of long-accumulated grievances: students and others now felt able to voice openly the condemnation of the depredations of the Suharto family and other senior regime leaders that had long circulated in a subterranean fashion. Condemnation of corruption also moved to the center of the demands of the *reformasi* protests because of the way that the financial crisis unfolded. That crisis became particularly severe in Indonesia precisely because the country's economy was so entangled in politics, and with the fate of the president, in particular. Moreover, Suharto's children and other cronies publicly and openly resisted IMF-imposed measures designed to dismantle some of their monopolies and other privileges, worsening capital flight and deepening the economic crisis.

Opposition to "corruption, cronyism and nepotism" was stamped on the new *reformasi* order as a sort of founding credo. All political forces, if they wanted to play an influential role in the post-Suharto order, had to at least claim to be doing whatever they could to advance the anticorruption agenda. This was even the case for groups such as Golkar, the former electoral vehicle of the Suharto regime, which was now rapidly trying to reinvent itself by burnishing its commitment to *reformasi* goals. At the same time, the myriad new social movements thrown up by the tumult of the *reformasi* period was infused with an anticorruption sensibility: organizations founded to advance almost any agenda—labor or land reform, local political reorganization, human rights, to name just some of the obvious examples—incorporated anticorruption themes and campaigns.

However, in the immediate aftermath of the resignation of Suharto in 1998, a *distinctive* anticorruption movement began to cohere, for the first time since the early 1970s. Over preceding decades, the logic of anticorruption politics had tended to draw protagonists toward more generalized anti-regime activism. There had been little point in opposing corruption in isolation when the entire regime was set up in order to enable it. Now that major democratic reforms were finally under way, several major NGOs, such as the Indonesian Legal Aid Foundation (Yayasan Lembaga Bantuan Hukum Indonesia), "refocused their attention so as to address anticorruption issues, to which they had given little emphasis previously" (Setiyono and McLeod 2010, 352). With the foundations for accountable government being laid down through processes of governmental reform, it became a logical and realistic option for activists to establish specialized anticorruption groups. This was part of a general shift in social movement politics, with the anti-Suharto movement dissipating in the aftermath of his removal from power, being replaced by thousands of new varieties of more focused and specialized social movement activism. Numerous liberal and leftist activists now believed that opposition to corruption had to be a strategic priority: they wanted both to ensure that the gross corruption of the Suharto regime would be punished and to root corruption out from the new democratic order—which they could see would be a priority given that so many leading political actors from the Suharto regime were successfully reinventing themselves and maintaining positions of authority and influence in that order.

The main organizational form adopted by the new anticorruption movement was the NGO: a small professional or semi-professional organization with paid staff as well as, typically, volunteers to assist in its activities. In Jakarta, the anticorruption movement became especially professionalized, with the formation of high-profile and specialized anti-corruption organizations, such as Indonesia Corruption Watch (ICW) and Transparency International Indonesia (TII). Well funded by international agencies and led by accomplished NGO activists, lawyers, and other professionals, these groups became "media favorites" and their leaders "national celebrities" (Hsieh 2016, 116). A good part of their public profile resulted from their investigatory work—and their willingness to name public officials involved in corruption scandals and sometimes to expose them by releasing private documents. At the same time, an array of specialist local anticorruption NGOs were formed in the regions, often by former student activists or others who had been engaged in antigov-ernment activism earlier during the democratic transition. In 2001, the Indonesian Society for Transparency (MTI) published a list that indicated that the total number of anticorruption NGOs in Indonesia was 158, with many of these located in regional centers (Hsieh 2016, 130). However, the numbers of such organizations tended to fluctuate, given that, "in many places, CSOs are born and die following changes in socio-political circumstances and in line with the availability of funding" (Setiyono and McLeod 2010, 353). Many of the local groups were certainly much more ad hoc and transitory than the peak organizations in Jakarta, and very often they were little more than loose coalitions of activists who would come together for a particular campaign and then disperse. Moreover, as already alluded to, it should be stressed that one of the key enabling conditions of this flourishing of anticorruption NGOs was the sudden influx into Indonesia of financial support from international development agencies and NGOs for good governance and civil society programs: a large proportion of anticorruption NGOs were funded, directly or indirectly, by foreign donors.

Coinciding and interacting with this changing civil society landscape was an equally rapid evolution of the formal institutional structure for corruption eradication. From the turn of the millennium, successive post-Suharto governments responded to the public pressure by introducing a series of anticorruption reforms. This new institutional context has been described in detail elsewhere (Butt 2012) and can be summarized briefly here. The major reforms can be divided into two categories: first, introduction of new investigatory, punitive, and enforcement institutions that seek to identify and punish wrongdoing; and, second, supply-side interventions that are supposed to reduce opportunities and incentives for corruption by introducing greater transparency and predictability to government and by reducing the scope for exercise of discretionary authority on the part of officials.

With regard to the investigatory and judicial agencies, by far the most important steps were the introduction in 2002 of a Corruption Eradication Commission (KPK) and a specialist Corruption Criminal Court (Tipikor, Pengadilan Tindak Pidana Korupsi). Armed with special investigatory and prosecutorial powers, with well-paid staff operating under a strict code of ethics, the KPK was bound by special rules that were designed to ensure it conducted its investigatory role with zeal (for example, once it had declared an official investigation and named a suspect, the KPK was required to proceed to prosecution—removing the possibility of suspending the investigation in exchange for bribes, a technique frequently used by police and prosecutors—to considerable profit). Over subsequent years, the KPK amazed and titillated the Indonesian public with a series of dramatic arrests and trials of high-ranking politicians and officials, including several ministers, the head of the largest party in the ruling coalition, and the chief justice of the Constitutional Court. The KPK exclusively sent its cases to the Tipikor—a specialist court set up for this purpose in Jakarta, which included a large proportion of "ad hoc" judges drawn from outside the country's notoriously corrupt judiciary. The institutions had an extraordinary record of success: the Tipikor court convicted 100 percent of the approximately 250 suspects the KPK brought before it up to February 2011 (Butt 2011, 381).

With regard to supply-side governance reforms, Indonesia's efforts have been less spectacular but more broadly based. For example, Indonesia implemented a "big bang" process of decentralization, devolving extensive political powers and budgetary resources to (at current count) approximately five hundred district governments around the country. Though this reform had additional purposes, its proponents believed it would help to control corruption by bringing government decision-making down to a level where it could be more closely monitored by citizens, who would be empowered to vote out corrupt local government leaders and parliamentarians. Significant reforms have been introduced in government procurement, including by requiring open tendering of all but small and emergency projects, introducing online bidding mechanisms and establishing special bodies to decide on bids and monitor decision-making. There have been a host of e-government reforms, "one-stop" shops to reduce discretionary powers of bureaucrats in charge of business licensing, as well as reforms to systems for recruiting and promoting bureaucrats (see for example von Luebke 2009). Transparency is the new credo in Indonesia.

However, both sets of reforms—those focusing on enforcement and those on supply—have had questionable long-term effects. Indonesia's post-Suharto experience demonstrates that it can be equally difficult to establish islands of integrity within a sea of corrupt behavior as to reform underlying government systems in order to nudge the incentives toward universalism (Dick and Butt 2013; cf. Mungiu-Pippidi 2015). With regard to the former strategy, one obvious problem with the anticorruption strategy that focused on the empowerment of the KPK and Tipikor court is that these peak agencies had relatively limited reach. In 2014, the KPK reported it had 1,102 staff (compared to an estimated four hundred thousand in the national police). Accordingly, the vast majority of corruption cases continued to be handled as they always had been—by the police, prosecutors, and general courts. In 2014, for example, twenty-three corruption cases were handled by the KPK, as against 1,380 by general prosecutors (Butt 2015, 183). In part to address this problem (but perhaps also to dilute the specialized courts' effectiveness), the government established Tipikor courts in the regions. By doing so, the government opened the courts up to more career judges and therefore diluted some of the protections that had been included to prevent the original court from being drawn into the so-called "judicial mafia" that infests the general court system. Almost immediately, the new courts began to acquit defendants, and by March 2016 the KPK had arrested six judges from Tipikor courts on corruption charges related to cases over which they had been presiding (Kompas 2016). The KPK, meanwhile, has faced a concerted campaign to undermine its power, launched by a coalition of parliamentarians, police, and other officials. We explore this backlash in greater detail later in the chapter; at this point it is worth noting that the campaign has ebbed and flowed over the last decade, with strong media and public resistance often pushing back on attempts to amend the KPK law and strip it of powers. However, one serious blow came in December 2015, when the national parliament, many of whose members had been prosecuted by the KPK in the past, elected five new commissioners, choosing candidates who had stated they wanted to emphasize prevention rather than prosecution. Four of them had highly questionable backgrounds; one, a former judge, had acquitted the notoriously corrupt governor of Banten Province, Ratu Atut Chosiyah, when she had appeared before him.

The record of supply-side reforms has arguably been even less impressive. For example, with regard to decentralization, it is well established that rather than acting as a prophylaxis against corruption, devolution has instead encouraged its spread and entrenchment through the lower levels of government by distributing resources downward, along with greater discretionary power to determine their use and reduced scrutiny from higher authorities. Some scholars have argued that in fact Suharto practiced a "better class of corruption" because corruption was more centralized—and hence more predictable—in that earlier period (McLeod 2000). In contrast, the multiplicity of veto players and access points to state authority in the post-Suharto period has meant that officials in different institutions and at different levels of government often compete to extract resources from the same activities.

Overall, despite the public discourse and the best efforts of the new anticorruption agencies and movements, corruption rapidly adapted to the new political system, with new political players becoming enmeshed in new forms of the corrupt networks that had characterized the Suharto period. Suharto's centralized system of resource extraction and patronage distribution has been "democratized," allowing for the entry of many new players and encouraged by the fragmentation of sources of state resources (Aspinall 2013). Formal politics remains patronage oriented, with national government formed by a little-changing "cartel" representing most major parties, which use their access to public office to extract state resources (Slater 2004, 2014), a weak system of campaign finance regulation (Mietzner 2007, 2015), and widespread "money politics" in election campaigns

(Aspinall 2014; Aspinall and Sukmajati 2016). Numerous studies demonstrate the continuing pervasiveness of corruption in such institutions as the judiciary (Butt and Lindsey 2011), the police (Baker 2012) and military (Karensa 2016), and in sectors such as forestry and plantations (Smith et al. 2003), migration (Ford and Lyons 2011), and education (Widoyoko 2011), to name just a few.

Within this broader context of deeply pervasive corruption, the goals of most anticorruption campaigns and measures have remained framed by efforts at political institutionalization: reformers who have had an input into such new agencies as the KPK have striven to create new institutions that are insulated from political intervention and able to pursue corruption even among powerfully placed political figures. Most civil society actors have tried to deepen and defend this impulse. However, it should also not surprise us to learn that, in a system in which the boundaries between private and public interests are so intermeshed, private interests frequently also intervene, either to impede anticorruption efforts or to steer them. To delve further into how civil society groups have responded to this shifting context, the remainder of the chapter focuses on three main forms of anticorruption action that have come to the fore during the last decade or so.

Exposing Scandals and Working with the KPK

A major focus of most anticorruption NGOs, including major national organizations such as ICW, as well as most regional anticorruption NGOs, has been relatively straightforward: investigating and exposing corruption scandals and putting pressure on the government and law enforcement agencies to arrest, charge, try, and punish the wrongdoers. In the months and years that followed the downfall of Suharto, much of the most vigorous anticorruption campaigning in the country involved street protests and media campaigns aimed at exposing instances of malfeasance by particular government officials or agencies, both at the national level or locally—and a large number of both national and local officials have been forced out of office and even ended up in jail as a result.

To be sure, from the start, anticorruption NGOs recognized that this accusatory campaigning style had its limitations, and that it needed to be coupled with attempts to reform Indonesia's political system and to introduce legal institutions aimed at discouraging corruption and taking action against officials accused of participating in it. Accordingly, from very early in the *reformasi* period, a range of NGOs and think tanks engaged in policy lobbying, as well as training activities and participation in consultative processes with government, helping to encourage change within government itself. By doing so they helped to shape the formation of such institutions as the KPK and the Witness Protection Act (Setiyono and McLeod 2010, 355–360). Much of this policy lobbying has proceeded relatively quietly, because "NGOs that focus on bills and institutions appear to receive far less media attention" than public protest or denunciations of corruption scandals (Hsieh 2016, 116).

Despite the importance of such policy work, even now, almost twenty years after the end of the Suharto regime, the investigatory-cum-accusatory style remains by far the most common form of anticorruption campaigning in contemporary Indonesia. NGOs and allied groups using this approach typically focus in on a particular case or group of cases of corruption, release details to the media, often identifying perpetrators in the process, and demand that legal action be taken in response using a combination of street protests, media campaigns, and, increasingly, social media strategies. Some such groups—the most striking example is ICW—have developed significant investigatory, legal, and analytical capacity to look into particular corruption cases and to understand the structural roots of corruption as a general phenomenon. Such organizations have also developed significant media profiles, either nationally or at the local level, which means that whistle-blowers are sometimes inclined to contact them with leaks of material implicating corrupt officials.

Overall, the targeting choices of such NGOs have been largely nonpartisan. Though it is certainly possible to find many examples of particular anticorruption campaigns' being mobilized through the media and on the streets in order to harm partisan foes—for example, in 2010 there was a concerted and successful campaign to bring down the reforming finance minister, Sri Mulyani Indrawati, alleging her involvement in a bank bailout linked to corruption—those organizing such campaigns have tended to be politicians and their allies and agents. The major anticorruption NGOs such as ICW have on the whole been notably nonpartisan in their targeting, identifying perpetrators from all the major political parties and groups, in and outside of government, as well as in major state security agencies such as the police and armed forces. The overall thrust of such efforts, therefore, has been to extend the political institutionalization impetus of the early post-Suharto years of political transition.

This investigatory style of NGO campaigning has thus been greatly assisted by the formation of the KPK. A critical problem of anticorruption campaigning in the early post-Suharto period was that corruption cases would frequently die in the hands of police or prosecutors—indeed, officials in such agencies could use investigations for the purposes of extortion, threatening wrongdoers with prosecution in order to extract bribes from them. Anticorruption efforts were, in other words, thoroughly penetrated by private interests. The KPK, which was viewed by NGO activists as being highly effective and, at least initially, largely incorruptible, was thus a natural ally for such groups and a recipient of the results of their investigations. This pattern was set early on, from the time of the first successful prosecution by the KPK that seized national attention—that of Aceh governor Abdullah Puteh, who was sentenced to ten years in prison in March 2005 for taking a kickback in the purchase of a helicopter. The KPK brought a case against Governor Puteh only after a local NGO, the Aceh People's Solidarity against Corruption (Solidaritas Rakyat Aceh Anti Korupsi, SoRAK) reported the case to the commission, after another NGO had earlier reported it to the local police and prosecutors, who had failed to act (Setiyono and McLeod 2010, 361–362). From this time on, especially in cases of large-scale corruption, NGOs began to work increasingly closely with the KPK and to routinely report their findings to it. According to Doni Muhardiasyah, head of research and development at the KPK, a majority of corruption cases prosecuted by the agency were initially reported by civil society organizations, either to the KPK itself or to other law enforcement agencies (Muhardiasyah 2008, cited in Setiyono and McLeod 2010, 361). The KPK has recognized the value of this collaboration and has initiated various programs of formal cooperation with NGOs, for example, working with local anticorruption groups in the monitoring of court processes and decisions (Adha 2016).

It should also be noted that most NGOs have recognized that the investigatory and prosecutorial approach has limitations, especially given the KPK's limited capacity to take on cases. Most NGOs thus supplement such work with public education and publicity campaigns of various kinds; others have tried to encourage political rather than legal sanctioning of corrupt officials. As an example of the latter approach, in the lead up to the 2004 parliamentary elections, a coalition of NGOs created a movement aimed at encouraging citizens not to vote for "rotten politicians" (*politisi busuk*) (Hsieh 2016, 198–247). Modeled on a highly successful campaign that had been used in South Korea in 2000, the NGOs generated a list of sixty-one politicians they said were implicated in corruption and other problematic behaviors such as human rights abuses. They encouraged voters to boycott them in the forthcoming election, promoting this goal through a concerted media campaign. The campaign was, however, largely seen to be a failure. It was hampered in part by Indonesia's basically closed-list proportional representation election system, which meant that voters had little leeway for casting votes for individual politicians rather than for parties. Even so, though ICW has made similar efforts in subsequent elections (Hsieh 2016, 247–248) for which Indonesia has adopted candidate-centered elections, the campaigns are generally considered to have been failures. Such failures have tended to drive most NGOs back toward the investigatory model, and toward cooperation with the KPK.

Defending the KPK

As the KPK became increasingly effective, prosecuting a large number of politicians, bureaucrats, and law enforcement officials, a backlash against it from officialdom gathered momentum. Such pressure has included efforts to remove some of the KPK's special powers. Even more importantly, once the KPK began to arrest high-ranking police officers, police and prosecutors began to push back directly by using their own powers to investigate, arrest, and prosecute KPK commissioners and staff. This approach was effective not least because KPK commissioners who were charged or tried could be suspended or removed from their posts (Butt 2015, 180). The first major assault came in 2009 when police charged the head of the KPK with murder and two commissioners with extortion (for the details of this complex affair, see Butt 2011). Susno Djuadi, a police officer whose telephone was being tapped by the KPK and was later revealed as a central player in the attempt to undermine the commission, gave an angry interview in *Tempo* magazine where he likened the KPK's conflict with the police to an ineffectual *cicak* (gecko) trying to fight a *buaya* (crocodile), a nomenclature that was enthusiastically embraced by supporters of the commission. A similar confrontation came in 2012 and 2013 after the KPK charged Djoko Susilo, the national head of traffic police, for graft in the purchase of driving simulators. Police not only refused to cooperate with the KPK and withdrew twenty officers seconded to the commission but also attempted to raid the KPK office and arrest one of the commission's investigators who, despite having a police background, was looking into the case (McRae 2013, 298–299). A third wave came in late 2014 and early 2015 when incoming president Joko Widodo (Jokowi) refused to appoint Budi Gunawan, a senior police officer, to his cabinet. Budi Gunawan had come to national media attention in 2010 for having suspicious bank deposits of US$10.45 million. Jokowi used the KPK to screen ministerial candidates and the commission gave Budi a "red card." Budi's exclusion from the cabinet angered former president Megawati Soekarnoputri, Budi's major sponsor; to placate her, Jokowi subsequently nominated Budi as national police chief. The KPK immediately declared him a corruption suspect. In retaliation, the police launched another assault on the KPK, refusing to collaborate on the case, and arresting and investigating commissioners and investigators. For a time, the police all but crippled the KPK, with Jokowi failing to strongly defend the commission.

A major focus of civil society activism has thus been defensive, aiming to protect the KPK from these attacks. Such campaigns have tended to adopt a conventional social movement style, utilizing both traditional tactics of social movement politics, such as demonstrations and press campaigns, alongside newer approaches, notably reliance on social media. This approach reached an early peak during the so-called *cicak* versus *buaya* episode of 2009. At this time, the KPK garnered great public support. A broad coalition of civil society groups, the media, and liberal middle-class opinion backed the organization and the anticorruption effort it embodied. Within forty-eight hours of the two KPK commissioners' being charged by the police, 110,000 persons had joined a Facebook group defending the pair, with a million signing up within nine days. This was the first major social media political campaign in Indonesia. The electronic and print media also exploded into a frenzy of condemnation of the police, prosecutors, and government, and there were large demonstrations in major cities, with many protestors carrying posters or banners that depicted feisty geckos bravely facing off against fierce-looking crocodiles and otherwise using a variety of creative and satirical methods to defend the KPK and condemn its enemies. Meanwhile, ICW, TII, and other Jakarta-based NGOs formed a formal coalition, which they called the "Cicak" movement, using one of the acronym word plays so beloved of Indonesians—in this case, "Cicak" meant "Cinta Indonesia, Cinta KPK," "Love Indonesia, Love the KPK" (Hsieh 2016, 139). In the face of the public outcry, President Yudhoyono, who was generally very sensitive to public criticism, ultimately took action to protect the commission.

Similar efforts to defend the KPK have cohered in subsequent episodes of social-movement-cum-social-media activism when the agency has come under attack. The leaders of important anticorruption NGOs have consistently done whatever they could to stand up for the KPK and, especially, to defend its independence. They have generally been able to rely on strong media support when doing so, with the leaders of prominent groups such ICW having ready access to major television networks, newspapers, and online media outlets. These defensive mobilizations have typically also involved witty social media campaigns, including the widespread sharing of memes poking fun at those attacking the KPK and corruption in the political class more generally, and underlining the urban, educated, and largely middle-class backgrounds of those involved.

Throughout the period when the KPK has been under attack, the commission and its NGO allies have held one important strong card: the strength of public opinion. Through the post-Suharto period, public opinion polls have generally identified corruption as one of Indonesia's most important national problems, and the public has equally expressed repeated support for the KPK against its various adversaries. For example, during one recent bout of attacks on the agency mounted by prominent national politicians, one national survey institute found that 64.4 percent of respondents were willing to trust the KPK over the national parliament, while only 6.1 percent trusted the parliament more (Tribunnews.com 2017).

In this context, Indonesian anticorruption NGOs have been indefatigable in their defense of the KPK, but attempts to undermine the agency by the police, parliament, and other elements of the ruling elite have been equally relentless. Over time, as elements within the elite have chipped away at the KPK's integrity and independence, some of the civil society enthusiasm to defend the agency has arguably begun to wane. To be sure, the KPK and the battle against corruption still continue to enjoy strong public support, but the activists and their allies have faced an immensely wearying task, with each attempt to defend the institution not only requiring significant expenditure of energy and political capital, but the integrity of the institution itself slowly being whittled away. While the outright elimination of the KPK remains highly unlikely, the gradual diminution of its effectiveness seems much more likely. It is possible that, over time, Indonesian anticorruption activists will lose their most important ally, with antagonism to anticorruption efforts slowly wearing down the impetus of the broader institutional reform efforts that accompanied the transition to the post-Suharto political order.

Anticorruption Campaigns in the Regions

Another category of anticorruption activism has involved campaigning against corrupt local officials in the regions. As noted earlier, under decentralization policies introduced in 1999, considerable political authority and financial resources devolved to the regions. As is well known, such formal decentralization was accompanied by a decentralization of corruption, and many of the KPK's most notorious prosecutions have been of governors, district heads, or local legislators, or have otherwise involved local politics. As previously noted, the first KPK prosecution to grab national attention was that of Aceh governor Abdullah Puteh in 2005. The stunning arrest of the chief of the Constitutional Court, Akil Mochtar, in 2013, and his subsequent prosecution and conviction, turned on bribes he had received for settling local election disputes.

In the immediate aftermath of *reformasi*, a large number of specialist local anticorruption groups emerged, many of them established by former student activists or legal professionals. Other local groups—students, civil society groups, intellectuals, among others—are in many locations eager to expose malfeasance on the part of local politicians, but only occasionally do their campaigns attain significant momentum, attract national media attention, or result in successful prosecutions. As noted, one typical pattern in Indonesian corruption law enforcement is for cases to stall at the police or prosecutors' office, where they are often used to extract bribes from the accused. Accordingly, one critical component of local anticorruption campaigns is typically the effort to increase public pressure on local political elites and law enforcement agencies to follow through on reported cases of corruption.

One important early analysis of regional anticorruption campaigns was made by Jamie Davidson (2007). He focused on a critical case of civil society mobilization in Padang, West Sumatra, in 2002 that, he argues, triggered a sea change in investigation of corruption in regional legislatures throughout Indonesia. As he puts it: "In late 2002, some four years into the post-Soeharto era, hardly any regional assembly members in Indonesia were under investigation for corruption with respect to budgetary expenditures. Two years later, well over 1,300 such individuals from over 100 provincial and district legislatures were (or had been)" (Davidson 2007, 76). This dramatic change, Davidson argues, was inspired by the highly successful campaign in Padang that "inspired copycat movements across the country to press local prosecutors to investigate local legislative bodies" (Davidson 2007, 77). The Padang campaign was detonated by the members of the provincial legislature voting themselves a 400 percent increase in pay. In response, a loose coalition of local students, NGOs, and other activists, organizing under the auspices of ad hoc and flexible "coordination forums," pursued legal remedies, making use of some of Indonesia's new post-*reformasi* anticorruption legislation, and simultaneously used the normal protest repertoires of street demonstrations and media campaigns that the *reformasi* generation had honed during their campaigns against Suharto. The campaign resulted in forty-three of the legislators' being found guilty in court and a string of investigations and prosecutions elsewhere in the province and, as indicated earlier, other parts of Indonesia. The Padang case highlights the critical ingredients involved in such campaigning, including flexible use of both legal mechanisms and public pressure, savvy media campaigns, and the forging of broad coalitions among civil society groups, but also the creation of linkages with universities and intellectuals, members of the legal profession, and, where possible, politicians and law enforcement agencies.

As Davidson himself pointed out, there have been tremendous differences in political outcomes across Indonesia when local corruption scandals come to light. A report in late 2014 indicated that 325 regional heads and deputies had been charged, convicted, or declared suspects in corruption cases (Tribunnews.com 2014). Though this seems like a large number (there are about 540 districts and provinces in Indonesia), in fact, it points to the patchiness of such outcomes, given the near ubiquity of corruption, and even of anticorruption campaigns, across regional Indonesia.

One critical factor that makes a difference in terms of the outcomes of local anticorruption campaigns is local political ecologies: in some parts of Indonesia, especially in more industrialized regions and major provincial capitals, there are relatively large and independent middle classes and dense civil society networks, including vigorous local mediascapes, strong universities, and large numbers of students and legal professionals. Such settings provide more supportive conditions for local anticorruption campaigns to thrive than do more remote locations, such that in some parts of Indonesia local anticorruption campaigns are genuinely bottom up (rather than in countries such as China or Vietnam, where they are generally top-down affairs). In district capitals in primarily rural or natural-resource-producing regions, middle-class employment is largely centered on the civil service, local newspapers and lawyers depend on the local government for most of their business, and university students

generally want to become civil servants. People in such settings are
therefore much more reluctant to challenge local authorities—even when
their corruption is a public secret. To be sure, sometimes local groups can
short-circuit such local limitations by forging connections with national
NGOs, the KPK, and the national media, thus promoting nationalization
of local contentious politics (Djani 2013, 174). But these movements
generally find it hard to thrive in such social settings.

Another factor that differentiates these cases, however, is the
importance of formal politics: local anticorruption campaigns tend to
succeed when their goals coincide with rivals of the officials who are
their targets. Partisan interests, in other words, can and do sometimes
play a role in shaping the occurrence and targeting of such campaigns.
In the case of the Padang investigations that led to viral replication
across Indonesian regions, a major factor was the fact that the interior
minister at the time (who was aligned with the PDI-P, Partai Demokrasi
Indonesia-Perjuangan) saw the case as "an opportunity to take a swipe
at rival parties in a decidedly non-PDI-P bailiwick" (Davidson 2007,
77). In Luky Djani's account of the successful anticorruption campaign
in Garut, West Java, which led to the removal from office of the sitting
bupati, or district head, and his sentencing to seven and a half years in
jail, efforts by local anticorruption group GARASI (Gerakan Rakyat anti
Korupsi, People's Movement against Corruption) to forge alliances within
the local political elite and with local business actors, helped produce a
positive outcome. These local elite actors were willing to join the campaign
against the *bupati* in part because he had hoarded patronage rather than
distributing it widely through the local elite (Djani 2013, 173–214). As
Clark has put it, when identifying which instances of corruption end up
being prosecuted in regional Indonesia,

> the mobilisation of corruption laws is, more often than not,
> a means to an end. For local politicians and bureaucrats it is
> an opportunity to extract concessions from the executive or
> potentially remove a political opponent; for local civil society
> organisations it is an opportunity to gain resources from the
> local government; for local political entrepreneurs it is an
> opportunity to transition into politics or senior government;
> and for the central government it is an opportunity to inter-
> vene in local politics for political advantage. (Clark 2013, 75)

Inevitably, therefore, such campaigns have tended to require local anti-corruption NGOs to forge alliances with a wide array of other actors, including political elites at the local and national levels. Such anticorruption groups inevitably run risks of being drawn into power struggles among rival political actors, sometimes resulting in their being tarnished by such associations, or even of being depicted as playthings of this or that elite faction. The fact that NGO actors are themselves often on the lookout for patronage (indeed, a few local anticorruption NGOs are themselves in the extortion business) sometimes makes such accusations plausible. Such campaigns thus face the constant risk of being pulled into the patronage morass at the local level. The availability of allies in the shape of national-level anticorruption NGOs, and the presence of the KPK as the ultimate recourse in cases of large-scale local corruption, has been one check on this tendency though, as we have seen, this check may be losing its force.

Conclusion

Over recent decades, the nature of anticorruption campaigning by social movements and civil society groups in Indonesia has evolved dramatically. During the Suharto years, corruption was integral to the structure and functioning of the regime. But it was risky for civil society actors to raise it as a political problem, at least in ways that frankly confronted its true nature and extent. Moreover, many critics of the government eventually concluded that it would not be possible to eliminate corruption without dramatically changing the shape of the regime, especially by providing guarantees of free expression and other human rights that would enable citizens to honestly assess the extent of governmental misbehavior and enforce accountability on officials who engaged in it. In this way, the struggle against corruption became inseparable from the wider struggle to end, or at least reform, the Suharto regime itself. There were occasional outbursts of public protest about corruption—notably as part of the student movement of the 1970s—but this convergence of goals reached its final expression in the *reformasi* movement of 1998–1999, in which democratization was presented as both a means and a prerequisite for ending corruption.

    In the post-Suharto period, the political structures became, at least theoretically, much more supportive of efforts to eliminate abuse of office for personal gain. The opening of political space, plus the establishment of mechanisms for democratic accountability and greater human rights protection, allowed citizens and social movements to investigate corruption and provided them with avenues to remove corrupt officials from office. As we have seen, a raft of new anticorruption rules and institutions were established, notably a highly regarded specialist Corruption Eradication Commission (KPK). As a result, the struggle against corruption gained much greater public legitimacy; indeed, it became an integral part of the new *reformasi* order. At the same time, the struggle to end corruption was also particularized and professionalized: a new generation of specialist anticorruption movement organizations came into being, many of them NGOs, and an array of public campaigns were launched that did not merely present corruption as a general problem but focused on a myriad of particular cases or sites of corruption.

As we have seen, with this change of regime, new forms and modes of anticorruption campaigning emerged. An investigatory or accusatory style became dominant, in which particular anticorruption groups—sometimes the professionalized NGOs, but sometimes more ad hoc campaign groups in the regions—identified particular cases of corruption and then campaigned to exert public pressure to ensure that they were prosecuted. The emergence of a new range of official mechanisms for eradicating corruption—notably the KPK—greatly assisted such campaigns, and cooperation with the KPK became critical to many of the most important anticorruption groups. Accordingly, when the KPK itself came under attack from officials who were threatened by the commission's investigations, some of the most important civil society coalitions of the post-Suharto period coalesced in defensive campaigns aimed at arresting the backlash and protecting the KPK. Finally, the devolution of political authority, financial resources, and corruption itself to the regions prompted a parallel decentralization of anti-corruption campaigning, with a host of coalitions and protest campaigns being organized in the regions in an attempt to bring down this or that corrupt local leader. Such campaigns have frequently involved extensive coalition building, both among broader networks of civil society actors but also within the state apparatus and ruling political elites.

These distinct fronts of anticorruption campaigning have achieved many successes in post-Suharto Indonesia. The formal institutional context has changed greatly, with new anticorruption institutions such as the KPK themselves arising in part as a result of civil society campaigns. Numerous corrupt officials have been exposed, removed from office, and punished. Corruption has become a major focus of the media, and anticorruption campaigns continue to enjoy broad public support. Even so, in many respects the struggle against corruption in the post-Suharto period has been a Sisyphean task. Despite all the energy expended, and all the achievements, progress toward systemic change remains elusive. Corruption remains deeply embedded in the informal networks and practices that underpin state power, and it is difficult to conclude that all the efforts of the post-Suharto period have substantially changed this situation or that there has been a significant reduction in the overall quantum of corruption. Many efforts to curtail corruption themselves remain hostage to private interests. Certainly, in some parts of the country, and in particular institutions, progress has been recorded, but in such key institutions as the courts, the parliament, and the police it is difficult to see signs of major improvement. Overall, in the words of ICW, corruption remains "chronic and dangerous" (ICW 2016, 5) in the post-Suharto period.

After almost two decades of democratization, these problems have fed widespread alienation among social movement activists with the entire political class and with the state apparatus. Anticorruption groups have struggled to hit upon a strategy that they themselves find satisfying: everyone talks about "systematically" targeting the "roots" of corruption, but, in fact, many anticorruption groups fluctuate among proposing piecemeal policy reform, exposing particular corrupt officials, and ineffectually promoting broad "cultural change." Activists in such groups demonstrate tremendous commitment and have a sense of deep strategic patience. Their energy is renewed by their frequent successes in galvanizing public opinion in support of their campaigns. Overall, however, serious questions remain about their ability to sustain themselves in a political climate that seems to be turning decisively against them.

Notes

1. It should be noted that critics of the KPK have frequently focused on its cooperation with anticorruption groups such as ICW, suggesting that such work violates official guidelines (Firmansyah 2017).

Bibliography

Adha, Bayu Agustari. "Pantau Peradilan Korupsi di Riau, KPK Gandeng 22 LSM Lokal." *AntaraRiau*, May 26, 2016. Retrieved from https://www.antarariau.

com/berita/73411/pantau-peradilan-korupsi-di-riau-kpk-gandeng-22-lsm-lokal (accessed 24 November 2017).

Aspinall, Edward. *Opposing Suharto: Compromise, Resistance and Regime Change in Indonesia*. Stanford: Stanford University Press, 2005.

Aspinall, Edward. "A Nation in Fragments: Patronage and Neoliberalism in Contemporary Indonesia." *Critical Asian Studies* 45, no. 1 (2013): 27–54.

Aspinall, Edward. "Indonesia's 2014 Elections: Parliament and Patronage." *Journal of Democracy* 25, no. 4 (2014): 96–110.

Aspinall, Edward, and Mada Sukmajati, eds. *Electoral Dynamics in Indonesia: Money Politics, Patronage and Clientelism at the Grassroots*. Singapore: National University of Singapore Press, 2016.

Aspinall, Edward, and Gerry van Klinken, eds. *The State and Illegality in Indonesia*. Leiden: KITLV Press, 2011.

Baker, Jacqueline. "The Rise of Polri: Democratisation and the Political Economy of Security in Indonesia." PhD dissertation. London School of Economics and Political Science, 2012.

Butt, Simon. "Anti-Corruption Reform in Indonesia: An Obituary?" *Bulletin of Indonesian Economic Studies* 47, no. 3 (2011): 381–394.

Butt, Simon. *Corruption and Law in Indonesia*. Abingdon: Routledge, 2012.

Butt, Simon. "The Rule of Law and Anti-Corruption Reforms under Yudhoyono: The Rise of the KPK and the Constitutional Court." In *The Yudhoyono Presidency: Indonesia's Decade of Stability and Stagnation*, edited by Edward Aspinall, Marcus Mietzner, and Dirk Tomsa, 175–195. Singapore: Institute of Southeast Asian Studies, 2015.

Butt, Simon, and Tim Lindsey. "Judicial Mafia: The Courts and State Illegality in Indonesia." In *The State and Illegality in Indonesia*, edited by Edward Aspinall and Gerry van Klinken, 189–213. Leiden: KITLV Press, 2011.

Clark, Samuel. "Enforcing Corruption Laws: The Political Economy of Subnational Prosecutions in Indonesia." Unpublished PhD dissertation. University of Oxford, 2013.

Crouch, Harold. "Patrimonialism and Military Rule in Indonesia." *World Politics* 31, no. 4 (1979): 571–587.

Davidson, Jamie S. "Politics-as-Usual on Trial: Regional Anti-Corruption Campaigns in Indonesia." *The Pacific Review* 20, no. 1 (2007): 75–99.

Dick, Howard, and Simon Butt. "Is Indonesia as Corrupt as Most People Believe and Is It Getting Worse?" Policy Paper. Centre for Indonesian Law, Islam and Society. Melbourne, 2013.

Djani, Luky Djuniardi. "Reform Movements and Local Politics in Indonesia." Unpublished PhD dissertation. Murdoch University, 2013.

Firmansyah, Teguh. "Romli Kritisi 'Kedekatan' KPK-ICW." *Republika*, July 11, 2017. Retrieved from http://nasional.republika.co.id/berita/nasional/hukum/

17/07/11/osxc8m377-romli-kritisi-kedekatan-kpkicw (accessed 24 November 2017).

Ford, Michele, and Lenore Lyons. "Travelling the Aspal Route: Grey Labour Migration through an Indonesian Border Town." In *The State and Illegality in Indonesia*, edited by Edward Aspinall and Gerry van Klinken, 107–122. Leiden: KITLV Press, 2011.

Hsieh, Shang-po. "Nongovernmental Organisations and Corruption Prevention in Democratising Indonesia (1998–2008)." PhD Dissertation. Australian National University, 2016.

ICW (Indonesia Corruption Watch). *Annual Report 2016 Indonesia Corruption Watch: Menyemai Semangat Antikorupsi.* Jakarta: ICW, 2016.

Karensa, Edo. "Indonesia's Defense Sector at High Risk of Corruption: Transparency International." *Jakarta Globe*, January 21, 2016. Retrieved from http://jakartaglobe.beritasatu.com/news/indonesias-defense-sector-high-risk-corruption-transparency-international/.

Kompas. "JP, Hakim Tipikor Keenam yang Ditangkap KPK." *Kompas Online*, May 24, 2016. Retrieved from http://nasional.kompas.com/read/2016/05/24/07295841/jp.hakim.tipikor.keenam.yang.ditangkap.kpk.

Mackie, J. A. C. "The Commission of Four Report on Corruption." *Bulletin of Indonesian Economic Studies* 6, no. 3 (1970): 87–101.

McLeod, Ross H. "Soeharto's Indonesia: A Better Class of Corruption." *Agenda* 7, no. 2 (2000): 99–112.

McLeod, Ross H. "Institutionalized Public Sector Corruption: A Legacy of the Soeharto Franchise." In *The State and Illegality in Indonesia*, edited by Edward Aspinall and Gerry van Klinken, 45–64. Leiden: KITLV Press, 2011.

McRae, Dave. "The Indonesian Student Movement of 1998." Working Paper 110. Centre of Southeast Asian Studies. Monash University, 2001.

McRae, Dave. "Indonesian Politics in 2013: The Emergence of New Leadership?" *Bulletin of Indonesian Economic Studies* 49, no. 3 (2013): 289–304.

Mietzner, Marcus. "Party Financing in Post-Soeharto Indonesia: Between State Subsidies and Political Corruption." *Contemporary Southeast Asia* 29, no. 2 (2007): 238–263.

Mietzner, Marcus. "Dysfunction by Design: Political Finance and Corruption in Indonesia." *Critical Asian Studies* 47, no. 4 (2015): 587–610.

Muhardiasyah, Doni. "Strategi, upaya, dan tantangan TPK dalam perspektif KPK" [Strategies, efforts and challenges of the Corruption Eradication Team from the perspective of the Corruption Eradication Commission]. Presentation at discussion forum on Nationalism and Corruption Eradication, Semarang, August 28, 2008.

Mungiu-Pippidi, Alina. *The Quest for Good Governance: How Societies Develop Control of Corruption.* Cambridge: Cambridge University Press, 2015.

Persson, Anna, Bo Rothstein, and Jan Teorell. "Why Anticorruption Reforms Fail: Systemic Corruption as a Collective Action Problem." *Governance* 26, no. 3 (2013): 449–471.

Raillon, François. *Politik dan Ideologi Mahasiswa Indonesia: Pembentukan dan Konsolidasi Orde Baru 1966–1974.* Jakarta: LP3ES, 1989.

Reeve, David. "Political Jokes." *Inside Indonesia* 81 (2005). Retrieved from http://www.insideindonesia.org/political-humour.

Robison, Richard, and Vedi R. Hadiz. *Reorganising Power in Indonesia: The Politics of Oligarchy in an Age of Markets.* London: Routledge Curzon, 2004.

Setiyono, Budi, and Ross H. McLeod. "Civil Society Organisations' Contribution to the Anti-Corruption Movement in Indonesia." *Bulletin of Indonesian Economic Studies* 46, no. 3 (2010): 347–370.

Slater, Dan. "Indonesia's Accountability Trap: Party Cartels and Presidential Power after Democratic Transition." *Indonesia* 78 (2004): 61–92.

Slater, Dan. "Unbuilding Blocs: Indonesia's Accountability Deficit in Historical Perspective." *Critical Asian Studies* 46, no. 2 (2014): 287–315.

Smith, J., K. Obidzinski, S. Subarudi, and I. Suramenggala. "Illegal Logging, Collusive Corruption and Fragmented Governments in Kalimantan, Indonesia." *International Forestry Review* 5, no. 3 (2003): 293–302.

Synnerstrom, Staffan. "The Civil Service: Towards Efficiency, Effectiveness and Honesty." In *Indonesia: Democracy and the Promise of Good Governance,* edited by Ross H. McLeod and Andrew MacIntyre, 159–177. Singapore: Institute of Southeast Asian Affairs, 1993.

Tidey, Sylvia. "Corruption and Adherence to Rules in the Construction Sector: Reading the 'Bidding Books.'" *American Anthropologist* 115, no. 2 (2013): 188–202.

Tribunnews.com. "Sejak Otonomi Daerah, 70 Persen Kepala dan Wakil Kepala Daerah Terjerat Korupsi." *Tribunnews.com,* December 25, 2014. Retrieved from http://www.tribunnews.com/nasional/2014/12/25/sejak-otonomi-daerah-70-persen-kepala-dan-wakil-kepala-daerah-terjerat-korupsi.

Tribunnews.com. "Survei SMRC: Masyarakat Lebih Percaya KPK Daripada DPR." *Tribunnews.com,* June 15, 2017. Retrieved from http://www.tribunnews.com/nasional/2017/06/15/survei-smrc-masyarakat-lebih-percaya-kpk-daripada-dpr.

von Luebke, Christian. "The Political Economy of Local Governance: Findings from an Indonesian Field Study." *Bulletin of Indonesian Economic Studies* 45, no. 2 (2009): 201–230.

Widoyoko, J. Danang. "The Education Sector: The Fragmentation and Adaptability of Corruption." In *The State and Illegality in Indonesia,* edited by Edward Aspinall and Gerry van Klinken, 165–188. Leiden: KITLV Press, 2011.

Part II

Anticorruption Driven by Party Loyalty

3

(Anti-)Corruption and Partisan Bias
in Taiwan's Newspapers

CHRISTIAN GOEBEL

Judged by major corruption measures, Taiwan has not made significant progress in fighting corruption. Taiwan's scores in the Transparency International (TI) Corruption Perceptions Index (CPI) and the World Bank's World Governance Indicators, are not much higher than they were in 1996 (Transparency International 2018; World Bank 2014). However, experts disagree with this gloomy verdict—for example, the Bertelsmann Transformation Index (BTI) gives Taiwan the top score for "prosecution of office abuse" (Stiftung Bertelsmann 2016). And while many people complain about corruption, few have actually experienced it (Transparency International 2011). In fact, the Taiwanese government has been intensifying its fight against corruption, although the overwhelming majority of people, despite having not experienced corruption themselves, think that the situation has not improved at all.

This paradox illustrates the pitfalls of judging the extent of corruption by perception-based indicators, at least in countries where bribery and other forms of "abusing public office for private gain," the World Bank's definition of corruption, are not conducted openly. Here, perceptions are shaped by the very instances where anticorruption works well: the arrest and conviction of politicians and businessmen. While it is sad that several high-level officials, judges, legislators, and even the former president have been found to be corrupt, that their own administrations indicted them is a reason for optimism. That these are obviously not cases of political revenge implies that ethical universalism, that is, the government's equal and fair treatment of everyone (Gewirth 1988), is on the rise in Taiwan. No matter how widespread corruption really is, the chance that corrupt activities will be detected, investigated, and punished has increased significantly in the last two decades (Goebel 2016).

Since Taiwan became democratic in 1992, and especially after the change in ruling parties in 2000, the passage of new laws and the reform of existing ones has defined more clearly than ever what constitutes "corrupt" behavior. Legal changes have followed international norms. Moreover, since the change in ruling parties, the Taiwanese government has guaranteed judicial independence and considerably strengthened anticorruption agencies. Despite the fact that there is still corruption, and that the institutional configuration of Taiwan's anticorruption agencies is far from optimal, these are major achievements.

Taiwan combines elements of two patterns in the typology the introduction to this volume presents. On the one hand, the goal of political institutionalization has driven anticorruption efforts. Ma Ying-jeou, for example, quickly turned against the clientelist base of the ruling Kuomintang (KMT) party after he was appointed minister of justice from 1993 to 1996. When the Democratic Progressive Party (DPP) was voted into government in 2000, newly appointed minister of justice Chen Ding-nan implemented sweeping reforms that landed politicians of his own party, including former president Chen Shui-bian, in jail (Goebel 2016). On the other hand, however, there have always been accusations of a political bias in Taiwan's anticorruption initiatives. The KMT and the DPP are deeply divided; the DPP accuses the KMT of not being able to break with its corrupt past, while the KMT counters with what has come to be known as "whataboutism." Each party blames the other for being one-sided in their enforcement of anticorruption, an accusation that scholars have been unable to confirm so far (e.g., Wu 2012). While individuals in either party have contributed to the deepening of political institutionalization, both parties have so far failed to publicly recognize the significant achievements made by the other side and instead blame each other for problems that continue to exist.

Hence, political discourse on anticorruption does not align with Taiwan's actual experience, which might explain Taiwan's citizens' negative perceptions of political corruption. According to one explanation, Taiwan's partisan media deserves much of the blame for this predicament. Instead of contributing to moderation by critically engaging with Taiwan's anticorruption discourse, they are said to amplify "their" party's position.

Allegedly all newspapers, broadcasters, and television stations display a clear bias toward one of Taiwan's two major political camps. For example, the *United Daily* is believed to side with the KMT, while the *Liberty Times* is regarded as a DPP newspaper. The *China Times* was long seen as a pro-KMT newspaper but is now said to have a pro-China bias after being taken over by Want Want Holdings, which resides in Shanghai. In addition, previous research has found that Taiwan's newspapers are more prone to negative than positive reporting (Fang and Feng 2004). Taken together, Taiwan's vitriolic political discourse, amplified by partisan media, might be responsible for creating the false impression that anticorruption in Taiwan is largely ineffective as well as driven by partisan politics, as Chen and Weiss outline in their introduction.

This chapter explores the veracity of these perceptions by looking at the role of partisan-linked media in reporting on corruption and anticorruption in Taiwan. Methodologically, this chapter presents a quantitative content analysis. All articles on the subject of corruption in Taiwan published in the four major newspapers and available online were collected and analyzed by means of two different techniques. First, the analysis applied unsupervised machine learning in the form of a topic-modeling algorithm to the whole corpus to extract the range of topics covered and to see which topics each newspaper was more likely to cover. Augmenting this document-level analysis is a corpus comparison on the sentence level, comparing all sentences making statements about corruption in the four newspapers by means of a word-embedding analysis.

In terms of the newspapers' partisan bias, the results are less clear-cut than expected. At the aggregate level, the analysis does find a slight partisan bias in three of the four newspapers' reporting, but these biases are weaker than initially assumed. Editorials and other opinion pieces might take a strong stand for or against one of the parties, but there is no evidence of a strong systemic partisan bias permeating the whole corpus. What the chapter does confirm, however, is the propensity of Taiwan's newspapers for negative reporting. None of the newspapers seem to give previous anticorruption efforts much credit and all are prone to exaggerate the seriousness of political corruption in Taiwan.

Regarding the theoretical issues the introduction to this volume raises, this study finds that the combination of partisan bias and propensity for negative reporting serves to reinforce the simplistic impression that Taiwan's anticorruption has been futile and driven by party loyalty, while neglecting the contribution of individuals in both parties to actual improvements in Taiwan's anticorruption regime.

Political Attitudes and the Media in Taiwan

THE PERCEPTION OF CORRUPTION

As noted earlier, indicators that measure corruption based on the perceptions of professionals and ordinary citizens suggest that the situation
has not improved over the last decade. However, these findings stand
in marked contrast to assessments by specialists. For example, the 2016
BTI country report states that corruption "is prosecuted rigorously under
criminal law" (Stiftung Bertelsmann 2016), and official statistics on anticorruption efforts in the public sector support this judgment.

Data from the TI Global Corruption Barometer also illustrate that
perceptions are not a good indicator of actual levels of corruption. For
instance, more than 60 percent of those surveyed for that report found
parliament, police, and civil servants to be corrupt or extremely corrupt,
but only 7 percent of all respondents in the 2010/2011 TI Global Corruption Barometer reported having paid a bribe (Transparency International
2011). Interestingly, perceptions of corruption were above world averages,
but the actual encounter of corruption in these institutions were far
below them. In addition, the fact that only a minority of cases reported
by the general public qualify for in-depth investigation lends credibility
to the assumption that corruption is perceived as worse than it actually
is. Out of 1,632 allegations of corruption members of the general public
filed in the second half of 2011, only ninety-one, fewer than 6 percent,
were substantial enough to qualify for in-depth investigation (Ministry
of Justice 2012). Finally, there is a partisan dimension to the perception
of corruption: as opinion surveys conducted by Taiwan's Agency against
Corruption (AAC) show, those in the population who support the KMT
are significantly less likely to perceive corruption as a problem than those
supporting the DPP (Ministry of Justice 2016). Existing perception-based
indicators do not account for this fact.

THE MEDIA AND POLITICAL POLARIZATION

Where does this partisan bias come from? As most of those involved in
political corruption hail from the KMT, it is possible that KMT supporters
see corruption as a necessary means to achieve their party's political ends
(Chin 2003). An alternative explanation is based on differences in cultural
values across the population. Some people might consider giving a gift to

a politician or being paid for their vote as part of the Chinese culture of establishing relationships by means of gifts (Xin and Pearce 1996). Others might embrace a different set of values and detest that very same practice (Fell 2005b). Quite possibly, those with more "traditional" values might find themselves drawn toward the KMT, while those who question this aspect of the Chinese "tradition" are more likely to support the DPP (see Lee 2007; Liu, Huang, and McFedries 2008). After all, the DPP was formed in opposition to the authoritarian KMT regime that had ruled Taiwan between 1947 and 1992, with opposing corruption consistently among the most prominent items on the party's campaign agenda (Fell 2005a).

Both explanations suggest that the divergent perceptions of corruption in Taiwan are rooted in different discourses regarding the phenomenon. The fact that KMT supporters and DPP supporters not only hold different opinions about corruption and anticorruption efforts in Taiwan but also differ in which media sources they use to inform themselves about politics support this assumption (Ministry of Justice 2016). KMT supporters tend to watch news on the Zhongshi, TVBS, and Zhongtian television stations; DPP supporters prefer the news programs of the Minshi, Sanli, Niandai, and Taidianshi channels; and nonpartisan citizens tend to watch news infrequently or not at all. In terms of newspapers, KMT supporters are overwhelmingly more likely to consume the *Apple Daily* (*Pingguo Ribao*), the *United Daily News* (*Lianhe Bao*), and the *China Times* (*Zhongguo Shibao*) than DPP supporters. In contrast, DPP supporters tend to favor the *Liberty Times* (*Ziyou Shibao*), which is decidedly unpopular with readers leaning toward the KMT.

The political affiliations of these media are said to reflect their ownership. For example, the former owners of the *United Daily* and the *China Times* were members of the KMT's core leadership body, the KMT Central Committee, and the KMT directly or indirectly controlled three television stations (Rawnsley 2004). The *China Daily* and the Zhongtian television station were later sold to Mainland Chinese investors. The *Liberty Times* was founded by a Taiwanese businessman and politician.

It is very likely that consumers of political news choose those outlets that most closely match their preferences. As various studies point out, media bias tends to converge with ideological and political cleavages in the population (see for example Chiang and Knight 2011; Endersby 2011; Gentzkow and Shapiro 2010; Hirschman and Thompson 1997; Prior 2013). Conservative news organs produce news for a conservative audience, and individuals with a conservative mindset are more likely to consume reports produced by conservative news organs. In simple terms, different media organs produce content aimed at different audiences, who, by consuming such content, feel that their values are affirmed. However, media not only affirm the values of their readership, but they might also shape them (Chong and Druckman 2007; Druckman 2004). For example, media might offer explanatory frames for the interpretation of specific events in the present or past and thereby influence their consumers' opinions.

If the correlation between individuals' partisanship and media choice is indeed caused by ideological polarization, this polarization should become apparent in a comparison of various news sources. We would expect to find very different narratives regarding corruption and anticorruption in Taiwan across news sources. News consumed almost exclusively by KMT supporters should be more forgiving of corruption, either as a general principle or when it affects politicians of their own party. In contrast, news consumed by DPP supporters should be directed against the KMT.

In practice, a media organ's ideological standpoint could be expressed in selection and statement bias (Groeling 2013). Selection bias occurs when news organs repress or cover certain events less intensely, presumably because they challenge the values and beliefs that outlet has come to stand for (McCarthy, McPhail, and Smith 1996). For example, a pro-KMT newspaper might feature fewer, shorter, or less prominently placed articles on the conviction of a KMT politician than its pro-DPP counterpart. Whereas selection bias concerns the frequency, length, and placement of news stories, statement bias refers to the language used to discuss a certain event (D'Alessio and Allen 2000). For example, a newspaper might portray a conviction on corruption charges as a witch hunt by the government or vindicate the involved politician's act by explaining it in the context of traditional values. Alternatively, the newspaper might feature examples of corruption in the opposition party to make the point that corruption affects all parties similarly. Those with a corruption-averse audience might display the opposite of a selection bias by giving not only convictions but also investigations prominent coverage. In terms of narratives, investigations and convictions alike could be cast as evidence that Taiwan is as corrupt as it has ever been and that anticorruption efforts are essentially futile. This approach would explain why there is a strong public perception that partisan loyalty is driving anticorruption efforts in Taiwan, even though these initiatives have made clear progress in political institutionalization.

METHOD AND DATA

The present analysis engages with these issues by conducting a content analysis of all available news articles on corruption and anticorruption efforts in four major newspapers: the *Apple Daily*, *United Daily News*, *China Times*, and *Liberty Times*. The choice of examining newspapers instead of television channels was made for pragmatic reasons: transcripts of all corruption reports by the nine main news channels were not available to the author. In addition, while all news stations have either a predominant KMT or DPP audience, one newspaper, the *Apple Daily*, draws an audience from both support groups. If news producers and their audience indeed converge ideologically, the content of that newspaper should give an indication as to why it appeals to both groups. The following paragraphs briefly introduce the four newspapers, which are Taiwan's most popular and together reach more than eight million people, equaling roughly one-third of Taiwan's population (Taiwan Government Entry Point 2012).

CASE SELECTION

The *Apple Daily* (2.33 million readers), read by 23.9 percent of all KMT supporters (Ministry of Justice 2016), is a tabloid owned by the Hong Kong Next Media group and has become famous for its investigative journalism, its criticism of China, and its sensationalist reporting (Lee 2007). It should display less of a partisan bias than the other newspapers. The ideological position of the *United Daily News* (1.65 million readers), read by 19.2 percent of KMT supporters, is said to align most closely with those in the KMT who support Taiwan's unification with China (Lee 2000). As mentioned earlier, it was owned by a member of the KMT's Central Standing Committee (Rawnsley 2004, 212). The *China Times* (1.49 million readers), with a readership of 7 percent of all KMT supporters, is also believed to be close to the KMT, though less so than the *United Daily News*. The *China Times* was also owned by a KMT Central Standing Committee member (Rawnsley 2004) but later sold to Chinese Want Want Holdings. Now, it allegedly supports the Chinese Communist Party (Hsu 2014), which might explain the comparatively low percentage of readers even among KMT supporters.

The *United Daily News* and the *China Times* are clearly unpopular with DPP readers, of whom only 2.2 percent read the former and 1.5

percent the latter newspaper. DPP supporters are overwhelmingly drawn toward the *Liberty Times* (*Ziyou Shibao*, 2.81 million readers), a pro-DPP newspaper (Kuo and Nakamura 2005) that boasts a readership of 34.6 percent of that group and is read by only 3.3 percent of those who feel close to the KMT. With a readership of 14.5 percent of all DPP supporters, the *Apple Daily* is the second most popular newspaper among DPP readers.

ASSEMBLING THE CORPUS

An attempt to source articles on the subject by relying on the newspapers' search function met with limited success, because the *Liberty Times* only allows searches three months into the past, and the archive of the *China Times* is difficult for non-Taiwanese nationals to access. A limited number of archive searches are available for registered and paying customers, but the site supports no international methods of payment.

However, a large number of articles published by these newspapers are also indexed on Google. I queried the search engines by using the following search pattern: "site:'[newspaper domain url]' AND 台灣 AND [search term]." The first keyword, consisting of the domain URL of each newspaper, ensures that only articles hosted by the four newspapers are returned, whereas the second keyword, 台灣 ("Taiwan"), limits the number of results containing reports on corruption in other countries. Finally, I employed the following eleven search terms: "corruption" (貪瀆 and 貪污), "serious corruption" (肅貪), "depraved" (腐敗, a more condemning term than 貪瀆), corrupt and depraved (貪腐), "bribe" (賄賂), "black gold" (黑金, denoting the relationship between organized crime and business but also often used in the context of political corruption), and A金, another way to write "black gold" (here, *a* is used as a transliteration of 黑 *hei*). For anticorruption efforts, I searched for the terms "anticorruption" (反貪) and "corrupt and depraved" (貪腐), as well as 掃黑, which translates literally as "sweeping out the black [gold]." Although the last seems to denote the fight against organized crime, the Chen Shui-bian administration has used it as a slogan for its anticorruption activities and has maintained this connotation. As Boolean searches employing both AND and OR operators did not return satisfactory results, I performed twenty-eight searches (seven terms times four newspapers), then eliminated duplicate results. I downloaded the html source code for all links thus obtained and appended them to the database. Besides the full text of the news items, each entry contains linked texts, advertisements, user comments, and other content not directly related to the content.

A first analysis revealed that a significant number of these articles covered very different topics, mentioning corruption only in passing or only providing links to articles on the subject. Hence, I reduced the sample to articles in which any combination of the eleven search terms appeared at least three times. This reduced the corpus to 3,103 articles. With the exception of the *United Daily News*, which is represented with 1,385 articles, the results are spread evenly: 656 articles appeared in the *Apple Daily*, 550 in the *Liberty Times*, and 492 articles in the *China Daily*.

UNSUPERVISED MACHINE LEARNING

I processed the articles for analysis by first cleaning them of all html code, white spaces, and non-Chinese characters using regular expressions. The resulting block of Chinese characters was segmented using the Python module jieba,[1] which uses a dictionary to insert white spaces between combinations of Chinese characters that make up a word (Levy and Manning 2003). In the Chinese language, most words consist of two Chinese characters. However, in contrast to alphabetic languages, in which white spaces separate words, in Chinese, the reader must glean these spaces from their relation to other words. All machine-learning algorithms work only with clearly demarcated words, which makes this procedure necessary (Chang, Galley, and Manning 2008). Fortunately, the results of simulations of segmentation modules on large Chinese-language corpora testify that this method reveals exact results, achieving F-Scores of 0.95 and above (Manning 2010).

To get a better understanding of the content of these articles and to prepare for the examination of the ideological differences among the four newspapers, I classified the corpus into topics by means of Latent Dirichlet Allocation (LDA) (Blei, Ng, and Jordan 2003). LDA parses the articles in a corpus to extract clusters of words based on the likelihood of their appearing together across all documents. The decision of how many such word combinations, called "topics," the algorithm should extract depends mainly on the desired granularity of the results. Up to a certain point, increasing the number of topics provides a more fine-grained analysis of the corpus; exceeding that point results in overfitting. For the analysis at hand, I used the Java-based software "Mallet" to extract topics (McCallum

2002).[2] Experimentation with different numbers of topics revealed that 150 topics captured the content of the corpus without the same issues' loading on different topics.

The procedure also elicited website content not related to the article, such as linked texts and advertisements; I excluded those terms not related to the topic of interest then reran the model. The wording of most of the resulting 150 topics is coherent. However, many of these topics, while including the key terms of this study, are nevertheless not related to the topic of corruption. For example, the corpus contains topics on food poisoning ("corrupt" also translates as "rotten"), and "black gold" is also used to refer to coffee. Yet other topics are historical treatises of Taiwanese or Chinese history that, among other things, discuss corruption in the Republic of China of the 1930s and 1940s, or Taiwan's involvement in international anticorruption efforts. Most of these topics would coappear in the same article as those of interest to this study. Finally, common expressions or particular writing styles also cluster in individual topics. Since these topics are not relevant to the analysis, I excluded them, leaving us with 104 topics directly related to corruption and anticorruption in Taiwan. Since some of these topics relate to different aspects of the same phenomenon, I reclassified them by adding up their topic scores under one label.

It should be noted that the exclusion of topics does not equal the exclusion of articles but the removal of noise from the existing articles, similar to selecting only those variables from a data set needed to test a particular hypothesis. The resulting data set consists of scores denoting the weight of each topic in a particular article.

Partisan Bias in the Taiwanese Media

THE DISCOURSE ON CORRUPTION AND ANTICORRUPTION

As can be seen from figure 3.1, the resulting topics cluster into five strong groups.

- Twelve of the 104 topics contain terms related to investigations of corrupt acts. Some topics focus on alleged perpetrators, others on institutions or investigators. They tend to relate

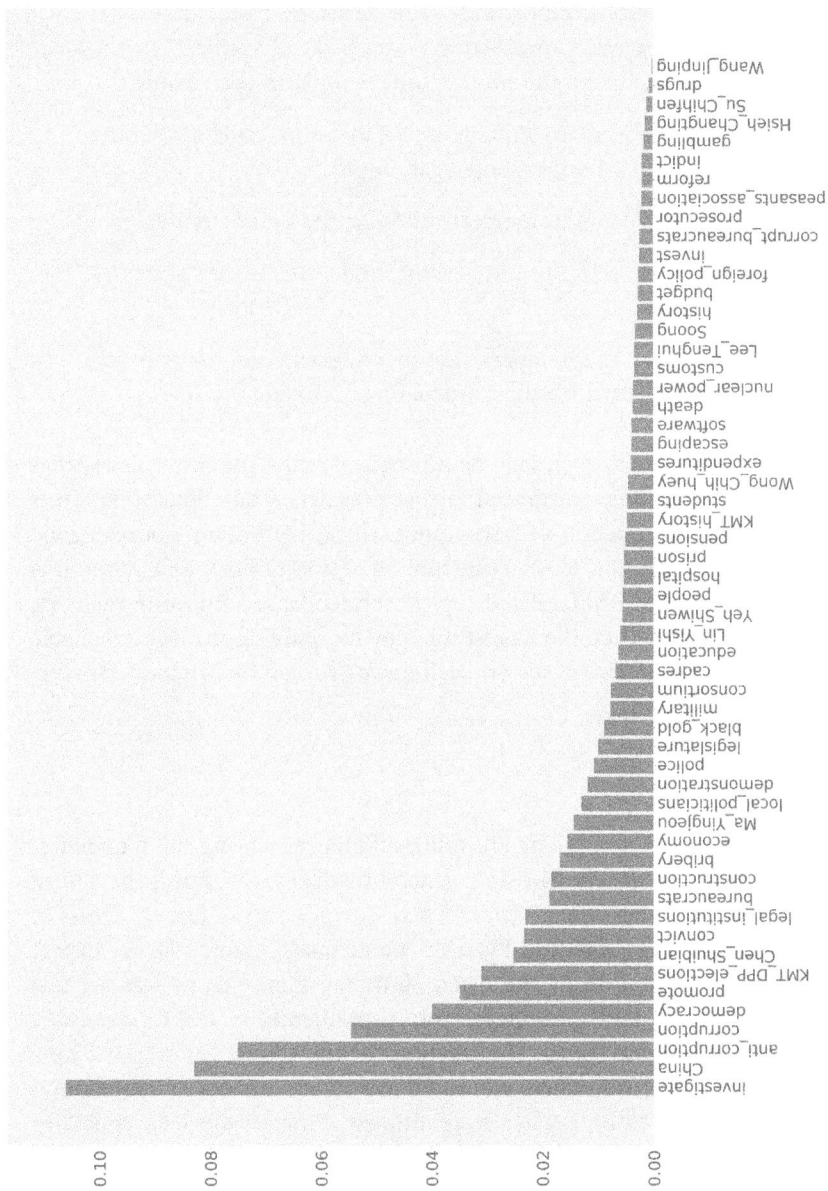

Figure 3.1. Topics in the corpus.

to descriptions of how individual cases are handled, including investigation, prosecution, and judicial verdicts. In the aggregate, this is the most frequent topic in the corpus.

- Ten topics relate to anticorruption in China, constituting the second most frequent aggregate topic.

- Six topics relate to anticorruption actors and activities.

- Four topics relate to terms associated with corrupt activities and actors.

- Democracy and democratization, represented in three topics, constitute the fifth most frequent category.

Fairly self-explanatory topics fill the subsequent ranks: the two major parties in relation to elections, disgraced former president Chen Shui-bian, terms related to the conviction of perpetrators, legal institutions, bureaucratic corruption, corruption in the construction sector, bribery, and so on. It is noteworthy that if KMT-related topics were collapsed into one category, that category would be the largest topic by far. Judging from the available corpus and irrespective of the outlet, Taiwan's corruption discourse mainly centers on the KMT.

Selection Bias

If the preceding assumptions are valid, differences among the four newspapers should be observable. As a general tendency, we expect the *United Daily News* and the *China Times* to play down, and the *Liberty Times* to emphasize, corrupt activities by KMT politicians. In contrast, we expect accounts of corruption by the Chen Shui-bian family as well as accusations against the DPP to appear more prominently in the *United Daily News* and the *China Times*. If allegations of the *China Times'* pro-China stance are valid, this is where we would expect accounts of anticorruption efforts in China to be especially prominent. Finally, given its appeal to both political camps, we expect the *Apple Daily* to be less condemning of either party than the other newspapers. Given its emphasis on investigative and sensationalist reporting, the coverage of crackdowns, gangsters, bribery, fraud, private-sector corruption, and judicial manipulation should be especially prominent in Taiwan's best-selling tabloid.

The correlation matrix (figure 3.2) nicely displays which topics are related to each other and which ones are not. Some topics are more likely

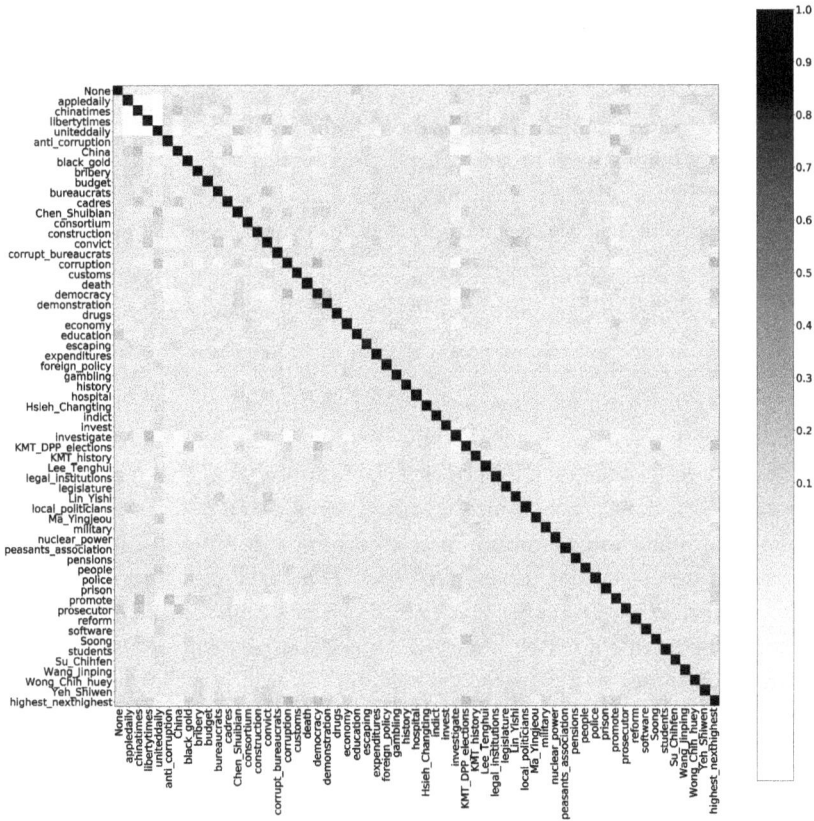

Figure 3.2. Correlation matrix of topics in the corpus.

than others to co-occur in one document. Most of these relations are not surprising. For example, the topic containing words related to the conviction of perpetrators correlates with topics related to bureaucratic corruption, former president Chen Shui-bian, investigations, local politicians, and Lin Yi-shih, a high-ranking politician who was sentenced to thirteen years in prison on charges of bribery. Perhaps more interesting is the fact that topics relating to democracy and democratization correlate significantly with the "corruption" topic. This pattern relates to a commonly made observation in Taiwanese media that corruption has worsened after the advent of democratization.

To probe for selection bias in Taiwan's news outlets, I included a dummy variable for each newspaper in the correlation plot. If the topic is more prevalent in one newspaper than others, Pearson's r will be positive and significantly different from zero. A negative correlation would suggest that a topic tends to be less prevalent in that newspaper. Finally, a value near zero would suggest that a topic is neither more nor less prevalent in that newspaper than in the others.

As can be seen, the four newspapers do indeed display significant differences with respect to the topics emphasized in them.

UNITED DAILY NEWS

The results visualized in figure 3.2 indicate that the expectations put forward earlier are met only in part. The *United Daily News* comes closest: compared to the three other newspapers in the sample, topics that negatively implicate the DPP are especially prominent. This newspaper is more likely to print reports on the corruption scandal of former president Chen Shui-bian and his family and accusations of an anti-KMT bias in investigating corruption cases. On KMT-related stories, the newspaper also performs just as expected. The likelihood that topics highlighting corruption in the KMT will surface in the *United Daily News* is lower than for all other newspapers.

Also, in comparison to the other papers, the *United Daily News* is far more likely to use variations of the term "corruption." In addition, it refers more frequently to legal institutions, invokes "the people," and mentions former president Ma Ying-jeou. Ma served as minister of justice under President Lee Teng-hui. Because he had no connections to local factions, cracked down on corruption, and cleaned up local financial institutions, he long enjoyed the image of a clean politician. Against this background, it is interesting that the topics of anticorruption, bribery, convictions, and investigations are less prominent here than in the other newspapers. This lack might suggest a tendency to complain about corrupt politics without mentioning specific individuals, perhaps because many of these people have KMT backgrounds. Chen Shui-bian, the disgraced former president, is the obvious exception.

LIBERTY TIMES

Looking at the other side of the spectrum, we see that the *Liberty Times* is especially likely to score high on topics related to the investigation of cases, which overwhelmingly affected KMT politicians. We find a weaker, yet positive correlation between the *Liberty Times* and topics pertaining to credits, corruption in the construction sector, demonstrations, education, government expenditures, and issues related to hospitals, elections, police, prison, and the conviction of Lin Yi-shih. These observations conform to the liberal and populist tendencies of this newspaper, which sees itself as a watchdog against government corruption and the abuse of power.

Apple Daily

The *Apple Daily* performs nearly as had been expected. Readers are indeed more likely to find articles on human-interest topics such as the anticorruption drive in China, investigations against corruption, corruption in local politics, and the scandal involving the legislator Wong Chih-huey. The last finding is surprising, because it would have been logical for such articles to appear in the *Liberty Times*, which is closer to the DPP than the other newspapers. Other topics, like bribery, the budget, convictions, the escape of convicted politicians from Taiwan, and two more politicians mired in scandals are less prevalent in the newspaper but still evident there. The findings are in line with the hypothesis that the newspaper does not showcase a strong bias toward either party—the odds of topics related either to the Chen Shui-bian family or KMT politicians' appearing in this newspaper are close to the sample average.

China Times

Finally, the *China Times* is somewhat similar to the *Apple Daily* in that the likelihood of many topics' appearing in that newspaper is close to the mean of the whole sample. Also, similar to the *Apple Daily*, the paper emphasizes topics related to China's anticorruption efforts. This finding seems to support the allegation that the *China Times* is more oriented toward China than, for example, the *United Daily News*.

Interestingly, the *China Times* covers anticorruption efforts not only in China but also in Taiwan—topics related to activities designed to rein in corruption and to the prosecution of individuals are especially prominent here, as is the "bribery" topic. This finding is surprising, because most of these activities affected the KMT. We find weaker, yet still positive correlations for topics related to anticorruption, black gold, historical issues, and the politician Soong Chu-yu, a member of the old guard of the KMT with strong connections to local factions. These are topics we would rather have expected the *Apple Daily* or the *Liberty Times* to cover. Judging from the topics, *China Times* does not seem to have an anti-DPP bias, but, like the *Apple Daily*, seems to select its stories based on human interest.

FINDINGS

The available sample reveals the expected pro-KMT and anti-DPP reporting bias only in the *United Daily News*. The findings are less clear-cut for the *Liberty Times*, where reporting bias does exist but less obviously than in the *United Daily News*. For example, the *Liberty Times* does not differ much from the pro-KMT newspapers in its coverage of corruption cases involving the KMT.

Similarly, the *Apple Daily* performs as expected with regard to being more or less neutral toward the two political camps, reports on indicted KMT politicians notwithstanding. The *China Times* deviates furthest from my initial expectations, because it is even more likely than the other newspapers to report on the conviction of KMT politicians. Noteworthy, however, is its predisposition to report about anticorruption efforts in China. That the newspaper is now owned by a Chinese investor might explain this finding, if that change in ownership has led the newspaper to change its standpoint from pro-KMT to pro-China.

STATEMENT BIAS

The following section examines the evidence for statement bias in the four newspapers' reports on corruption and anticorruption efforts in Taiwan. In particular, it analyzes whether newspapers are more likely to frame certain persons, institutions, and organizations than others negatively, and if such frames conform to the expectations outlined earlier. Specifically, I expect the *United Daily* and the *China Times* to frame the KMT positively and the DPP negatively, and the *Liberty Times* to frame the DPP positively and the KMT negatively. This pattern should hold true not only for the parties themselves but also for organizations either of the parties control. For example, I expect the *Liberty Times* to frame the government, presidency, or the Legislative Yuan negatively when controlled by the KMT. The opposite should hold true for the *United Daily* and the *China Times*.

I tested for the presence or absence of statement bias with the help of a word-embedding analysis. Word-embedding analysis transforms words into numeric vectors within a multidimensional space. The more frequently particular words co-occur, the more proximate they are in the vector space. The proximity of words can be estimated by calculating their cosine distance.

SELECTION OF TERMS

Because how newspapers frame not only individual parties but corruption as a whole is of interest, the analysis examines the framing of a broad variety of organizations, individuals, and institutions. My selection of terms was guided both by the literature on corruption in Taiwan and items included in surveys to measure "confidence" in national (political) organizations such as parliament, the government, or the courts.[3] The former provides insight into how the different newspapers frame corruption and anticorruption efforts in Taiwan, the latter into how media frame the impact of corruption on Taiwan's political fabric. A high association between "KMT" and "corruption" would be an example of the former; close proximity between "government" and "corrupt," of the latter.

Two main terms are of interest. The first is "corrupt." As previously described, there are several Chinese translations for the term "corruption." As this analysis is concerned with statement bias, I chose the term *fubai*, which translates as "corrupt" and also as "rotten, putrid, decayed." The term not only indicates that someone has engaged in an act of corruption but also that this person is morally reprehensible.

The second term is "incompetent." I include this term to establish if reports on corruption are associated with the notion that particular individuals or organizations are considered incompetent, either because they are unable to reduce corruption or because corruption is associated with incompetence. News media's frequent characterization of individuals or organizations as corrupt or incompetent might explain why the Taiwanese do not give the government credit for its success in fighting corruption.

As for terms associated with corruption and incompetence, I chose the following words to represent parties, politicians, other actors, and institutions related both to corrupt networks and to anticorruption activities and organizations in Taiwan:

- Political parties: KMT, DPP, PFP, TSU

- Politicians: Lee Teng-hui, Chen Shui-bian, Ma Ying-jeou, Tsai Ying-wen (presidents); Lin Yi-shih, Yeh Sheng-mao (high-level KMT and DPP politicians convicted of corruption)

- Actors and institutions in corrupt networks: "black gold," "farmer's association," "consortium," "party assets," "local factions," "triads"

- Anticorruption institutions: "AAC," "Sweeping out Black Gold program"

To shed light on how the individual newspapers assess Taiwan's political institutions more broadly, I chose the following terms:

- Political community: "Taiwan," "nation," "society"

- Political organizations: "government," "Legislative Yuan," "(County) Assembly," "political party," "police," "elections"

- Political roles: "president," "leader," "legislator," "mayor," "speaker," "councilor," "civil servant," "judge"

- Values: "justice," "morality," "democracy," "work style of government"

Finally, I included the term "worsen" to establish whether the newspapers indicate that corruption has become a more serious problem than before. To account for the impact of changes in government, I performed separate analyses for each administration and each of the newspapers.

CHEN ADMINISTRATION

Figure 3.3 presents the results for articles published in the Chen Shui-bian era (2000–2008). As can be seen, the results do not confirm the expectations laid out earlier: the cosine distances between the term "corrupt" and the other words do not differ significantly for most of the newspapers. For example, the level of association between "corruption" and "DPP" is nearly the same as the association between "corruption" and "KMT" for each of the newspapers. As for the names of the presidents, especially Chen Shui-bian and Ma Ying-jeou, figure 3.3 shows that the *Liberty Times* associates corruption more with Chen Shui-bian than with Ma Ying-jeou, which suggests that the newspaper does not tend to whitewash the accusations against Chen Shui-bian. The *China Times* associates Ma Ying-jeou, but not Chen Shui-bian, with the word "corruption," which can probably be explained by the fact that the *China Times* carried several reports on

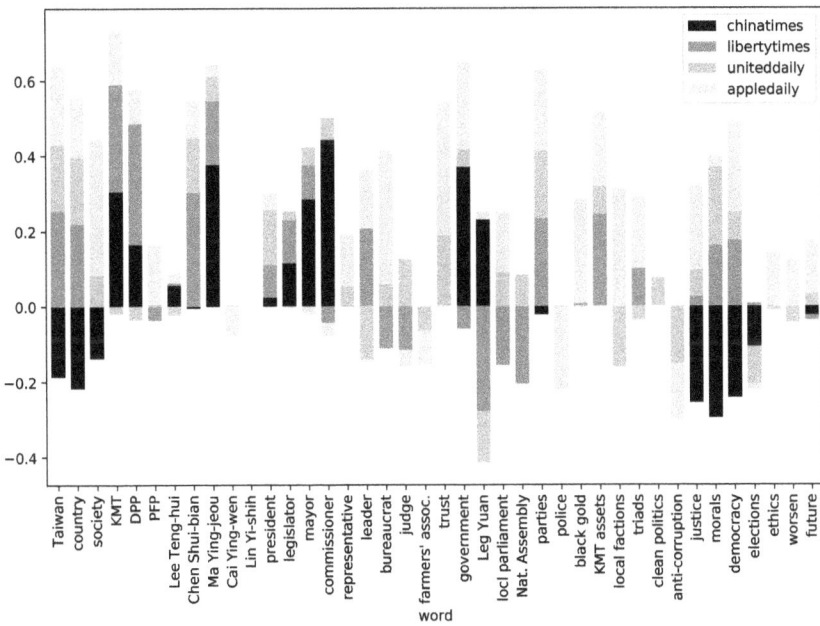

Figure 3.3. Cosine similarity between "corrupt" and selected terms, 2000–2008.

the establishment of Taiwan's anticorruption agency under Ma Ying-jeou after a number of high-level corruption cases. Also, only very few *China Times* articles are available for this time span, so the scores for this time period and newspaper should be treated with caution. The association of other terms for the individual newspapers does not seem to follow a consistent pattern; they display mostly similar values for terms such as "Taiwan," "nation," "KMT" and "DPP," "President Chen Shui-bian," and "KMT general secretary and Taipei mayor Ma Ying-jeou." The same is true for the terms "party" and "democracy."

These results suggest that all newspapers associate important concepts and organizations with corruption, independent of their partisan background. In other words, no matter which newspaper one reads, the reader is likely to be confronted with the same associations, which are very critical of the general political environment in Taiwan, irrespective of which political party has the power to set the agenda.

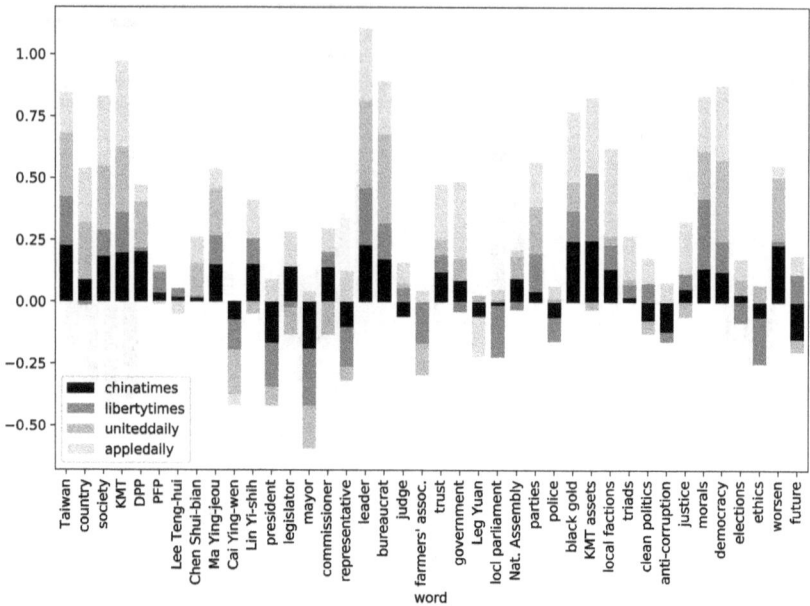

Figure 3.4. Cosine similarity between "corrupt" and selected terms, 2008–2016.

Ma Administration

The findings are similar for the Ma Ying-jeou administration (2008–2016), but with important differences. Most notably, newspapers tended to focus more in this era on negatively framing the KMT than the DPP. However, once more, the results do not confirm my expectations. The *United Daily*, for example, associates both political parties with the term "corruption." In the *Liberty Times*, the KMT's score is higher than the DPP's, but the values are very small. Only the *Apple Daily* displays a marked difference in scores, which might be explained by the fact that the tabloid has reported eagerly on the corruption scandals that occurred in the Ma Ying-jeou administration. "Leaders" and "administrators" are also likely to be associated with the term "corruption."

The newspapers used the term "incompetent" so sparsely between 2000 and 2008 that meaningful analysis is not possible. For the Ma Ying-jeou administration, the results yet again display similar tendencies to what we observed with respect to the term "corruption." The four newspapers do

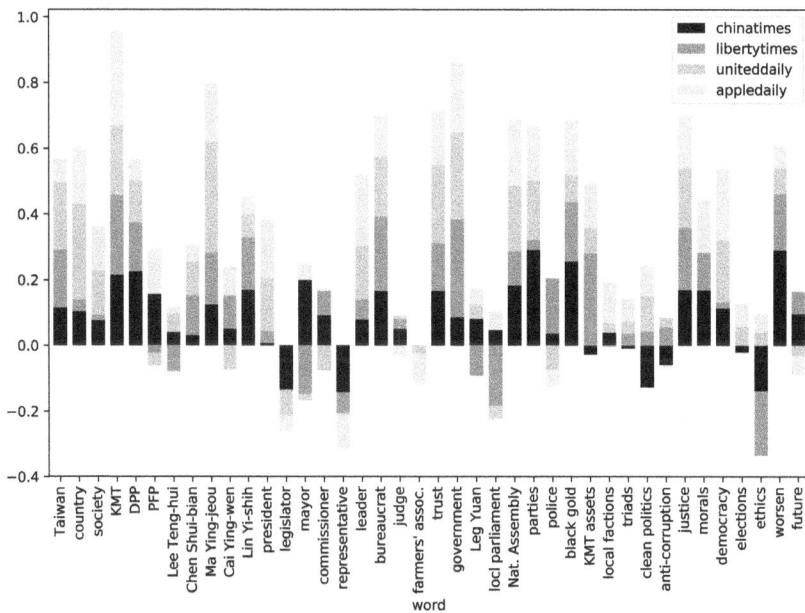

Figure 3.5. Cosine similarity between "incompetent" and selected terms, 2008–2016.

not differ much in their association of the term "incompetent" with "KMT,"
"Ma Ying-jeou," "public servants," and "government." The term "financial
consortium" also correlates strongly with "incompetent," which might be
a result of the global financial crisis. Also significant is the fact that terms
like "justice," "morality," and "democracy" are strongly associated with
"incompetence," and that "incompetence" is strongly associated with the
word "worsen" for all but one newspaper. Again, this result suggests that
in the aggregate, the newspapers do not so much display partisan biases
as they are prone to negative reporting. Almost unanimously, they seem to
associate major political institutions with both corruption and incompetence.

Although patterns of word-embedding differ somewhat from administration to administration, that difference pertains mainly to the level of
association between the different words and the two core terms and less to
differences across newspapers. It is remarkable that, although the samples
are completely independent of each other, all four newspapers display
similar trends regarding the terms that are associated with corruption or
incompetence.

Conclusion

Do Taiwanese newspapers differ in how they report on corruption and anticorruption efforts? If so, does the displayed bias correlate with the alleged ideological positions of these newspapers? The findings are mixed. As regards selection bias, the *United Daily News*, commonly associated with being close to the KMT, comes closest to meeting our expectations. We find the *China Times* to be less a mouthpiece for the KMT than expected, and the *Liberty Times* also seems to be more balanced than its alleged pro-DPP stance would lead one to anticipate. Although not directly related to the research question addressed in this chapter, it is remarkable how much space the *China Times* and the *Apple Daily* devote to anticorruption initiatives in China. For the *China Times*, this tendency might reflect attempts to promote a positive image of China, whereas the *Apple Daily* is perhaps more interested in the sordid details of China's ongoing anticorruption campaign. In its reporting on corruption in Taiwan, the *Apple Daily*'s large KMT-affiliated readership does not prevent it from reporting on KMT scandals.

The results are less conclusive for the analysis of statement bias. I found no evidence that any of the newspapers systematically accuse certain politicians or parties of being corrupt or incompetent. Rather, there seems to be a tendency to portray the polity at large as being negatively affected by corruption. Little evidence suggests positive reporting on the progress that undoubtedly has been made in fighting corruption. In other words, the newspapers do not differ much in that they all paint a rather bleak picture of the state of politics in Taiwan. This finding confirms previous research on the propensity of Taiwan's newspapers for negative reporting. Given how cynical the Taiwanese population is when it comes to politics, newspaper editors might be afraid that good news will not sell well.

It follows that despite numerous, though as of yet unsubstantiated, accusations that both parties use anticorruption efforts mainly to fight their political opponents, Taiwan's existing anticorruption framework has been mainly driven by a goal of political institutionalization. Despite remarkable achievements in eliminating corruption by both parties, Taiwan's vitriolic political discourse, amplified by the news media, contributes to the perception that anticorruption efforts have largely failed. Although the newspapers do not overtly blame the opposition, they help create the impression that Taiwan's political environment—which is, after all, characterized by bipartisanism—is not conducive to fighting political corruption. Hence, it is likely that Taiwan's news media bear at least part of the responsibility for the difference between popular perceptions and experiences of corruption.

However, these findings need to be taken with a grain of salt. First, the biggest limitation of the present study is my not having access to the full-text archive of the four newspapers. It is therefore not possible to say whether the selected articles constitute a representative sample or if only certain articles are published online.

Second, the present analysis does not account for the influence of the articles examined. All articles figure equally in the analysis, regardless of whether they are printed on the front page or the inside of a newspaper, if they have had many or few readers, or if they are discussed widely or not. By its very nature, quantitative content analysis can only grasp general trends; it is likely to overlook single, very influential articles.

Third, I have been able to establish that the four papers do indeed differ in their ideological disposition, but I cannot make any claims on how relevant these newspapers are for shaping the values and beliefs of their readers. Relatedly, newspapers are only one, and perhaps not even the most popular, medium of political information for Taiwan's citizens.

While the present analysis has taken a first step in analyzing the relationship between the ideological disposition displayed by Taiwan's media and the values and beliefs of Taiwanese citizens, it will be necessary to conduct similar analyses for other media, as well. In addition, the relationship between media exposure and political attitudes would have to be established by means of experiments or surveys.

Notes

1. Https://github.com/fxsjy/jieba.

2. Mallet applies Gibbs Sampling, a Markov Chain Monte Carlo (MCMC) algorithm classified as "Bayesian." Mallet outperforms all LDA solutions offered in the R statistical programming language in terms of speed—I tried the packages Topic Models (Hornik and Grün 2011) and STM (Roberts, Stewart, and Tingley forthcoming)—and yields better results than, for example, the Python Gensim module (Řehůřek and Sojka 2011), which seems to work better with English-language texts than with Chinese sources.

3. See for example the World Values Survey (http://www.worldvaluessurvey.org).

Bibliography

Blei, David M., Andrew Y. Ng, and Michael I. Jordan. "Latent Dirichlet Allocation." *Journal of Machine Learning Research* (January 2003): 993–1022.

Boudin, F. "A Comparison of Centrality Measures for Graph-Based Keyphrase Extraction." International Joint Conference on Natural Language Processing (IJCNLP), 2013, 834–838.

Chang, Pi-Chuan, M. Galley, and C. D. Manning. "Optimizing Chinese Word Segmentation for Machine Translation Performance." *Proceedings of the Third Workshop on Statistical Machine Translation* (2008): 224–232.

Chiang, Chun-Fang, and Brian Knight. "Media Bias and Influence: Evidence from Newspaper Endorsements." *The Review of Economic Studies* 78, no. 3 (2011): 795–820.

Chin, Ko-lin. *Heijin: Organized Crime, Business, and Politics in Taiwan*. New York: Routledge, 2003.

Chong, Dennis, and James N. Druckman. "Framing Public Opinion in Competitive Democracies." *American Political Science Review* 101, no. 04 (2007): 637–655.

D'Alessio, Dave, and Mike Allen. "Media Bias in Presidential Elections: A Meta-Analysis." *Journal of Communication* 50, no. 4 (2000): 133–156.

Druckman, James N. "Political Preference Formation: Competition, Deliberation, and The(ir) Relevance of Framing Effects." *American Political Science Review* 98, no. 4 (2004): 671–686.

Endersby, James W. "Fair and Balanced? News Media Bias and Influence on Voters." August 1, 2011. Retrieved from https://papers.ssrn.com/sol3/papers.cfm?abstract_id=1920620.

Fang, Nien-hsuan, and Chien-San Feng. "Press Coverage of Post-Presidential Election Turmoil: Not Yet Hate Speech, but Reinforcing Resentments." *Issues and Studies* 40, nos. 3 and 4 (2004): 354–361.

Fell, Dafydd. *Party Politics in Taiwan: Party Change and the Democratic Evolution of Taiwan, 1991–2004*. New York: Taylor & Francis, 2005a.

Fell, Dafydd. "Political and Media Liberalization and Political Corruption in Taiwan." *China Quarterly* 184 (2005b): 875–893.

Gentzkow, Matthew, Jesse M. Shapiro. "What Drives Media Slant? Evidence from US Daily Newspapers." *Econometrica* 78, no. 1 (2010): 35–71.

Gewirth, Alan. "Ethical Universalism and Particularism." *The Journal of Philosophy* 85, no. 6 (1988): 283–302.

Goebel, Christian. "Taiwan's Fight against Corruption." *Journal of Democracy* 27, no. 6 (2016): 124–138.

Groeling, Tim. "Media Bias by the Numbers: Challenges and Opportunities in the Empirical Study of Partisan News." *Political Science* 16, no. 1 (2013): 129–151.

Hirschman, Elizabeth C., and Craig J. Thompson. "Why Media Matter: Toward a Richer Understanding of Consumers' Relationships with Advertising and Mass Media." *Journal of Advertising* 26, no. 1 (1997): 43–60.

Hornik, Kurt, and Bettina Grün. "Topicmodels: An R Package for Fitting Topic Models." *Journal of Statistical Software* 40, no. 13 (2011): 1–30.

Hsu, C-J. *The Construction of National Identity in Taiwan's Media, 1896–2012.* Leiden: Brill, 2014.

Kuo, Sai-Hua, and Mari Nakamura. "Translation or Transformation? A Case Study of Language and Ideology in the Taiwanese Press." *Discourse and Society* 16, no. 3 (2005): 393–417.

Lee, Aie-Rie. "Value Cleavages, Issues, and Partisanship in East Asia." *Journal of East Asian Studies* 7 (2007): 251–274.

Lee, Chin-Chuan. "State, Capital, and Media." In *De-Westernizing Media Studies,* edited by James Curran and Myung-jin Park, 124–138. New York: Routledge, 2000.

Lee, Ya-Ching. "Effects of Market Competition on Taiwan Newspaper Diversity." *Journal of Media Economics* 20, no. 2 (2007): 139–156.

Levy, R., and C. Manning. "Is It Harder to Parse Chinese, or the Chinese Treebank?" *Proceedings of the 41st Annual Meeting on Association for Computational Linguistics* 1 (2003): 439–46.

Liu, James H., Li-Li Huang, and Catherine McFedries. "Cross-Sectional and Longitudinal Differences in Social Dominance Orientation and Right Wing Authoritarianism as a Function of Political Power and Societal Change." *Asian Journal of Social Psychology* 11, no. 2 (2008): 116–126.

Manning, Christopher. "A Conditional Random Field Word Segmenter." 2010. Retrieved from https://philpapers.org/rec/MANACR.

McCallum, Andrew Kachites. "MALLET: A Machine Learning for Language Toolkit." 2002. Retrieved from http://mallet.cs.umass.edu.

McCarthy, John D., Clark McPhail, and Jackie Smith. "Images of Protest: Dimensions of Selection Bias in Media Coverage of Washington Demonstrations, 1982 and 1991." *American Sociological Review* (1996): 478–499.

Ministry of Justice. *Fawubu Lianzhengshu 100 niandu gongzuo baogao* [Agency against Corruption 2011 work report]. Taipei: Fawubu Lianzhengshu, 2012.

Ministry of Justice. *Fawubu Lianzhengshu 104 nian lianzheng mingyi dioacha di yi jieduan diaocha baogao: minzhong dui lianzheng guangan yu xunxi laiyuan* [Investigation report on the first stage of the 2015 public poll by the Agency against Corruption: The public's perception of integrity and their sources of information]. 2016. Retrieved from http://www.aac.moj.gov.tw/HitCounter.asp?xItem=423097&mp=289.

Prior, Markus. "Media and Political Polarization." *Annual Review of Political Science* 16 (2013): 101–127.

Rawnsley, Gary D. "Treading a Fine Line: Democratisation and the Media in Taiwan." *Parliamentary Affairs* 57, no. 1 (January 2004): 209–222. https://doi.org/10.1093/pa/gsh017.

Řehůřek, Radim, and Petre Sojka. "Gensim—Statistical Semantics in Python." 2011. Retrieved from EuroSciPyarchive.euroscipy.org/file/6477/raw/Radim_Rehurek.pdf.

Roberts, Margaret E., Brandon M. Stewart, and Dustin Tingley. "STM: R Package for Structural Topic Models." *Journal of Statistical Software*. Forthcoming.

Schult, D. A., and P. Swart. "Exploring Network Structure, Dynamics, and Function Using NetworkX." *Proceedings of the 7th Python in Science Conferences* (SciPy 2008) (2008): 11–16.

Stiftung Bertelsmann. Taiwan Country Report, Bertelsmann Transformation Index 2016. Retrieved from https://www.bti-project.org/fileadmin/files/BTI/Downloads/Reports/2016/pdf/BTI_2016_Taiwan.pdf.

Taiwan Government Entry Point. Print Media, 2012. Retrieved from http://www.taiwan.gov.tw/ct.asp?xItem=77852&ctNode=1916&mp=1001.

Transparency International. Global Corruption Barometer 2010/2011. Retrieved from http://www.transparency.org/gcb201011.

Transparency International. Corruption Perceptions Index 2018: Score Time Series since 2012. Retrieved from: https://www.transparency.org/cpi2018.

World Bank. Worldwide Governance Indicators. 2018. Retrieved from http://info.worldbank.org/governance/wgi/wgidataset.xlsx.

Wu, Chung-li. "Charge Me If You Can: Assessing Political Biases in Vote-Buying Verdicts in Democratic Taiwan (2000–2010)." *The China Quarterly* 211 (2012): 786–805.

Xin, Katherine K., and Jone L. Pearce. "Guanxi: Connections as Substitutes for Formal Institutional Support." *Academy of Management Journal* 39, no. 6 (1996): 1641–1658.

4

Rust Removal

Why Vietnam's Historical Anticorruption Efforts
Failed to Deliver Results,
and What That Implies for the Current Campaign

EDMUND MALESKY AND NGOC PHAN

A s we polish this chapter for submission, Vietnam is in the throes of an unprecedented anticorruption effort. On January 8, 2018, the corruption trial of Đinh La Thăng, the Vietnamese Communist Party secretary (VCP) of Hồ Chí Minh City and a Politburo member, began in Hà Nội. The trial, which also includes twenty-one subordinates of PetroVietnam, the state-owned oil company that Thăng led before entering government as the minister of construction, is unprecedented for two reasons. First, Thăng will be the first Politburo member to face trial and a certain long-term prison sentence. While four previous Politburo members have been disciplined (Thayer 2018b), two for corruption-related charges, these elites received reprimands or removal from higher office; they never faced criminal charges in a Vietnamese court of law. Second, in pursuing two related corruption cases, Vietnamese authorities have shown an unusual willingness to reach beyond their borders. In a plot worthy of spy novel, Germany accused Vietnam of allegedly kidnapping Trịnh Xuân Thanh, the former general director of PetroVietnam's Construction Corporation and Thăng's former subordinate, and smuggling him back to Vietnam before he was able to complete asylum procedures. Later, Phan Văn Anh Vũ, a property developer and former secret service officer, was found in

Singapore and, with the cooperation of local authorities who canceled his Singapore visa, was arrested by Vietnam's Ministry of Public Security for revealing state secrets.

As with the ongoing anticorruption effort in China (see Wedeman, chapter 7 in this volume), the campaign has swept up the high-profile tigers above as well as several flies who served in subordinate capacities to the corrupt elite officials. Thanh stands accused of causing US$150 million in losses to state assets and faces the death penalty, but his alleged crime is just the most egregious in a range of different offenses currently being prosecuted. At the other end of the corruption spectrum, the VCP inspectorate dismissed Nguyễn Xuân Anh, party secretary of Đà Nẵng, from his position and punished him for the relatively mundane violations of listing a doctorate from an uncertified university on his resume, using city cars for personal use, and falsifying addresses to hide the true extent of his real estate holdings (TuoiTre 2017b).

In this chapter, we attempt to make sense of these cases by putting them in the context of Vietnam's history of anticorruption efforts, including formal legislative and VCP efforts, as well as high-profile anticorruption cases. We argue that previous efforts have only been cosmetic, have never attempted to unwind the systemic elements that reinforce corruption in the country and were heavily influenced by elite political maneuvering (see Chen and Weiss, the introduction to this volume). International analysts have praised Vietnam's formal anticorruption legislation on paper, but implementation has been weak and internal contradictions have thwarted the laws' effectiveness. At the same time, connections to elite politics have tinged the legitimacy of anticorruption in the public eye. Finally, despite formal commitments from top leaders, there has been little effort to put in place institutional changes that might thwart future corruption. Vietnam has no independent anticorruption board, as in Hong Kong (Manion 2004; Fisman and Golden 2017), and the VCP's Anticorruption Commission has struggled to extricate itself from internal politics. Meritocratic promotion, although enshrined in principle through cadre evaluation, is weakened by payments for appointments to top government and state-owned enterprise positions, which has diminished public perceptions about the quality of public servants. Moreover, elite-level corruption has a ripple effect, as those same officials have incentives to allow corruption in their agencies in order to amortize their initial investment. Finally, transparency of budgets and public disclosure has remained tepid and weakly enforced.

The chapter proceeds as follows. In the first section, we discuss Vietnam's comparative standing in international indices of corruption and delineate the common modes of corrupt behavior that exist in the country using two nationally representative surveys of firms and citizens. In the second section, we outline Vietnam's formal anticorruption procedures. In the third section, we discuss high-profile anticorruption cases in Vietnam, demonstrating quantitatively and qualitatively their connections to elite political machinations. The fourth section discusses the 2017 elite corruption scandals and asks whether this particular effort is substantively different because of its greater focus on institutional reforms (see the introduction to this volume).

Corruption in Vietnam

In this section, we study international and domestic survey data to look at why corruption has remained persistent and even trended upward in Vietnam despite repeated anticorruption efforts. Research on Vietnam has highlighted corruption as a "systemic" problem and offered explanations for different forms of corruption that map quite well onto international typologies.

Thaveeporn Vasavakul (2008) characterizes these forms as: first, "grease" or "speed money" to fulfill basic tasks or services; second, the illegal privatization of state property; and third, the selling of state power. In addition, she argues that there is "a tendency in Vietnam to view public office as a vehicle for personal enrichment; secondly; a tendency to pay attention to servicing one's patronage network rather than working for some notion of the public good" (Vasavakul 2008). International typologies usually categorize Vasavakul's first category of grease money as petty or micro-corruption and the latter two categories as grand or macro-corruption.

In international comparisons, Vietnam ranks poorly when it comes to corruption. Most international measures rank Vietnam in the bottom 30th percentile, where low scores reflect poor efforts to combat corruption. For instance, Vietnam places 109th out of 144 countries in the World Economic Forum's (WEF's) Irregular Payments and Bribes Index (World Economic Forum 2017) and 113th out of 176 countries in Transparency International's Corruption Perceptions Index (CPI). Similarly, Transparency International's

Global Corruption Barometer reports that 44 percent of Vietnamese report paying a bribe of some form (Transparency International 2017).

At the same time, Vietnam ranks poorly in terms of what many analysts consider to be contributing factors to corruption. Its government regulations are burdensome and full of contradictions, creating opportunities for unscrupulous officials to hold up normal transactions. Vietnam ranked 101st out of 144 countries on WEF's 2016–2017 Burden of Regulation Index (World Economic Forum 2017). This puts Vietnam just behind Nigeria and Timor-Leste, while its fellow single-party regime China ranks 19th. Indeed, between 50 and 60 percent of Vietnamese firms have answered in the country's largest nationwide survey that the main purpose of regulation is not to protect employees and citizens, but to provide an excuse for extracting bribes from businesses (Malesky 2005–2017).

Furthermore, budgeting and policymaking occur in the dark, where illicit deals are common. WEF further ranked Vietnam 116th of 144 countries for the transparency of its government policymaking, directly behind Zimbabwe and Bangladesh and far behind China (ranked 33rd). The Vietnam Chamber of Commerce and Industry (VCCI) has also highlighted a trend toward worsening overall transparency in drafting new regulations in its annual report on ministerial efficiency (Malesky 2005–2017).

MEASURES OF CORRUPTION FROM VIETNAMESE SURVEYS

In addition to the international measures of corruption, Vietnam also has two national-level surveys that are useful for gauging corruption over time. The Provincial Competitiveness Index Survey, funded by the United States Agency for International Development (USAID) and administered annually by the Vietnam Chamber of Commerce and Industry (VCCI) since 2005, surveys the perceptions and experiences of owners and managers of Vietnam's domestic businesses. With an annual sample size of ten thousand private businesses in all sixty-three provinces, it is the largest and most highly regarded business survey in the country. In addition, the Provincial Administration Performance Index (PAPI) Survey, funded by the United Nations Development Program and implemented by the Vietnam Fatherland Front and Centre for Community Support and Development Studies (CECODES), annually gauges citizens' perceptions. It uses a nationally representative sample of about fourteen thousand respondents that includes sizable samples from every province in the country. Both instruments include questions that track both petty and grand corruption. Caution is in order, however: Such public opinion surveys capture petty corruption well because citizens experience this type of corruption directly. Macro-corruption is much harder to document. This qualification is important, because national campaigns have primarily targeted these harder-to-observe-and-analyze activities.

Figure 4.1 studies three questions from the PCI survey that have appeared in every iteration since 2006, allowing us to track corruption perceptions over time. The first two panels of figure 4.1 track estimates

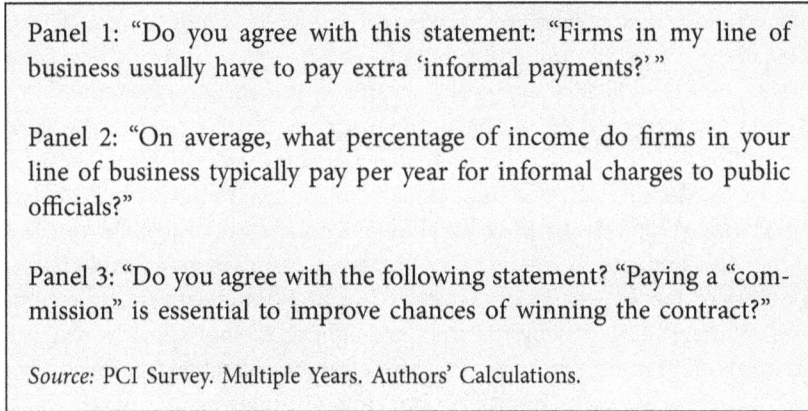

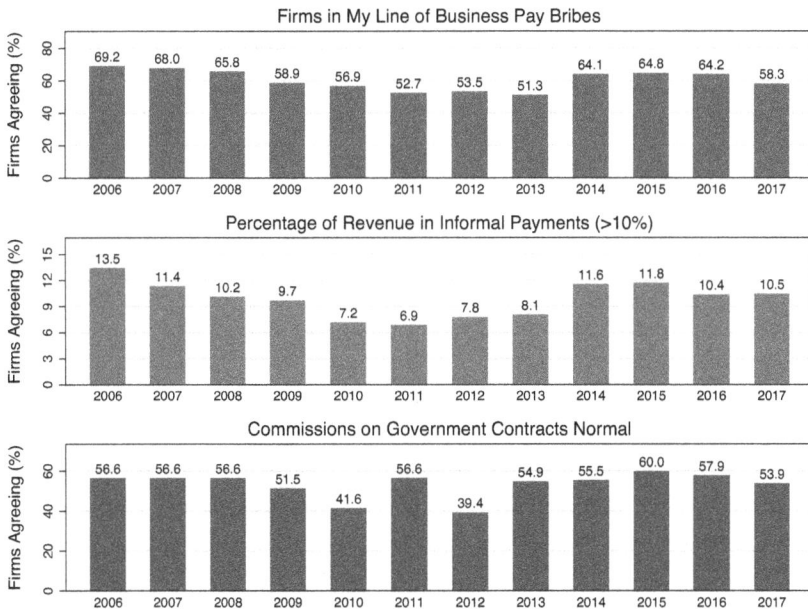

Panel 1: "Do you agree with this statement: "Firms in my line of business usually have to pay extra 'informal payments?'"

Panel 2: "On average, what percentage of income do firms in your line of business typically pay per year for informal charges to public officials?"

Panel 3: "Do you agree with the following statement? "Paying a "commission" is essential to improve chances of winning the contract?"

Source: PCI Survey. Multiple Years. Authors' Calculations.

Figure 4.1. Business perceptions of corruption over time.

of petty corruption, specifically whether firms believe others in their line of business pay bribes and the estimated size of those bribes. The second question looks at grand corruption by asking whether the small set of firms that compete for government procurement contracts feel the necessity of offering commissions, the Vietnamese euphemism for kick-backs, to be eligible to win. The first thing to notice about the graphs is that, while there are some perturbations over time, the general trend is that corruption has remained high. Between one-half and two-thirds of firms believe that corruption is common; between 7 and 12 percent pay exorbitantly high amounts of money in bribes; and well over half of the firms believe kickbacks are necessary for government procurement. In short, anticorruption efforts have not made much of a dent in business perceptions of corruption. Second, after declining marginally in the first half of the decade, all three indicators trended upward between 2011 and 2016, which coincides with the previous administration under Nguyễn Tấn Dũng. This finding is consistent with characterizations of his administration as open to the international economy but highly opportunistic (Vuving 2010; Vuving 2013). Finally, there is some light on the horizon. The recently completed 2017 iteration of the PCI survey shows marginal improvements on all three indicators. Trends are not down to their historic levels, high though those were, but there appears to be a blip in the right direction.

Figure 4.2 studies corruption from the perspective of Vietnamese citizens, by looking at the share of citizens who believe corruption is a problem in six dimensions of activity. Dimensions are ordered by the share of citizens agreeing that they present a problem. Two of these measures capture the facilitation form of grease money or facilitation payments, including accessing titles and construction permits. Two of the measures gauge petty corruption in public service delivery, specifically bribes to teachers and medical professionals. The final two measures capture aspects of grand corruption, including whether bribes are needed to seek state employment and whether local officials divert state funds for their personal enjoyment.

The first thing to notice about the graph is that there is a clear rank ordering of which dimensions of corruption are most pronounced in Vietnam. Citizens believe corruption in state hiring and access to health care are the most problematic, and they feel slightly less strongly about corruption in education and the diversion of state funds. The final dimension is probably underestimated due to its opacity. Next, as with the PCI, the corruption perceptions remained stubbornly high and again trended upward over the course of the previous government administra-

I am going to read several statements about events that occur sometimes. When I read them to you, please think about your own experience and tell me how much you agree with each statement. That is to say, you agree completely (2), you agree somewhat (1), you disagree or you disagree completely (0).

- In order to get a job in the government, people have to pay a bribe.

- People like me have to bribe to receive medical treatment in the district's hospitals.

- People have to pay bribes in order to obtain a land title.

- In my commune/ward, officials divert funds from the state budget for their personal benefit.

- Parents have to pay bribes to teachers for their children to receive more attention at the primary school nearest to my house.

- In my commune/ward, officials receive kickbacks in exchange for approval of construction permits.

Note: Data from 2011 to 2017 Provincial Administrative Performance Index Survey (http://papi.org.vn/eng/). Calculations by authors.

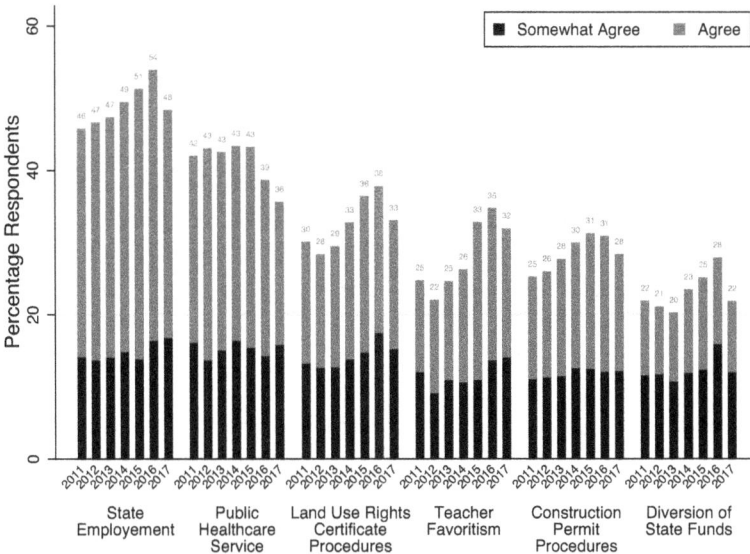

Figure 4.2. Citizen perceptions of corruption over time.

tion (2011–2016). Again, in every indicator, a distinct downward blip is notable with the incoming of the new administration in 2017.

Before we delve into the 2017 downturn, which may be illusory, we first need to deal with the general trend. Why has corruption remained persistent and even trended upward in Vietnam? In the next section, we tackle this question by taking a careful look at Vietnam's anticorruption efforts.

Anticorruption Policies

Analysts of Vietnamese politics are familiar with the persistence and upward trend of corruption over the past five years. Thayer (2018a) has described corruption as rust eating away at the legitimacy of the VCP. Zachary Abuza, another well-known analyst, has further argued that failing to deal with corruption makes "a mockery of authority" and described corruption as an "existential threat" to the VCP (Pennington 2017). At multiple points over the past decade, the VCP leaders have agreed with this assessment and have engaged in well-publicized anticorruption efforts. In fact, Vietnam's 2009 Anticorruption Strategy demonstrated a high degree of awareness of these dangers and practices, acknowledging that the very survival of CPV rule is at stake, while noting:

> [Corruption is] leading to adverse effects in many ways, eroding the confidence of the people in the leadership by the party and the management of the state, giving rise to potential conflicts of interest, social resistance, and protest, and widening the gap between the rich and the poor. Corruption has become a major obstacle for the success of *Doi Moi* and the fighting force of the party, threatening the survival of the regime. (Government of the Socialist Republic of Vietnam 2009)

Vietnamese leaders have long been concerned about the problems that corruption poses for economic development. According to Gainsborough and colleagues (2009), the current wave of efforts to address corruption and wrongdoing in the public sector revolves around five groups of solutions included in the National Anticorruption Strategy. These include: strengthening transparency of official functions to reduce opportunities for corruption; improving the performance of civil servants; perfecting economic management to ensure a fair and equal environment for business; increasing inspections, auditing, and subsequent punishment of corruption; and enhancing societal awareness to prevent and combat corruption.

Efforts to combat corruption go back to the early 1990s. Economic reforms that had started a few years earlier in 1986 started to expand economic activity and create legal gray zones that facilitated the rise of corruption and rent seeking. First, there was a wave of official legal normative documents including Decision No. 240/HDBT (1990) and Prime Minister's Decision No. 114/TTg (1992), which discussed the growing dangers of smuggling and corrupt activities that were growing in Vietnam. A second set of legislation took a more comprehensive approach and involved multiple ministries and agencies. These included the Anticorruption Ordinance of 1998, the revised Anticorruption Ordinance of 2002, the Law on Thrift and Anti-Waste of 2005, and the Law on Corruption Prevention and Combating of 2005. The resolution of the third Plenum of the Party Central Committee (tenth term) in August 2006 picked up the issue again. It focused specifically on the problem of corruption and finally led to Vietnam's Anticorruption Strategy in May 2009, followed by the ratification of the United Nations Convention against Corruption (UNCAC) in July 2009. Simultaneously, VCP decisions gave government officials authority to dismiss corrupt bureaucrats. In the wake of corruption scandals in 2006, the prime minister obtained the ability to dismiss malfeasant provincial People's Committee (PCOM) chairmen and ministers through the National Assembly (VietnamNet 2017).

In early and mid-2000s, Vietnam accelerated its integration into the world economy through agreements such as the 2001 US–Vietnam Bilateral Trade Agreement and Vietnam's accession to the WTO in 2007. Its anticorruption legal framework was developed to, at least partially, bolster the regime's legitimacy, in the wake of destabilizing distributional effects of trade, and satisfy demands from international partners and investors. The single most important part of that framework is the 2005 Anticorruption Law—the first of its kind in Vietnam—that criminalized several types of corruption, mandated asset disclosure requirements for public officials, and introduced whistle-blower protection (Transparency International 2012). In 2005, the National Assembly also passed the Law on Procurement. This was an important milestone, as public procurement is one of the sectors most susceptible to corruption. It is also sizable, affecting transactions with a total value of $20.47 billion (22% of national GDP) in 2009. In 2009, Vietnam revised both the Anticorruption Law and the Law on Procurement as well as ratified the UNCAC. In the same year, the government approved the National Strategy on Anticorruption, extending it to 2020, which recognized the role of transparency and openness, introduced an action plan, and proposed sector-specific approaches toward fighting corruption.

As a result of these efforts, Vietnam's legal framework against corruption is considered strong by the organization Global Integrity in their 2009 annual report. The government also introduced supporting regulations to supplement anticorruption laws. In 2006, then prime minister Nguyễn Tấn Dũng issued Decree 26/2006/CT-TTg, which prohibited the use of public funds for personal gifts. Decision 137 in 2009 aimed at raising awareness of corruption by mandating compulsory anticorruption training at all educational levels. Regarding asset declaration, Decree 68/2011-ND-CP required public officials to disclose their personal property and assets.

In addition to enacting formal legislation, the VCP has built elite institutions to measure and combat corruption. On February 1, 2013, the party established a Central Steering Committee on Anticorruption, which was headed by the general secretary himself (Central Committee of the Communist Party of Vietnam 2013). The party also reestablished the Central Department for Internal Political Affairs to support this committee (Central Committee of the Communist Party of Vietnam 2012). In a significant political move, Nguyễn Bá Thanh, a rising star in the party and the immensely popular party secretary of Đà Nẵng, the country's fastest growing and best governed city, was summoned to Hà Nội to manage the department (Malesky 2005–2017).

Despite the well-regarded laws, implementation has fallen considerably short. The same 2009 Global Integrity Report lamented the implementation gap of the 2005 Anticorruption Law. For instance, despite whistle-blower protection, citizens denouncing corruption were obligated to report the case to the head of the agency they are accusing, which immediately undermines the legal protections. Moreover, whistle-blowers have to give their full names and addresses as well as provide documentation to support the claim, according to Decree 47. Asset disclosures by public officials are largely nominal. Regarding the National Strategy on Anticorruption, little information is publicly available on specific policy initiatives and the results they intend to bring. In addition, policymakers pay little attention to regulations on access to information and post public employment.

Beyond specific issues of implementation, there are two other reasons that anticorruption efforts in Vietnam have fallen short of their goals. First, little effort has been made to unwind the systemic nature of Vietnamese corruption. While petty and grand corruption are theoretically separable, in practice in Vietnam they are thoroughly intertwined. Appointments to positions at top government agencies usually require some form of bribe payment that can reach into the millions of dollars (San Juan 2016). Interested parties must raise money, often taking loans from family and friends in order to be eligible. Once they have purchased their offices, these individuals have very little incentive to rein in corrupt behavior. In fact, some officials pressure subordinates into corrupt activities and pass shares of rents upward to them to amortize the former's investment (VietnamNews 2017).

Second, unlike countries that were more successful at reducing corruption, Vietnam has never engaged in systematic auditing or corruption investigations in a particular ministry, agency, or business sector. There has also been little effort to build sets of institutions that make corruption less likely. Anticorruption efforts in Vietnam have been reactive and cosmetic, responding to incidents of corruption that were uncovered through rare and idiosyncratic investigations that exploded into public consciousness through scandals or major bankruptcies of SOEs rather than proactively seeking to detect and eradicate corruption. We describe these high-profile incidents in the following section to give a sense of how anticorruption efforts have proceeded in Vietnam.

The History of High-Profile
Corruption Cases in Vietnam (1996–2016)

While Vietnam has made little headway on systematic anticorruption efforts, there has been a large number of high-profile cases that captured the public's attention and attempted to signal government resolve. This section summarizes anticorruption pushes in Vietnam from the mid-1990s until today. The timing and nature of these episodic cases suggest underlying political motivation. They often reflected intra-elite infighting rather than a systematic goal of uprooting corruption in the relevant sectors. We cannot properly classify them as campaigns, because they lacked systematic efforts to investigate and prosecute malfeasance in the country as a whole or even particular sectors or arenas. Before we delve into the individual details of the case, it is useful to begin with some suggestive evidence of the connections between anticorruption and elite politics.

Using Google trends dating back to 2004, figure 4.3 presents the difference between two common search terms: (1) Party Inspectorate (Ban Kiểm tra Trung ương) and (2) Party Economics Committee (Ban Kinh tế Trung ương). We chart the total number of searches for the two terms, which provides a very good sense of what the Vietnamese public was interested in during this time. As the absolute number of search terms can be confusing and inflated by growing internet access over time, it is helpful to standardize the searches to a common scale allowing for more valid comparisons. Google's methodology presents a standardized 100-point scale with 100 representing the highest number and 0 the lowest number

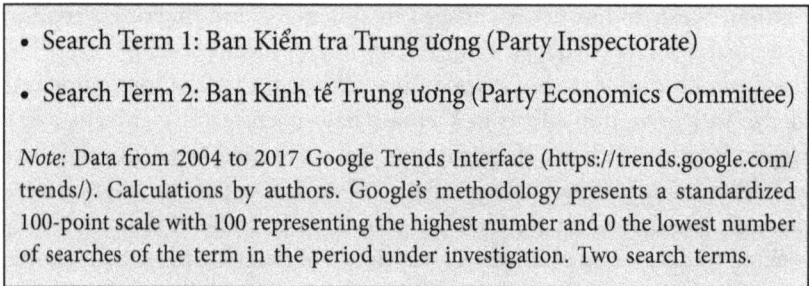

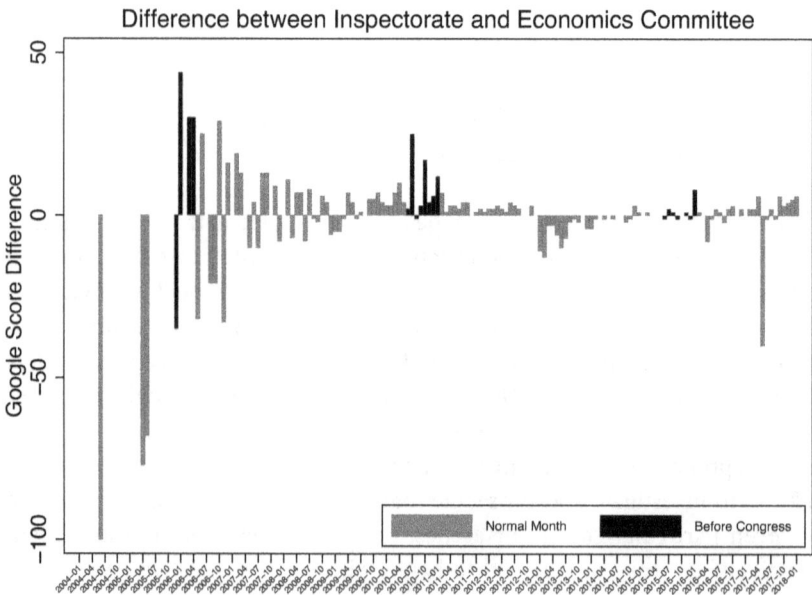

- Search Term 1: Ban Kiểm tra Trung ương (Party Inspectorate)

- Search Term 2: Ban Kinh tế Trung ương (Party Economics Committee)

Note: Data from 2004 to 2017 Google Trends Interface (https://trends.google.com/trends/). Calculations by authors. Google's methodology presents a standardized 100-point scale with 100 representing the highest number and 0 the lowest number of searches of the term in the period under investigation. Two search terms.

Figure 4.3. Relationship between anticorruption cases and elite politics.

of individual searches of the term in the period under investigation (2004 to present). The Party Inspectorate is the body charged with investigating and punishing high-profile corruption cases. The Party Economics Committee is charged with writing the Socioeconomic Plan presented at the Party Congress and with setting the agenda for economic reforms and government investment decisions for the next six years. For our analysis, Party Economics Committee serves to standardize our analysis of trends in the Party Inspectorate, ensuring that we do not mistakenly confuse increased internet usage or activity in preparation for the Party Congress every five years as a trend.

The graph presents two shades. Gray bars represent periods six months prior to and including the month in which the Party Congress was held. Black bars represent all other months, including the sixth months after a Congress and years in which no Congress took place. We present the difference between the two scores (inspectorate–economics).

The graph shows very clearly that at precisely the times when we would expect to see the greatest attention to the Economics Committee—when it is preparing the plans that will shape economic activity for the next five years—there is a severe bias in favor of Google searches for Party Inspectorate. In short, VCP investigations into corruption spike right at the period when provinces and ministries are choosing delegates for the Party Congress and scheming about the next leadership, implying a political logic to the onset and publicity of investigations. This result is consistent with qualitative evidence that corruption cases have typically been used to eliminate or cow competition before the Party Congress (Gainsborough 2003b) and quantitative evidence presented by Malesky and colleagues (2011) for the 1996–2006 period. In both periods, most corruption investigations and prosecutions occurred in the months prior to Congresses with far less anticorruption activity immediately after or in between Congresses.

While the quantitative evidence is suggestive, in the following sections we discuss a high-profile corruption scandal from the period before each subsequent Party Congress to further establish the reactive nature of anticorruption cases in Vietnam and their inextricable link to elite political machinations.

TAMEXCO (1996)

The first major corruption scandal during the economic reform (Đổi Mới) period was the case of Tamexco in 1996. Tamexco, known in full as Tân

Bình Production Service Trading and Export Company, was a general trading company connected to the Hồ Chí Minh City's Tân Bình District's People's Committee. Through importing fertilizers and construction materials and exporting seafood, the company quickly prospered and expanded.

In 1996, Hồ Chí Minh City police arrested Phạm Huy Phước, Tamexco's director. The charges included bribery, contravening state regulations, gambling, and exploiting his public position. In the end, Phước and three others, including a government official, received death sentences. In connection with the case, the party's Standing Committee in Hồ Chí Minh City censured and fired the chairman of Tân Bình's People's Committee (Gainsborough 2003a). Tamexco went bankrupt not long after the charges in 1999.

Gainsborough (2003a) argued that the motivation behind the prosecution of Tamexco was largely political, suggesting that the central government used anticorruption as an instrument to rein in local interests who were spiraling away from the former's control. Alternative explanations, such as the government's determination to punish graft or Tamexco's large debts, are not credible, since the company's practices and debt size were relatively common at the time. Gainsborough speculated that Tamexco's fall was connected to higher politics: Nguyễn Hà Phan, a Politburo member, head of the party's Central Economic Committee and reportedly a close ally of Phước, was expelled from the party by the Central Committee in 1996, right before the eighth Party Congress (BBC 2017a).

NĂM CAM (2003)

The investigation and prosecution of Năm Cam was a major corruption and criminal case in the early 2000s, affecting leadership decisions before the 2001 Party Congress. This was the first crackdown on a mafia-style criminal network whose tentacles reached deep into the police and the justice system. The case was so deeply imprinted into the popular culture that a hit television show was created around a character in Năm Cam's image.

Năm Cam, or Trương Văn Cam, was a mobster who ran his illegal operations from Hồ Chí Minh City, the biggest and most economically important city in Vietnam. His activities included organization of gambling, racketeering, and the lucrative business of hotels and brothels. Năm Cam and his subordinates carried out these activities with relative impunity, resorting to harsh and cruel force in their competition with other criminal groups. Although he had been arrested once before, Năm Cam escaped serious charges and penalties. It turned out that the first arrest itself prompted him to build a protection network, partly by bribing the local police to cover his operations and, more importantly, thanks to his deep connections to people in high positions in the government and the Communist Party. Năm Cam's stranglehold on Hồ Chí Minh City was so tight that, when he was arrested the second time in December 2001, the police force from Tiền Giang Province in the Mekong delta was used instead of HCMC officers to ensure that the planned operation would not be leaked to him (Người Lao Động 2001; Công An Nhân Dân 2015).

As a result, when Năm Cam was finally tried in October 2003, the case brought down an entire network of criminals, police, and public officials. There were 155 defendants in total, including thirteen police officers, three officers in the procuracy, five other public officials, and seventeen Communist Party members. The Supreme People's Court gave Năm Cam and four of his subordinates the death penalty. Trương Tấn Sang, the party secretary of Hồ Chí Minh City, Politburo member, and future president of Vietnam, may have been admonished for not providing sufficient oversight to thwart such high-level corruption (Thayer 2018a).[1]

PMU 18 (2006)

PMU 18 was one of the biggest corruption scandals in Vietnam during the mid-2000s and the one with the most severe international implications. PMU 18 (Project Management Unit 18) was an agency created in 1993 to manage construction projects for the Ministry of Transport. Between 1993 and 2006, PMU 18 managed around $2 billion worth of projects sponsored by the World Bank, Japan, and some European countries. Especially in Japan, the revelation of widespread wrongdoings at PMU 18 called into question the effectiveness and appropriateness of official development assistance (ODA) for Vietnam.

In January 2006, three months before the April Party Congress, police in Hà Nội arrested Bùi Tiến Dũng, the executive director of PMU 18. Allegedly, he made the mistake of walking into a local coffee shop that doubled as an illegal gambling den and coincidentally placed a half-million-dollar bet right in front of two police officers. The charges leveled against him included the embezzlement of $1.8 million for gambling on football matches and hiring prostitutes. Upon searching PMU 18's computers, the police uncovered evidence that two hundred of its employees were also involved in illegal gambling. Dũng's arrest also affected bigger fish in the ministry. The media suspected his predecessor, Nguyễn Việt Tiến, who was working as the deputy minister of transport at the time, of possible involvement. In April 2006, the police arrested Tiến on several charges, including the use of public vehicles for private businesses.

Bùi Tiến Dũng's case indirectly brought down other government officials. On April 13, 2006, the major newspaper *Tiền Phong* reported that Dũng's men had met several high-level officials five days before his arrest, possibly for collusion. The VCP subsequently removed Cao Ngọc Oánh, head of the Investigative Agency under the Ministry of Public Security, from his post, in addition to forcing his abstention from participation in the 2006 Party Congress. Oánh, a rising star at the time, had been expected to be elected into the party's Central Committee and take the position of deputy minister of public security. His candidacy was ultimately thwarted by the revelations. Also implicated were the then general secretary's son-in-law and an assistant in the prime minister's office.

After eighteen months of investigation, the case ended in May 2008. Hà Nội's People's Court convicted Bùi Tiến Dũng and five subordinates of "intentionally contravening state rules" and embezzlement, and they sentenced the former to thirteen years in prison. At the end, the cases against Nguyễn Việt Tiến and Cao Ngọc Oánh were dropped. Speculation was rife in the country that trail of corruption reached much higher into the party-state hierarchy and further investigations were forthcoming. Rumors circulated about the future of the children of high-ranking officials who either worked in PMU 18 or had extensive contracting relationships with the office.

Those investigations never happened. After political equilibrium was established and punishments were meted out for the most obvious perpetrators, state efforts instead focused on burying the story. In fact, a legal backlash was undertaken against the journalists who broke the original story and the policemen who investigated the case. In October 2008, the Supreme People's Court convicted two reporters from *Thanh Niên* and *Tuổi Trẻ* of "abusing democratic freedom" and propagating "false information" when covering the case. They each received two years in prison. Hà Nội's People's Court charged Major General Phạm Xuân Quắc, head of the formal investigation, with "disclosing work secrets," because of his communication with the journalists (Ba Kien 2010). In August, the minister of information and communication revoked seven reporters' journalist licenses for their role in the inaccurate reporting, including those of major editors at *Thanh Niên* and *Tuổi Trẻ*.

Despite having major domestic and international implications, PMU 18 did not lead to any systematic purge of construction projects in the Ministry of Transport. Furthermore, no institutional reform took place in terms of audits of the sector or greater transparency. Media coverage of the case was stifled after a few months: The VCP ordered media outlets to focus instead on the government's new anticorruption policy. Some observers suggest that the case was a front for intra-elite infighting in the months leading up to the Communist Party's tenth National Congress in April 2006. The investigation served its purposes of weakening one of the competing elite blocs and winning the leading bloc seats in the central committee. Having gained a significant political power advantage, the winning elites saw no benefit in prosecuting the case further.

Vinashin and Vinalines (2011–2012)

In the early 2010s, Vietnam saw a flurry of corruption cases surrounding big state-owned conglomerates. Breaking out before and around the tenth Party Congress in 2011, these cases severely weakened Prime Minister Nguyễn Tấn Dũng—the architect of the economic development strategy based on Korean-style conglomerates. Dũng signed the decision to experiment with this form of economic organization in May 2006 (Prime Minister of the Socialist Republic of Vietnam 2006). Importantly, as a result of previous reforms of the state sector in 1995, the prime minister position maintained control of several of these big corporations, with the authority to appoint presidents and chairpersons of boards of directors. The decision to pursue a strategy of conglomerates was a critical one, and it significantly altered the balance of power in the Vietnamese Politburo and among the leading troika (general secretary, president, prime minister). With separate patronage and financial channels outside the traditional party hierarchy due to his authority over the conglomerates and administrative control of the Ministry of Finance, Dũng had amassed tremendous ability to influence voting decisions in the Central Committee and Politburo (Abrami, Malesky, and Zheng 2013; Malesky, Abrami, and Zheng 2011). Leading political commentators openly wondered whether Dũng, technically a state and not a party official, was now the most powerful political actor in Vietnam, which would be highly unusual in a single-party system where the party secretary generally reigns supreme. Dũng's competitors for power, including President Trương Tấn Sang, General Secretary Nguyễn Phú Trọng, and their allies, began searching for ways to push back against the concentration of authority before the next Party Congress. Their main approach was to undercut the enormous rents produced by the state conglomerates and simultaneously chip away at the patronage pyramid that Dũng headed.

The first brick to fall was the shipbuilding conglomerate Vinashin. From the mid- to late-2000s, following high national GDP growth and in the midst of the conglomerate frenzy, a large amount of capital was injected by the Vietnamese government into large state-owned corporations. For example, in 2005, the government issued $750 million worth of bonds to finance Vinashin's projects (VnExpress 2005). Vinashin, however, did not focus on its expertise in shipbuilding but instead made reckless investments in non-core businesses such as banking, real estate, and thermal power (Pincus, Anh, and Le Thuy 2008). Eventually, these investments lost money and Vinashin failed to fulfill shipment on several vital international shipbuilding contracts, forcing the company into a deep financial hole. The government was forced to bailout the company, taking on its bad debt rather than allowing it to go bankrupt. Consequently, in 2011, the Supreme People's Court convicted Phạm Thanh Bình, the chairman of the board of directors and president of Vinashin, of the exploitation of his public position and deliberately contravening state regulations leading to severe loss of state assets.

Vinalines was another example of a state-owned conglomerate going awry. Also with newly infused state capital, Vinalines' leaders approved the purchases of old, out-of-service vessels, which eventually led to the company's defaulting on five loans worth $1.1 billion (Vuving 2013, 328). The State Appellate court found that these were too frequent and egregious to be mere accidents, finding Vinalines' leaders to have engaged in a systematic effort to transfer state resources into private hands. In particular, the court focused on the purchase of a floating dock from a Singaporean firm for US$9 million, despite the fact that the Singaporean firm had only recently acquired the float from a Russian operation for $2.3 million. The sale violated Vietnam's Marine Code articles on government procurement, because the dock was clearly out of date and could not be used in operations. Consequently, the court found that Vinalines' leaders were guilty of a tacit kickback agreement with the Singaporean vendor.

Eventually, in February 2012, the police arrested four lower-level Vinalines bosses for embezzlement. The big fish came later in May 2012 when they attempted to arrest Dương Chí Dũng, former chairman of Vinalines' board of directors and the head of the Vietnam Maritime Administration. Causing great public sensation, Dũng seemed to have been warned of the impending arrest and managed to escape to Cambodia (Tromme 2016). After his capture in September, Dũng implicated Phạm Quý Ngọ, the deputy minister of public security, as his informant. Adding to the mystery surrounding the case, Ngọ died shortly after, with cancer being the putative cause.

On December 16, 2013, the Hà Nội People's Court sentenced Dương Chí Dũng to death for intentionally contravening state rules to embezzle $1.6 million. The case of Vinalines was another blow to Prime Minister Nguyễn Tấn Dũng as it further discredited his vision and exposed the failings in his management of the economy.

Prime Minister Nguyễn Tấn Dũng was now in a well-documented fight for his political career after the bankruptcy of Vinashin, the state-owned shipbuilding company (Koh 2012). His troubles would come to a head in sixth plenum of the Central Committee (October 1–15, 2012), when the Politburo unanimously recommended consequences for its own serious mistakes in management of the country and "a comrade of the Political Bureau" was to be singled out for particular criticisms. The Central Committee would eventually reject the Politburo recommendation and PM Dũng would emerge unscathed. Dũng finally left politics after the next Party Congress in 2016, after not being able to amass enough votes to remain in the Politburo as general secretary.

DISCUSSION OF ANTICORRUPTION EFFORTS BEFORE 2017

Several themes are noteworthy from the discussion of high-profile cases before 2017 that are important to understanding anticorruption policy in Vietnam. First, none of the cases emerged from systematic and preplanned investigations or audits. Each case arose due to external incidents, such as arrests for illegal gambling or poor performing SOEs that inadvertently revealed malfeasance in a subset of top leaders. Thus, in every case, the response of the Vietnamese leadership was reactive, investigating the specific allegation and doling out punishment to the perpetrators.

Second, each burst of anticorruption activity occurred just prior to either a Party Congress or important VCP plenum and damaged the prospects of some officials that were contending for higher government or party office. These cases add texture to figure 4.3, showing how there is a political cycle to corruption allegations as Chen and Weiss highlight in the introduction to this volume.

Third, the pattern of punishments illustrates Gainsborough and colleagues' (2009) assertion of the systemic nature of Vietnamese corruption. In each case, a top official was sanctioned, but the subsequent trials included dozens of subordinates who played a role in the scheme. Noticing this pattern is important, because it provides the theoretical bridge between grand and petty corruption. At the top echelon, we have elite officials pocketing millions of dollars from the abuse of public office. Below those officials, however, are multiple subordinates carrying out petty corruption and funneling the money upward. Taking the PMU 18 case again as an example, we see grand corruption in the kickbacks on procurement and the large payments to receive a management position in one of the projects running through the office. This malfeasance, however, led directly to misbehavior on the part of lower-level officials. Companies that paid to win government procurement bids sought to limit their bribe costs by overcharging the Vietnamese government for construction materials (charging for grade A cement, while using grade C, for instance) and charging for ghost workers who received compensation but did no work. Lower-level officials who saw these budgets and chose not to act were committing petty corruption stimulated by the original kickback. Similarly, PMU 18 leaders who paid for positions in the rent-producing body also felt compelled to amortize their investment by finding additional sources of rents in construction licenses and construction permits and by creating a culture where bribes accepted at the lower level were shared with higher-level authorities. Again, these cases, classified as involving grease money, were not isolated. The demand for these rents was precipitated by the original grand corruption of payment for office.

Fourth, none of the cases led to downstream investigations in the industry (i.e., government procurement in construction) where the violations took place. Further, little institutional reform accompanied the discoveries. In fact, in three of the cases, after the assignment of punishment, significant efforts were made to limit further discussion on the topic, including, in the case of PMU 18, the arrests of the officers who had uncovered the crimes in the first place. It is extremely difficult to prove a negative—that there were little systematic anticorruption efforts. As we noted earlier, Vietnam has a host of formal anticorruption legislation, including clearer rules for procurement auctions. If the cases described were what precipitated the anticorruption legislation, however, we would expect the subsequent reform efforts to be more specific, targeting the specific rules, agencies, and industries, where problems had been uncovered. This has rarely been the case.

The Vinashin and Vinalines cases, however, represent a subtle shift in anticorruption activity. Whereas the previous cases touched on elite politics by implicating connected officials directly or indirectly, cases like Nam Cam and PMU 18 did not appear to be emanate from deep-seated political rivalries and did not seem to target those connected to particular elite leaders. While they still fit within the broad anticorruption typology of private interests, these cases appear to harbinger events to come in two ways. First, they point to more strategic political targeting and a willingness to work up the food chain from low-level subordinates to the elite echelons to score political points. Second, the investigation was less tied to the political calendar and more focused on routing out malfeasance that was costing the Vietnamese government vital resources and damaging legitimacy. We probe how the strategic alternations become more pronounced in the next section.

A Shifting Approach in Vietnam's 2017–2018 Anticorruption Drive

Since the new administration took office at the beginning of 2017, anti-corruption campaigns against government bigwigs have increasingly taken center stage. An intertwined cluster of grand corruption cases that attracted a lot of public attention is that of PetroVietnam, OceanBank, and PetroVietnam Construction Joint Stock Corporation, described in more detail later. The timing of these cases is clearly different from the previous efforts, occurring at the beginning of the term rather than in the six months prior to the next party elections. This indicates clearly that political jockeying before important Central Committee votes is a less important reason for the effort and signals an effort to attack malfeasance more thoroughly. As we noted in the introduction to this chapter, the new leadership is also demonstrating greater willingness to punish the very elite, including Politburo members, and pursue anticorruption efforts internationally. After reviewing the cases, we return to whether the current effort signals a radical break from previous anticorruption policy.

PETROVIETNAM (PVN), OCEANBANK, AND PETROVIETNAM CONSTRUCTION JOINT STOCK CORPORATION (PVC) (2016–2017)

In 2017, a VCP investigation felled the biggest tiger of any anticorruption campaign. Đinh La Thăng served as the chairman of the board of directors of PetroVietnam, the national petroleum conglomerate, under Prime Minister Dũng. With his knack for publicity, adept use of the media, and a dash of showmanship and populism that is novel in the context of Vietnam, Thăng rose rapidly in the party. A Central Committee member since 2006, he was promoted to minister of transport in 2011. In the next Party Congress in 2016, fellow VCP delegates elected Thăng to the Politburo and assigned him to the post of party secretary of Hồ Chí Minh City, effectively making him one of the most powerful men in the country.

After Dũng's failed bid to become the party secretary, however, Thăng fell along with his patron. In May 2017, the party's Central Committee removed Thăng from the Politburo and his position in Hồ Chí Minh City for mistakes and wrongdoings during his time in charge of PetroVietnam. On December 8, 2017, the police arrested Thăng for his role in troubles at OceanBank and PVC. This particular charge centered around the awarding of public contracts to connected companies without public tendering or competition.

PETROVIETNAM AND OCEANBANK

The beginning of the end for Thăng came when the police started looking into wrongdoings by his subordinates at OceanBank. OceanBank was a small private bank that had previously only operated in rural areas. At the end of 2008, PetroVietnam (PVN), at that point still under the leadership of Đinh La Thăng, bought stocks in OceanBank and became a major shareholder. PetroVietnam leadership installed Nguyễn Xuân Sơn, previously the CEO of PetroVietnam Finance Corporation (PVFC) under PVN, as OceanBank's president.

Being a small, new, and relatively unknown player in the finance industry, OceanBank faced great difficulties in attracting depositors. PetroVietnam's investment and Sơn's appointment opened the door for the bank to access promising clientele in the energy sector. Hà Văn Thắm, OceanBank's chairman, authorized Sơn to pay higher interest rates than legally allowed by the state bank to attract lenders in the petroleum and natural gas sector in an attempt to raise funds. OceanBank would then recoup these unofficial expenditures by charging borrowers and buyers of foreign currencies extra fees, which the company did not specify in official contracts. The latter would pay these fees by purchasing fake "services" from BSC Vietnam—a company connected to OceanBank—which would funnel the money back to Thắm and Sơn (CafeF 2017; Viet Duc 2016).

The wrongdoings attracted the authorities' attention partly due to mismanagement that led to the bank's disastrous business performance: a bank with authorized capital of only 4 trillion VND (US$178 million) ended up with a loss of 10 trillion VND ($US444 million) and bad debts of more than 15 trillion (US$666 million) (DanTri 2017). In October 2014, the state bank suspended Hà Văn Thắm as chairman of OceanBank. The police arrested Thắm the same day for violations of regulations in lending, exploitation of public position resulting in serious damages, and intentional violation of state regulations. In April 2015, the state bank nationalized OceanBank, ended all rights and privileges of its shareholders, and put it under special management. Three months later, Nguyễn Xuân Sơn was also arrested with the same charges.

After two years, in 2017, the police additionally charged Nguyễn Xuân Sơn with embezzling PVN assets and changed the charge of "exploitation of public position resulting in serious damages" to "exploitation of public position to embezzle assets." The investigators concluded that Sơn pocketed 49 billion VND (US$2.3 million) from the 246 billion (US$11.2 million) that Thắm gave Sơn to pay the unofficial interest rates to lenders in the energy sector. As PetroVietnam—a state-owned entity—held 20 percent of OceanBank's stocks, these are considered state funds so, legally, Sơn was stealing money from the government (BBC 2017b). In late September, the People's Court in Hà Nội gave Hà Văn Thắm a life sentence and, to Nguyễn Xuân Sơn, the death penalty. They both appealed the decision.

Soon after, the Police Investigative Agency of Corruption and Economic Criminals (C46) under the Ministry of Public Security arrested Đinh La Thăng for intentional violation of state rules resulting in serious damages for the loss of the 800 billion Vietnamese dong (US$36 million) that PVN invested in OceanBank. According to the charges, during the three times that PetroVietnam injected capital into OceanBank, Thăng repeatedly bypassed PetroVietnam's board of directors, ignored orders from the prime minister's office, and broke the 2010 Law on Credit Institutions (Ba Chiem 2017).

PVC

Concurrently, the end also crept on to Đinh La Thăng from another direction with the case of Trịnh Xuân Thanh, chairman of the board of directors of PVC. In 2010, Thăng, as chairman of PetroVietnam's board of directors, awarded PVC with contracts in the construction of a new thermal power plant, despite the fact that PVC did not have the relevant expertise and in disregard of state rules requiring formal public tendering. In addition, Thăng ordered his subordinates at PetroVietnam to transfer US$6.6 billion upfront to PVC before the latter acquired official legal contractor status. Trịnh Xuân Thanh went on to use this money for other purposes, causing a loss of 119 billion Vietnamese dong (US$5.4 million) to the state (Tam Lua 2017).

In September 2016, the Police Investigative Agency of Corruption and Economic Criminals (C46) charged Thanh with intentional violation of state regulations resulting in serious damages of 3.2 trillion VND (US$145.5 million) (CafeF 2016). Thanh, however, managed to escape to Germany after taking some days off work for "health issues." The case took a sensational turn ten months later, on July 31, 2017, when Vietnamese authorities announced that Thanh had turned himself in. The German Ministry of Foreign Affairs contested this version of events, accusing Vietnam of kidnapping Thanh in Berlin when he was taking a walk in the park, before smuggling him back to Vietnam through the Czech Republic (TuoiTre 2017a). The events subjected Vietnam-Germany diplomatic relations to unprecedented strain. Germany demanded that Vietnam return Thanh immediately and deported one employee at the Vietnamese embassy.

On December 28, 2017, the Supreme People's Procuracy additionally charged Trịnh Xuân Thanh with the embezzlement of 14 billion Vietnamese dong in another project at PVC. As for Thăng, he went to trial on January 8, 2018, under the charge of intentional violation of state rules leading to severe damages. At the time of writing, his future remains unclear.

Discussion: Is the 2017–2018 Effort Different?

Speculation is rife in Vietnam's coffee shops about whether the Thăng trial and the related anticorruption push will be more effective than previous efforts (Hutt 2017; Pennington 2017) As with previous high-profile cases that we documented in this chapter, connections to elite political machinations have cast doubt among Vietnam analysts about whether the trials are more about scoring political points against former rivals than rooting corruption out of the system.

Of the cases that have grabbed newspaper headlines in Vietnam in 2017 and 2018, all of the accused had personal and professional relationships with Nguyễn Tấn Dũng, the prime minister of Vietnam between 2006 and 2016, who presented himself as an economic reformer and exploited the position's control of bureaucratic appointments and state-owned enterprises to amass tremendous decision-making power as well as personal rents (Le Hong Hiep 2015; Schuler and Ostwald 2016; Vuving 2017). The cases of OceanBank and PVC appear to be preparations for official corruption cases against bigger fish, such as Đinh La Thăng and Nguyễn Tấn Dũng, now that Dũng's authority in the party leadership has been weakened (Hutt 2017).

It is not just who has been targeted that has bred skepticism. Paying extralegal interest rates is unfortunately a common problem in the Vietnamese state banking sector. According to Trần Đình Triển, the deputy chairman of the Hà Nội Bar Association, the problem is not only with Hà Văn Thắm but the entire banking system (BBC 2016). Why was OceanBank singled out for the practice? Similarly, the dismissal and trial of Nguyễn Xuân Anh stands out, because his violations as party secretary of Đà Nẵng seem so ordinary. Because illegitimate diplomas and use of corporate cars are relatively minor and common offenses, speculation has turned to the fact that Xuân Anh's father is Nguyễn Văn Chi, a former Politburo member and close associate of Prime Minister Dũng (Pennington 2017). In 2016, PM Dũng was defeated in his effort to consolidate power and seek the position of party general secretary, by what retired diplomat David Brown referred to as "an anything but [Prime Minister Nguyễn Tấn] Dũng coalition" led by the incumbent general secretary, Nguyễn Phú Trọng. With Trọng's leadership secured, some analysts have argued that the corruption cases represent his attempt to entrench power by punishing the associates of a former rival (Brown 2017). Chen and Weiss call this anticorruption motivated by private interests in the introduction to this volume.

This explanation may be too pessimistic; there are reasons to be more sanguine about the current efforts. First, Vietnam, unlike China, has never had fixed factions (Thayer 2018b). Coalitions of top leaders have shifted over time and by issue area. Some top leaders currently listed as part of Trọng's coalition, such as current prime minister Nguyễn Xuân Phúc and Nguyễn Thiện Nhân, Thăng's replacement as party secretary of

Hồ Chí Minh City, were formerly listed as members of Dũng's coalition by the very same analysts, Vuving (2013) and Thayer (2013). The lack of entrenched factions means that it is possible to unify the new administration around an anticorruption coalition.

Second, use of criminal cases and court procedures are important to highlight, because they involve the use of an institutional punishment rather than the simple sidelining of a political foe and the return to business as usual before too much information on the case is revealed to the public. Relatedly, the use of criminal courts and sanctions indicates an empowerment of state judicial institutions over internal party mechanisms.

Third, the latest challenge to a high-ranking leader is not an isolated event, as in previous cases, but it coincides with a recent spree of changes in government and VCP policy to attack corruption and institutional changes to limit corruption in the future. This shift suggests Vietnam has moved from sporadic prosecution to an organized campaign, motivated by a unified Politburo, to address corruption proactively. Carlyle Thayer describes the anticorruption efforts as the largest in scope since Vietnam was reunified in 1976 (Thayer 2018b). Trọng has been extremely vocal on the topic of corruption. He famously said, "Corruption is like scabies, very annoying," in 2013 (BBC 2013), and, more recently, "Once the oven is heated up, even wet twigs and branches will catch fire" (VietnamNet 2017).

The new administration's approach appears to rest on three pillars: monitoring, access to information, and changing bureaucratic incentives.

With regard to monitoring, one of Prime Minister Nguyễn Xuân Phúc's first acts when he entered office in 2017 was to appoint VCCI and CECODES to use the PCI and PAPI surveys, respectively, to monitor changes in corruption for the government with a new battery of more specific questions and propose policy solutions (Government of the Socialist Republic of Vietnam 2016).

Second, under the new administration, the National Assembly has approved a number of important legislative documents that strengthen citizens' roles and capitalize on citizens' interest in governance and public administration. Among them was a Law on Access to Information, to be implemented in 2018, after preparation of necessary bylaws. The new law follows the Chinese Open Governance Initiative (OGI) in mandating that a range of government documents, such as legal documents, budgets, as well as land and infrastructure plans be placed online at every level of government (Horsley 2007). In addition, the new law contains provisions allowing citizens to request information not specifically outlawed, and mandates that agencies reply within a mandated time frame. Stromseth and colleagues (2017) have shown the effectiveness of the Chinese OGI in reducing misuse of public funds, and Vietnamese authorities seem to be heading in the same direction.

Finally, the new leadership is experimenting with a range of civil service reforms. At the sixth plenum of the twelfth VCP on October 11, 2017, the same meeting where the charges against Nguyễn Xuân Anh were announced, Trọng elucidated a set of party and civil service reforms that he explained would decrease corruption and increase accountability. These included reforms streamlining party institutions, by eliminating the overlapping executive functions of the party secretary and People's Committee chairman at the district and commune levels of government. On the government side, the goal is to reduce the size of the civil service by 25 percent and simultaneously increase the competitiveness and remuneration of remaining officials. The hope is that increasing meritocracy and the rewards of office will give civil servants incentives to reduce corruption. Skepticism remains about whether higher bureaucratic salaries will actually reduce corruption, but the National Assembly acted on the plenum's guidance and passed a resolution (with 94% affirmative votes) that will allow Hồ Chí Minh City to pilot the reforms. Draft resolutions are in place to streamline the Hồ Chí Minh City bureaucracy and increase the salaries of civil servants (TuoiTreNews 2017).

In short, the 2017 anticorruption efforts, while clearly touching on political tensions, appear to be part of a broader strategy than previous endeavors. Rather than simply arresting top officials, the recent legislation includes institutional reforms that are at least aimed at warding off future corrupt behavior through better monitoring, access to information, and bureaucratic incentives.

Whereas previous anticorruption activities were reactive and tainted by their connection to elite politics, the 2017–2018 efforts differ in that they center around a broader set of administrative reforms designed to preempt future corruption. These efforts do not respond to the discovery of corruption but are proactively designed policies that the party formally sanctioned and the Vietnamese parliament passed, and which are being filled out with implementing documents at the local level.

Of course, we must be cautious about being overly optimistic about the new efforts. A marginal one-year decrease in corruption trends can result from sampling error and be easily reversed. And as described earlier, Vietnam has a history of poorly implemented anticorruption laws. The

2017 batch may fall prey to the same inertia and intransigence. At this stage, it is very difficult to say with confidence that this time is different, even if the timing and content of the legislation suggests a new, more institutional than personal or opportunistic impetus.

Conclusions

As Thayer (2018b) has put it, corruption corrodes the legitimacy of the Vietnamese Communist Party. On paper, this fact has been acknowledged by top authorities, and consequently anticorruption has been a consistent theme of the Vietnamese leadership going back to the early mid-1990s. Despite numerous party documents, commissions, laws, and high-profile cases against perpetrators, including top officials, there has been little change in both international rankings and domestic surveys of Vietnamese firms and citizens regarding the incidence of corruption. Corruption has remained problematic and even trended upward during the previous administration of Prime Minister Nguyễn Tấn Dũng, reaching its zenith in 2016. Nor have systematic efforts to curb or draw attention to corruption been so visible a part of political rhetoric and strategy, either from the top or the ground, as they have in other countries in the region.

We argue in this chapter that corruption has remained stubbornly high, because implementation of anticorruption laws has remained poor and has been burdened by internal contradictions in the enactments themselves that undermined transparency and whistle-blower protections. Similarly, the targeting of journalists who pursue corruption investigations has scared off potential muckrakers. Moreover, the government's pursuit of corruption cases has been reactive and nonsystematic. To most Vietnamese analysts, high-level corruption cases appeared to be political score-settling or driven by private interests rather than party loyalty or efforts at institutional change (Chen and Weiss, the introduction to this volume). Cases disproportionately occurred in the month before the five-year party congresses, damaging the careers of particular leadership candidates. Once punishments were meted out, however, and political equilibrium restored, government officials made little effort to take anticorruption efforts further, to put in place institutions that would prevent further malfeasance. In fact, in some cases, restrictions were even placed on those simply trying to pursue more information about the original cases. Because of the lack of sincere commitment by authorities to anticorruption reform, the only documentable evidence of reductions in corruption have occurred among two groups: foreign investors subject to punishment in their home states for corruption committed abroad due to the OECD Anti-Bribery Convention (Jensen and Malesky 2017), and large and mobile domestic businesses who can evade bribe requests by threatening to shift their activities to other provinces (Bai et al. 2015). For other citizens and businesses, corruption has not declined and, in fact, has worsened over time.

While recent efforts suggest a shift in the political logic of anticorruption efforts, more systematically to address endemic corruption, any transformation seems partial and still uncertain. However, as we have pointed out, there are a few reasons to be cautiously optimistic that the current effort may be different. In contrast to previous efforts, however, investigators are prosecuting cases in the beginning of the term and not right before the Party Congress and, for the first time ever, are seeking criminal punishment against a Politburo member. Second, the campaign has been accompanied by several institutional reforms to promote greater monitoring, transparency, and meritocratic promotion. This set of reforms appears to be the onset of a proactive strategy to thwart the conditions for corruption rather than simply react to its consequences.

Notes

1. Although Thayer (2018a) cites a reprimand of Sang, we could not find any formal documentation of such discipline by the Central Committee. Several newspapers, however, claim a higher-level leader was punished. Only one, however, links the event to Sang, an overseas Vietnamese language newspaper called *Viet Bao* (2003).

Bibliography

Abrami, Regina, Edmund Malesky, and Yu Zheng. "Vietnam through Chinese Eyes: Divergent Accountability in Single-Party Regimes." In *Why Communism Did Not Collapse: Understanding Authoritarian Regime Resilience in Asia and Europe*, edited by Martin Dimitrov, 237–276. New York: Cambridge University Press, 2013.

Ba Chiem. "Vai trò của ông Đinh La Thăng trong vụ PVN mất 800 tỷ." *Zing News*, December 21, 2017. Retrieved from https://news.zing.vn/vai-tro-cua-ong-dinh-la-thang-trong-vu-pvn-mat-800-ty-post805674.html.

Ba Kien. "Tướng Quắc những ngày đi trong 'bão.'" *Tiền Phong*, February 17, 2010. Retrieved from https://www.tienphong.vn/xa-hoi/tuong-quac-nhung-ngay-di-trong-bao-186493.tpo.

Bai, Jie, Seema Jayachandran, Edmund J. Malesky, and Benjamin A. Olken. "Firm Growth and Corruption: Empirical Evidence from Vietnam." *The Economic Journal* (Wiley Online Library), 2015.

BBC. "TBT Trong: Tham Nhung Nhu Ngua Ghe." *BBC*, September 28, 2013. Retrieved from http://www.bbc.com/vietnamese/vietnam/2013/09/130928_nguyenphutrong_on_corruption.

BBC. "Truy to hang chuc bi can vu OceanBank." *BBC*, December 24, 2016. Retrieved from http://www.bbc.com/vietnamese/vietnam-38425576.

BBC. "Ủy viên Bộ Chính trị nào ở VN từng bị kỷ luật?" *BBC*, April 27, 2017a. http://www.bbc.com/vietnamese/vietnam-39736621.

BBC. "Vụ OceanBank: Nguyễn Xuân Sơn bị tuyên án tử hình, Hà Văn Thắm chung thân." *BBC*, September 29, 2017b. Retrieved from http://www.bbc.com/vietnamese/world-41438437.

Brown, David. "Vietnam's Conservatives Purge Former PM Dung's Allies." *The Sentinel*, September 8, 2017. Retrieved from https://www.asiasentinel.com/politics/vietnam-conservatives-purge-former-pm-dungs-allies/.

CafeF. "Tieu su Trinh Xuan Thanh." *CafeF*, December 28, 2016. Retrieved from http://cafef.vn/tieu-su-trinh-xuan-thanh-20160917081359441.chn.

CafeF. "Nhìn lại những phiên tòa xét xử đại án kinh tế năm 2017." *CafeF*, December 28, 2017. Retrieved from http://cafef.vn/nhin-lai-nhung-phien-toa-xet-xu-dai-an-kinh-te-nam-2017-20171228091333146.chn.

Central Committee of the Communist Party of Vietnam. "Resolution August 2006." 2006. Retrieved from http://tulieuvankien.dangcongsan.vn/cac-ban-dang-trung-uong/van-phong-trung-uong-dang/van-phong-trung-uong-dang-128.

Central Committee of the Communist Party of Vietnam. "Decision 162-QD/TW on Establishing the Central Internal Affairs Committee." 2012.

Central Committee of the Communist Party of Vietnam. "Decision 162-QD/TW on Establishing the Central Anticorruption Steering Committee." 2013.

Công An Nhân Dân. "Bí mật "điểm nổ" trong chuyên án triệt phá tập đoàn tội phạm Năm Cam." *Công An Nhân Dân*, August 10, 2015. Retrieved from http://cand.com.vn/Phap-luat/danh-sap-tap-doan-pham-toi-Nam-Cam-361299/.

Council of Ministers of the Socialist Republic of Vietnam. "Decision 240-HDBT on Anticorruption." 1990.

DanTri. "[Infographics]: Toan canh dai an Ha Van Tham va dong bon." *DanTri*, February 28, 2017. Retrieved from http://dantri.com.vn/kinh-doanh/info graphics-toan-canh-dai-an-ha-van-tham-va-dong-pham-2017022815092496.htm.

Fisman, Raymond, and Miriam A. Golden. *Corruption: What Everyone Needs to Know.* Oxford: Oxford University Press, 2017.

Gainsborough, Martin. *Changing Political Economy of Vietnam: The Case of Ho Chi Minh City.* New York: Routledge, 2003a.

Gainsborough, Martin. "Corruption and the Politics of Economic Decentralisation in Vietnam." *Journal of Contemporary Asia* 33, no. 1 (2003b): 69–84.

Gainsborough, Martin, Dang Ngoc Dinh, and Tran Thanh Phuong. "Corruption, Public Administrative Reform and Development: Challenges and Opportunities." In *Reforming Public Administration in Vietnam: Current Situation and Recommendations*, edited by Jairo Acuna-Alfaro, 318–376. Hanoi: UNDP, VFF and CECODES, 2009.

Government of the Socialist Republic of Vietnam. "Resolution 47/2007/ND-CP." March 2007. Retrieved from https://thuvienphapluat.vn/van-ban/ Bo-may-hanh-chinh/Nghi-dinh-47-2007-ND-CP-vai-tro-trach-nhiem-cua-xa-hoi-trong-phong-chong-tham-nhung-huong-dan-luat-phong-chong-tham-nhung-17978.aspx.

Government of the Socialist Republic of Vietnam. "Resolution 68/2011/ND-CP." August 2011. Retrieved from http://chinhphu.vn/portal/page/portal/ chinhphu/hethongvanban?class_id=1&mode=detail&document_id=151 216.

Government of the Socialist Republic of Vietnam. "Resolution on Anticorruption Strategy to 2020." May 2009. Retrieved from https://thuvienphapluat.vn/ van-ban/Bo-may-hanh-chinh/Nghi-quyet-21-NQ-CP-chien-luoc-quoc-gia-phong-chong-tham-nhung-den-nam-2020-88368.aspx.

Government of the Socialist Republic of Vietnam. "Resolution 35-NQ-CP on Support and Development of Enterprises by 2020." 2016. Article 4, Clause D.

Gueorguiev, Dimitar, and Edmund Malesky. "Foreign Investment and Bribery: A Firm-Level Analysis of Corruption in Vietnam." *Journal of Asian Economics* 23 (2012): 111–129.

Horsley, Jamie P. "China Adopts First Nationwide Open Government Information Regulations." *Freedominfo.org (Online)*, May 9, 2007. Retrieved from http://www.freedominfo.org/2007/05/china-adopts-first-nationwide-open-government-information-regulations/.

Hutt, David. "A Purge Too Far in Vietnam?" *Asia Times Online*, September 21, 2017. Retrieved from http://www.atimes.com/article/purge-far-vietnam/.

Jensen, Nathan M., and Edmund J. Malesky. "Nonstate Actors and Compliance with International Agreements: An Empirical Analysis of the OECD Anti-Bribery Convention." *International Organization* 72, no. 1 (2017): 33–69.

Koh, David. "The Sixth Plenum in Vietnam: Thunder without Rain." *ISEAS Perspective*, October 29, 2012.

Le Hong Hiep. "Vietnam's Leadership Transition in 2016: A Preliminary Analysis." *ISEAS Perspective*, 2015.

Malesky, Edmund. "The Vietnam Provincial Competitiveness Index: Measuring Economic Governance for Private Sector Development." 2005–2017. Retrieved from http://eng.pcivietnam.org/publications/full-report-2017/.

Malesky, Edmund J., Dimitar D. Gueorguiev, and Nathan M. Jensen. "Monopoly Money: Foreign Investment and Bribery in Vietnam, a Survey Experiment." *American Journal of Political Science* 59 (2015): 419–439.

Malesky, Edmund, Regina Abrami, and Yu Zheng. "Institutions and Inequality in Single-Party Regimes: A Comparative Analysis of Vietnam and China." *Comparative Politics* 43 (2011): 409–427.

Malesky, Edmund, Paul Schuler, and Anh Tran. "Vietnam: Familiar Patterns and New Developments Ahead of the 11th Party Congress." *Southeast Asian Affairs* (2011): 339–363.

Manion, Melanie. *Corruption by Design: Building Clean Government in Mainland China and Hong Kong.* Cambridge: Harvard University Press, 2004.

National Assembly of the Socialist Republic of Vietnam. "Ordinance 03/1998/PL-UBTVQH10 on Anticorruption." February 1998.

National Assembly of the Socialist Republic of Vietnam. "Ordinance 03/1998/PL-UBTVQH10 on Anticorruption." February 1998.

National Assembly of the Socialist Republic of Vietnam. "Law on Preventing and Combatting Corruption." November 2005a. Retrieved from https://thuvienphapluat.vn/van-ban/Bo-may-hanh-chinh/Luat-phong-chong-tham-nhung-2005-55-2005-QH11-6919.aspx.

National Assembly of the Socialist Republic of Vietnam. "Law on Thrift and Anti-Waste." November 2005b. Retrieved from https://thuvienphapluat.vn/van-ban/Tai-chinh-nha-nuoc/Luat-Thuc-hanh-tiet-kiem-chong-lang-phi-2005-48-2005-QH11-6923.aspx.

National Assembly of the Socialist Republic of Vietnam. "Law on Access to Information." April 2016. Retrieved from https://thuvienphapluat.vn/van-ban/Bo-may-hanh-chinh/Luat-tiep-can-thong-tin-2016-280116.aspx.

Nguoi Lao Dong. "Bai 5: Bat Nam Cam va dong bon: Nhung dieu it ai biet." *Nguoi Lao Dong.* December 28, 2001. Retrieved from http://nld.com.vn/thoi-su-trong-nuoc/bai-5-bat-nam-cam-va-dong-bon-nhung-dieu-it-ai-biet-81808.htm.

Pennington, John. "Is Vietnam's Clampdown Genuine." *ASEAN Today,* October 2, 2017. Retrieved from https://www.aseantoday.com/2017/10/is-vietnams-clampdown-on-corruption-genuine.

Pincus, Jonathan, Vu Thanh Tu Anh, and T. Le Thuy. "Vietnam: A Tiger in Turmoil." *Far Eastern Economic Review* 171 (2008): 28.

Prime Minister of the Socialist Republic of Vietnam. "Decision 114-TTg on Urgent Solutions to Prevent Corruption and Smuggling." November 1992. Retrieved from https://thuvienphapluat.vn/van-ban/Thuong-mai/Quyet-dinh-114-TTg-bien-phap-cap-bach-nham-ngan-chan-va-bai-tru-te-tham-nhung-buon-lau/38402/noi-dung.aspx.

Prime Minister of the Socialist Republic of Vietnam. "Decision 103/2006/QD-TTg on Experimenting with Establishing Vinashin." May 2006. Retrieved from https://thuvienphapluat.vn/van-ban/Doanh-nghiep/Quyet-dinh-103-2006-QD-TTg-De-an-thi-diem-hinh-thanh-Tap-doan-cong-nghiep-tau-thuy-Viet-nam-VINASHIN-11768.aspx.

Prime Minister of the Socialist Republic of Vietnam. "Decision 137/2009/QD-TTg on Anticorruption Education." December 2009. Retrieved from http://vanban.chinhphu.vn/portal/page/portal/chinhphu/hethongvanban?class_id=1&mode=detail&document_id=91928.

San Juan, Eric. "Jobs for Sale in Vietnam." June 24, 2016. Retrieved from https://www.equaltimes.org/jobs-for-sale-in-vietnam#.WlXZQqjXY2w.

Schuler, Paul, and Kai Ostwald. *Delayed Transition: The End of Consensus Leadership in Vietnam?* Singapore: ISEAS-Yusof Ishak Institute, 2016.

Stromseth, Jonathan R., Edmund J. Malesky, and Dimitar D. Gueorguiev. *China's Governance Puzzle: Enabling Transparency and Participation in a Single-Party State.* Cambridge: Cambridge University Press, 2017.

Tam Lua. "Truy tố ông Đinh La Thăng tội cố ý làm trái." *TuoiTre.* December 26, 2017. Retrieved from https://tuoitre.vn/truy-to-ong-dinh-la-thang-toi-co-y-lam-trai-20171226111723255.htm.

Thayer, Carlyle A. "Vietnam: Are Anticorruption and Factional Infighting Linked?" *Thayer Consultancy Background Brief.* January 5, 2018a.

Thayer, Carlyle A. "Vietnam: Anticorruption Campaign Assessed." *Thayer Consultancy Background Brief.* January 5, 2018b.

Thayer, Carlyle A. "Vietnam's 7th Plenum: New Leaders to Play Musical Chairs?" *Thayer Consultancy Background Brief.* May 16, 2013.

Transparency International. "Global Corruption Barometer 2017/2018." 2017. Retrieved from https://www.transparency.org/news/feature/global_corruption_barometer_citizens_voices_from_around_the_world.

Transparency International. "Overview of Corruption and Anticorruption in Vietnam." 2012. Retrieved from https://www.u4.no/publications/overview-of-corruption-and-anti-corruption-in-vietnam/.

Tromme, Mathieu. "Corruption and Corruption Research in Vietnam: An overview." *Crime, Law and Social Change* 65 (2016): 287–306.

TuoiTre. "Bo Ngoai giao lay lam tiec ve phat bieu cua Duc vu Trinh Xuan Thanh." *Tuoi Tre*, August 3, 2017a. Retrieved from https://tuoitre.vn/bo-ngoai-giao-lay-lam-tiec-ve-phat-bieu-cua-duc-vu-trinh-xuan-thanh-1363180.htm.

TuoiTre. "Cong bo vi pham cua Bi thu Da Nang Nguyen Xuan Anh." *Tuoi Tre*, September 18, 2017b. Retrieved from https://tuoitre.vn/ong-nguyen-xuan-anh-xai-bang-khong-hop-phap-20170918152501078.htm.

TuoiTreNews. "Vietnam's Legislature Passes Resolution on Special Mechanisms for Ho Chi Minh City Development." *TuoiTreNews*, November 25, 2017. Retrieved from https://tuoitrenews.vn/news/society/20171125/vietnamslegislature-passes-resolution-on-special-mechanisms-for-ho-chi-minh-city-development/42807.html.

UNDP, CECODES, and VFF. "The 2015 Vietnam Provincial Governance and Public Administration Performance Index (PAPI). Technical report." United Nations Development Program, 2015. Retrieved from https://www.undp.org/content/dam/vietnam/docs/Publications/PAPI%202015_REPORT_ENGLISH.pdf.

Vasavakul, Thaveeporn. "Recrafting State Identity: Corruption and Anti-Corruption in Doi Moi Vietnam from a Comparative Perspective." Rethinking the Vietnamese State: Implications for Vietnam and the Region, the Vietnam Workshop, August. 2008.

Viet Bao. "Tới Phiên Trương Tấn Sang Bị Kỷ Luật Vì Vụ Năm Cam." *Viet Bao*, January 23, 2003. Retrieved from https://vietbao.com/a21028/toi-phien-truong-tan-sang-bi-ky-luat-vi-vu-nam-cam (accessed February 18, 2018).

Viet Duc. "Hà Văn Thắm đã cấu kết với Nguyễn Xuân Sơn như thế nào?" *Voice of Vietnam*, October 7, 2016. Retrieved from https://vov.vn/vu-an/ha-van-tham-da-cau-ket-voi-nguyen-xuan-son-nhu-the-nao-557615.vov.

VietnamNet. "Tong bi thu: Lo nong len roi thi cui tuoi vao cung phai chay." *VietnamNet*, August 1, 2017. Retrieved from http://vietnamnet.vn/vn/thoi-su/chong-tham-nhung/lo-nong-len-roi-thi-cui-tuoi-vao-cung-phai-chay-387640.html.

VietnamNews. "Corruption Report Exposes Bribery." *VietnamNews*. September 20, 2017. Retrieved from http://vietnamnews.vn/politics-laws/394075/corruption-report-exposes-bribery.html#HATOiLGHzz4ZFWQ7.97.

VnExpress. "Vinashin nhan 750 trieu USD tien ban trai phieu." *VnExpress*, November 2, 2005. Retrieved from https://kinhdoanh.vnexpress.net/tin-tuc/vi-mo/vinashin-nhan-750-trieu-usd-tien-ban-trai-phieu-2683106.html.

Vuving, Alexander L. "Vietnam: A Tale of Four Players." *Southeast Asian Affairs* (2010): 366–391.

Vuving, Alexander L. "Vietnam in 2012: A Rent-Seeking State on the Verge of a Crisis." *Southeast Asian Affairs* (2013): 323–347.

Vuving, Alexander L. "The 2016 Leadership Change in Vietnam and Its Long-Term Implications." *Southeast Asian Affairs* (2017): 421–435.

World Economic Forum. "The Global Competitiveness Report." 2017. Retrieved from http://www3.weforum.org/docs/GCR2017-2018/05FullReport/TheGlobal CompetitivenessReport2017%E2%80%932018.pdf.

Part III

Anticorruption Driven by
Political Institutionalization

5

Anticorruption Politics in Thailand

From Regime Institutionalization to Sovereignty Wars

MICHAEL K. CONNORS

In their 1994 classic *Corruption and Democracy in Thailand*, which exposed the fraudulent means by which the public purse was gouged, Pasuk and Sungsidh (1994, 22) noted that what was at stake in competing networks of corruption was not so much a mere lining of the pockets as the "ability of each side to deploy this revenue to consolidate its relative political power." They painted a picture of interlocking networks of bureaucrats and politicians eager to use public positions to extract informal value, a partisan use of public office for private gain. In their account it was not the illegality of corruption that was most significant, but rather corruption's relation to a neopatrimonial logic that worked through the Thai state. Systemic corruption was a matter of power. They framed their conclusion, based on a historical survey of political development thinking and lessons from a history of Thai military rule, as a political axiom: "There are grounds to conclude that it is more harmful to have a society being dominated by an honest military than to have a parliamentary system with corrupt politicians. At least under a democratic framework there is the possibility of developing a civil society with the will to control corruption" (Pasuk and Sungsidh 1994, 24).

This was a widely held view that would come to influence the drafting of the broadly liberal 1997 Constitution. That Constitution legislated strong executive government, division of power, robust accountability agencies, and citizen participation within a strong rights framework (Connors 1999;

McCargo 2002). This hedge on liberal democratization that developed from the mid-1980s onward came at a challenging moment in Thailand's political opening that coincided with the political rise of provincial business notables. The latter's strong competition for the extractive potential of national and local political office led to intense vote buying and electoral and budgetary corruption tied to politicians (Pasuk and Baker 1993)—what was known as money politics. Grand corruption was also widespread, including procurement scandals tying bureaucrats and politicians; mega-project corruption such as the Klong Dan desalination plant, which involved massive graft and coercive tactics by a cabal of politicians and bureaucrats against citizens to acquire land that was then sold in turn to the project at an exorbitant price (Race 2010); and the nepotistic use of land reform policies under the Democrat Party–led government that led to its downfall in 1995.

For some observers, the Pasuk-Sungsidh axiom was disproven in the decade that followed Thailand's political opening. At the beginning, reformers wondered how to get "good people" into elected political power, by which they meant someone who had a demonstrable public interest and who would represent their constituency. At a bare minimum they sought the application of punitive costs, within the framework of a competitive political system, for "bad people" engaged in money politics. Indeed, the figure of the corrupt politician was prominent in the 1997 constitutional deliberations—and often the most critical were ex-politicians themselves who were aware of how the system worked. Consequently, several anti-politician elements were incorporated into the draft Constitution, including a directly elected but nonpartisan Senate that would play a role in selecting officeholders for the independent agencies of the state such as the Electoral Commission and anticorruption bodies. Originally, it was anticipated that the Senate would be selected via indirect means, but a majority of the Constitutional Drafting Assembly voted in favor of a direct vote. In the years that followed, many senators were seen as serving the government's agenda so that after the 2006 coup, liberals, conservatives, and reactionaries pushed for a mediated upper house that was not directly linked to the people's sovereignty and that presumably would be free of manipulation by politicians.

After the first elections held under the new Constitution in late 2000, the billionaire leader of the Thai Rak Thai party, Thaksin Shinawatra, became prime minister in early 2001. He gobbled up smaller coalition parties to ensure a firm parliamentary majority and began to attack the independent agencies of the state, including the National Anticorruption Commission that in 2000 found that he had deliberately misreported his assets as a political officeholder. After becoming prime minister, Thaksin appealed the decision and the Constitutional Court narrowly acquitted him. After this, Thaksin would subject the Senate and independent agencies of the state to significant political intervention, hindering their check, balance, and accountability role. Corruption did not decline. Indeed, under the Thaksin government, new scandals emerged that demonstrated that despite the formal apparatuses of anticorruption being in place there continued exorbitant procurement payments within the bureaucracy, favoritism to politically connected businesses, and efforts to obstruct the workings of the accountability agencies (McCargo and Ukrist 2005). In the face of Thaksin's challenge to the 1997 settlement, the antipolitician sentiment began to shift toward warranting extreme oversight of electoral institutions, politicians, and parliament by unelected "good people" who, being virtuous, would in turn represent and uphold national ideology and ethics. A foundational societal-wide normative shift occurred that substituted the conservative good official for the liberally conceived active citizen, the latter's spirit no longer judged capable of founding new norms. This was a development that emerged unevenly in the hybrid politics of the People's Alliance for Democracy (PAD) and its call for a royally appointed government (Connors 2008). First in 2005–2006 and more militantly in 2008, the PAD sought the overthrow of two elected governments deemed corrupt and treasonous. But street mobilization and strategic occupation by PAD were not enough. In the first instance a coup removed the government in September 2006 and in the second the courts removed two pro-Thaksin prime ministers in late 2008. Between 2009 and 2011 PAD's remnant elements protested the anti-Thaksin coalition government led by its erstwhile ally the Democrat Party—attacking both its toleration of corruption and its alleged weakness on a border dispute with Cambodia. Disillusionment with the Democrat Party paved the way for a significant number of activists to make a decisive break from electoral politics. The PAD's successor, the People's Democratic Reform Committee (PDRC), organized mass protests against the government led by Yingluck Shinawatra (2011–2014), Thaksin's sister, accusing it of mega-corruption. Its blockade of candidate registration and of polling booths foiled the February 2014 election and effectively paved the way for the May 2014 coup (Bencharat 2018). Thus it was that PAD and successor street movements and their elite backers injected into mass politics the ethical injunctions of virtue politics that had long had a mundane constituency among apparatchiks of Thailand's pedagogical state and its variegated supporters. "Virtue," aided by tanks and street politics, now loomed over elected politicians like a menacing proctor.

Although corruption occurs across all sectors, including the military, business, politics, and civil service, there clings to politicians a tailored opprobrium. If at first antipolitician sentiment around corruption had been mobilized selectively, over time it emerged as a structure of feeling that fed into the possibility of permanently dismantling democratic gains. Indeed, in 2016 a highly controlled referendum on the military junta's draft Constitution returned a healthy majority. Those who campaigned against the draft were subject to harassment and arrest. Prominent Thai analyst Thitinan Pongsudhirak argued that the 62 percent "yes" vote was a major shift in support of the anticorruption claims of the military and marked an endorsement of the move to control elected parliamentarians. Thitinan (2016) wrote with the hope that a decade-long violent polarization was dissipating: "This voter verdict suggests the Thai electorate is fed up with conventional politicians and corruption and graft. To be sure, the draft Constitution is lopsided and shifts power away from elected bases of legitimacy to unelected sources of moral authority. It was touted as anti-politician and anti-money politics on the premise that Thailand's political troubles emanate from elected politicians." In redescribing this remarkable concession to military rule, Thitinan captured Thailand's post-coup dominant antipolitics/anticorruption sentiment.

The authoritarianization process from 2006 to the present has seen political trust placed in the military and technocrats in a fashion that functionally parallels that of other authoritarian states. This enables the instrumental use of corruption politics to either marginalize potential political opposition or to bolster incumbent regime legitimacy. Such motivations are evident in the post-coup cases of corruption investigated by the National Anticorruption Commission against the coup-ousted Yingluk Shinawatra cabinet and Pheu Thai politicians for the rice subsidy scheme, and for introducing amnesty legislation in the 2013 parliamentary sitting. It is as if Thailand is back to the 1970s when statists contemplated how to build a party of the state in the face of rising leftist opposition, and a new generation, along with some lingerers, have now decided that the state captured and remolded by them is the best party to advance Thailand's technocratic-fueled economic and political development. And it is this politics that this chapter seeks to unpack by explaining how it is that Pasuk and Sungsidh's axiom was evidently turned on its head.

Chen and Weiss ask in the introduction to this volume, "What are the political motivations behind anticorruption efforts, across regime types? Whose interests do they advance or threaten? And what ramifications do these efforts have for government legitimacy, standards of accountability, popular engagement or cynicism, the nature of linkages between politicians and citizens, and regime durability?" Answering those questions in summary form is no easy task, given the contested nature of the corruption claims in the first place and the blunt but compelling democracy-authoritarian narrative that has accompanied Thailand's political crisis, as well as democratization studies more generally. This chapter seeks to contribute a framework that answers at least some of Chen and Weiss's questions by engaging with the political ambivalence at the heart of the Thai state. This move allows for greater understanding of the contradictory politics of the period—including in the realm of anticorruption politics. State ambivalence in Thailand is a condition of the failure of any force to effectively hold and direct the state in its integral sense, often leading to the resolution of conflict in the episodic return to decisionist regimes that invoke a state of emergency and rule dictatorially (Connors 2009).[1] Anticorruption politics have been impacted by state ambivalence and can only be understood in its light. By tracing how this is so, the limits, practices, and paradoxes of anticorruption politics within the parameters set by the structural power of different regimes may be situated. The state here is understood as an assembly of apparatuses that relationally reflects contending regime forces in political society that constantly seek to capture it either wholly or in parcels. This, in part, follows the strategic relational approach that Bob Jessop has developed in large part by a reading of Poulantzas (Jessop 2016). However, before pursuing that approach's relevance for understanding anticorruption politics, the chapter reviews select treatments of anticorruption moralism in relation to Thailand.

Interpreting Anticorruption Politics: Moralism?

In their wide-ranging study of Southeast Asia and critical intervention into literatures related to good governance, neoliberalism, and Southeast Asia since the Cold War, Rodan and Hughes (2014, 1) note the proliferation of organizations that have emerged to service the "new accountability agenda," including of "human rights commissions, auditing bodies with new investigative and monitoring powers, mandatory environmental

impact procedures, competition commissions, and judicial and administrative powers being extended into traditional policy domains. Initiatives
outside the state, or in partnership with it, involve a diverse array of civil
society actors. These range from watchdogs on corruption, transparency,
labor standards, corporate ethics, and electoral institutions to consumer
groups evaluating and monitoring state services." The authors see this as
part of the myriad of institutions that have emerged under global constitutionalism, a reform of the state that corresponds to and is driven by
a globalizing neoliberal project with local support and that social forces
adapted to, appropriated, and in the Thai case, transformed.

When Rodan and Hughes speak of accountability coalitions, they
focus on the political movement element, its domestic political form, rather
than the macro structures of global constitutionalism. They are discerning
in noting that such movements and institutions are influenced by political
economy of context and the national political struggles relevant to each
state and its contenders. Their basic argument, which has relevance for
the Thai context, is summarized as:

> Struggles over accountability reform are more influenced by
> moral conservatism than democratic assertiveness. Morally
> conservative approaches to accountability may be promoted,
> often in alliance with liberal approaches, to challenge or co-opt
> incipient democratic movements. The relative strength of dif-
> ferent ideologies reflects historical legacies and contemporary
> political economy relationships. Ideological categories differ
> over where political authority ought to rest in the accountability
> relationship and therefore have differential appeal to groups
> of varying interests. The issue is not whether accountability
> is diluted or not but whose authority is championed through
> accountability reforms. (Rodan and Hughes 2014, 3)

In relation to Thailand, their consideration of the immediate years after
the 1997 Constitution was promulgated fits an account of institutionalization as the driving force of anticorruption politics (see later discussion).
But as opposition grew against Thaksin for both the apparent benefit his
companies enjoyed by their proximity to political power and his cen-
tralization of political power, that opposition shifted from critiques of
authoritarianism and the need for due process to a politics of monarchism
and nationalism, and a critique of Thaksin's alleged ethics deficit: "Moral

ideologies thus dominated the coalition that sought to oust Thaksin, as erstwhile liberals allied tactically with, or reverted to, a moral ideology of royalist conservatism that bore little resemblance to classical liberalism" (Rodan and Hughes 2014, 171). Ignoring for the moment that classical liberalism was (and remains) capable of high moralism on citizen capacity, Rodan and Hughes's observation of the shift in antipolitics discourse is important. For their critical focus in interpreting these shifts is not the veracity or otherwise of contending claims about who is corrupt, but the manner in which anticorruption politics reflected broader underlying ideological conceptions of the problems and consequences of corruption. Their critical task was to ask of the different anticorruption positions that played out across Southeast Asia what underlying ideological position they advance and thereby determine the dangers or possibilities of such politics in the broader field. Such questions do a lot of work in illuminating the apparently unintended consequences of much political development work around corruption. As others have, Rodan and Hughes read the Thai case as an example of the mobilization of moral discourses that have delegitimated politicians and led to a conservative antidemocratic politics that obliterates accountability.

Similarly, Aim Sinpeng (2014) notes that the moral discourses of the anticorruption movements that emerged in the 2000s in Thailand were present in the 1990s reform project. She shows how some actors took what she describes as a behaviorist approach to corruption—an argument that corruption was a moral failing of individuals. While in competition with other approaches to corruption such as functionalism (where corruption is simply abuse of public office) that required institutional and legal responses, by the mid-2000s, these "behaviorist" ideas were ascendant and shaped the anti-Thaksin movement's royal nationalism, as did arguments about the inadequate moral basis of electoral democracy issuing from some Buddhists' adherence to Dhammocracy (the rule of Dhamma) and judging politics through it. While recognizing that institutionalist perspectives also informed the movement against Thaksin, Aim argues that the issue became a normative one about Thaksin's failings—a "moral issue." This framing moved the opposition to a different register, highlighting the dangers to nation and monarchy if Thaksin's state capture were allowed to continue. She writes that the movement succeeded in

> transforming corruption into an issue of "morality," "nation-alism," and "royalism." Such a conceptualization underlies

the importance of context- and value-based understandings
of corruption. In the minds of the PAD, it also reflects the
failure of the "institutional approach" in tackling corruption
issues through constitutional and institutional engineering.
Three major discourses on corruption marked the early stages
of PAD mobilization: (i) policy-based corruption; (ii) good
people; and (iii) electoral corruption and dharma democracy.
These discourses approached corruption from normative, not
functionalist perspectives. They all revealed the importance
of the norms of nationalism, royalism, and morality embedded within how the Yellow Shirts understood corruption and
political reforms. (Aim Sinpeng 2014, 531)

What emerges in these representative accounts is a narrative of conservative
moralism that delegitimated politicians by portraying them as unethically
corrupt. This pejorative view of politicians, not necessarily based on conservative politics, was longstanding. Major surveys have demonstrated low
public trust in politicians' ethics from 1999 to 2011, with minor variations, including minor improvements during the Thaksin years, and then
a subsequent decline, but not reaching the nadir of 2000 (Quah 2011).
Such mistrust is spread across state institutions, but not evenly. Transparency International's Global Corruption Barometer of 2011 shows almost
equally high levels of perceived corruption among the military, political
parties, police, and civil servants. Interestingly, before the next wave of
mass mobilization in 2013, but in the presence of further antipolitician
rhetoric during the premiership of Yingluck Shinawatra, the barometer
shows a rise in perceptions of corruption in political parties and the police
and a decline in perceived corruption in the military (with the civil service still nevertheless considered highly corrupt). In 2017, Transparency
International (TI) reported that Thailand had a net 72 percent reading of
favorable views on the military government's efforts to combat corruption
(interviews conducted in 2016). In its summary of the findings in table
5.1, TI notes perceptions of political parties as among the most corrupt
institutions as widely shared and not unique to Thailand.

Moreover, World Bank (WB) indicators that show a steady decline
in the rule of law (relative to other countries), from a highpoint in 1996
to a low point in 2009, with 2014 showing a major decline from the base
point of 1996, provide further evidence of the persistence of corruption.
Indicators for control of corruption show a similar decline from a highpoint

Table 5.1. Corruption perceptions of Thai institutions (5 = extreme corruption)

	Military	Civil Service	Political Parties	Police
2007	3.0	NA	4.2	4.0
2010–2011	3.5	3.7	3.6	3.6
2013	2.8	3.7	4.0	4.0

Source: Transparency International (n.d). Taken from TI's online reports and tables available at https://www.transparency.org/.

in 1998 to near-equal low points in 2006–2007 and 2014—coterminous with the political crises that climaxed in coups-d'état (World Bank 2015). While WB indicators cannot speak of absolute rises or declines in corruption specific to Thailand, they confirm that, despite its involvement in the global governance reform project, Thailand has gone backward. Thailand's Corruption Perceptions Index has steadily declined over the decade, despite the range of institutions and social campaigns against corruption. And although public discourse in relation to corruption has largely centered on scandals of the political class, this focus has not been exclusive. It is worth noting that the accountability industry is typically overworked with cases concerning the civil service, which form the bulk of anticorruption agency work, both of the NACC and other bodies (Research Institute for National Development 2015). And these efforts would seem to have had some impact. Pasuk (2015) reports a significant percent decline in citizen reports of having to pay bribes (petty corruption) to midlevel bureaucrats from 1999 to 2014. If actual corruption declined in the middle bureaucracy while grand political corruption was perceived to have risen we have a piece in the jigsaw puzzle of Thitinan's claim of popular support for the 2016 draft Constitution, and the significant willingness of many to disinvest their sovereignty into an authoritarian state.

Authoritarianism: Enabling Corruption and Anticorruption Politics

We have to ask, if moralism or moral judgment of politicians' failings (predominantly viewed as corrupt) has always been present, why did it come to possess rhetorical efficiency to move national sentiment in an authoritarian direction? And there is also the puzzle of disproportionate scorn poured on politicians while merely dabbed on civil servants, despite the ubiquitous trans-sectoral base of corruption. The antipolitician bias of anticorruption politics is worth dwelling on. On the one hand, citizens viewed bureaucratic corruption within the register of institutionalization as manageable and subject to investigation by the accountability mechanisms of the state, supported by media exposure and civil society. On the other hand, within the context of regime battles between pro- and anti-Thaksin forces, citizens came to view political corruption as an existential threat to political order because it could occupy or subvert those agencies as a function of its power capacity and hold over other institutions. Here lies a clue as to the political ramifications of antipolitician rhetoric. The administrative and the political are seen as two different orders of the corruption problematic. A coup group has never overthrown a bureaucracy, only a government. This differential value on the harm done by the different orders of corruption, and the antipolitician campaigning around it, dynamically shifted moral authority in favor of decisionist rather than parliamentary politics.

Given the nature of the argument to follow, some conceptual clearing is necessary. This chapter attempts to map a framework through which anticorruption politics can be understood beyond the democracy-authoritarian continuum. It attempts to specify regime structure at different moments in order to illuminate the enabling/disabling conditions for specific types of anticorruption politics. It begins from the premise that authoritarianism is a feature of all forms of political rule. Rather than situating authoritarianism in specific institutional sites (though it surely resides there—see table 5.2), it suggests that an enabling condition for the exercise of authoritarian power is the failure to establish and consolidate rules for the exercise of power as a consequence of Thailand's specific "democratic transition" that entailed a liberal and security settlement based on repression of progressive democratic forces, and the entrenchment of the monarchy at the center of a national power bloc that sought to stabilize the field (Connors 2009, 358–359; Connors 2007). That tentative settlement left competing groups of strategic elites in Thailand in a permanent state of insecurity; they have continually reverted to authoritarian modes to secure their position, even as liberalism ideologically deepened its reach in the 1990s. This was the insecurity condition for the continuance of neopatrimonial politics in a formally liberal state structure. As will be shown, authoritarian capacities wielded by political actors in conditions of insecurity enabled a thwarting of those instrumentalities that would deal with corruption.

If we accept that authoritarianism is as much about a certain exercise of power as it is about regime appellation, then it may be conceived that it will be a feature of all regimes. Regimes here are understood as specific patterns of power articulated to an ideology and a social base, whose protagonists seek control over state apparatuses. All the regime types described later in this chapter had authoritarian features, including those designated as liberal. The approach breaks through liberal pretension, enabling a recognition of the politics of liberal decisionism and authoritarianism (see Connors 2019). However, it is necessary to distinguish an authoritarian regime by design from the prevalence of authoritarian modes of power in a formally nonauthoritarian regime. In the former, regime structures are intentionally made to serve the illiberal coalition of interests embedded in and enabled by the regime control of state apparatuses. In the latter, the ambivalent nature of state power, its openness to different purpose, and its manipulation by authoritarian and liberal currents create a political landscape of insecurity that reinforces authoritarian choice. And if we follow the opening observation that grand corruption in Thailand relates to networks of power, we may also note that each regime shapes the possibilities of corruption and the grounds for its resistance.

Paralleling and borrowing from Linz, but wanting to separate state and regime, I have previously argued that an "authoritarian state is one in which an apparatus of arbitrary power (what may be called an ensemble of dictate) exerts control, and often undirected influence, over physical life and/or a social field defined by imposed limited, hierarchical pluralism. Although patterned, the deployment of power is arbitrary by virtue of its relative unaccountability/un-responsibility, and though pluralism is sometimes "controlled . . . it is not obliterated. An authoritarian state tends to exert coercive force in the extension of its quasi-legitimacy" (Connors 2008, 3–4).[2] In the following, I elaborate aspects of this definition so as to bring into focus types of authoritarian assemblage, marked by the varied configuration of the four attributes noted, that may attach differently to regime types.

Un-Responsible Power[3]

All states feature un-responsible power, full accountability being a sustaining myth of political community. The exercise of arbitrary and un-responsible power over the spheres of human existence and association entails the perversion of the relatively free range of collective political possibilities that might exist in an open public field.

UNIVERSAL CLAIMS

When applied to national-level state-society formations, "authoritarianism" entails that, on balance, the exercise of power is illiberal and based on the authority of those who hold the center (either formally or obscurely), and to those to whom they delegate or defer. State authority is variously legitimated by democratic, authoritative, and mythic claims to universal representation, or some combination of all (see Malloy 1992, 232). Institutional configurations within a regime do not match such universal claims. What enables those who exercise power at the center of a state are varied legitimating claims to demobilize opposition through mechanisms of repression, co-option, toleration, enduring strategies of depoliticization, plebiscitary gestures, democrasubjection, or even electoral mandates and parliamentary majorities.

HIERARCHY OF LINKAGES

Authoritarian states will be differentially marked by vertical and sectoral linkages between different levels of power, mediated by actors who react to and shape the institutional features of the existing regime, according to prevailing incentive and disincentive patterns and the domain of intervention (health, education, industry policy, etc.). This variation provides room to move. Authoritarian state institutions can articulate to various regime types, as can liberal institutions. While political typologists will rightly characterize regimes according to the dominant impulse at work in the center (democratic, authoritarian, totalitarian, etc.), most regimes are complex, multilevel systems marked by contradictory impulses within and across their respective domains. State institutions in any particular regime form can defy regime framers' hegemonic projects (see below). Within an authoritarian regime may be found liberal state institutions; within a liberal regime may be found authoritarian state institutions.

PROPENSITY TO COERCION

The deployment of coercive force is not unique to the authoritarian state, but the logic of exclusion by which such states operate does provide a marked propensity to coerce. Authoritarian states are rarely wholly legitimate, meaning they supplement universal claims by marks of their failure—the use of force. They tend to work on the principle of a dual exclusion: of dissident or oppositional forces subjected to legal or repressive measures, and of some social element by virtue of which the national citizenry may be formed over and over again.

Providing that one or more elements of this assemblage are present, authoritarianism emerges fully when, on average, a state's hierarchical organization of power over, and its actions toward, the social body it claims to represent is un-responsible and coercive in direction or consequence. Authoritarianism within different regimes, from those that are explicitly dictatorial to those that are constitutionally liberal, may be measured by the intensity of specific authoritarian assemblages. To speak of "intensities" allows that in any authoritarian assemblage, particular instances of sub-regime liberalism may persist and help authoritarianism endure. It is also possible to speak of an apparatus of dictate within liberal regimes, referring to sub-regime levels. This latter observation follows Schmitter (1995, 556–558), who suggested, in looking at democratic consolidation, paying attention to the multiple sites in which different structures of behavior are processed in relations between the state and society; he called these sites "partial regimes."

Table 5.2 on page 152 matches key Thai political institutions against the four attributes of authoritarianism and makes truncated observations on those institutions related to corruption. Table 5.3 on page 156 then seeks to identify the institutional configuration at the center of different regime forms and schematically indicates the anticorruption politics within each of the regimes. To the extent that different regimes periodically reconfigure the institutions above through the institutional flux that marks Thailand's formal political history, the Thai state necessarily expresses ambivalence, as no enduring hegemonic project and its regime protagonists capture the state. Table 5.3 brings the institutions into an ideal type regime configuration, allowing an approximation of the degrees of authoritarian power present in each regime. It presents a compact matrix through which to consider the context of anticorruption politics that this chapter seeks to interpret.

The State of Ambivalence:
From Institutionalization to Sovereignty Wars

The schematic analysis of the authoritarian assemblage mapped in table 5.3 illuminates the impact of structural authoritarian power on anticorruption

Table 5.2. Authoritarian features of Thai state institutions, 1980s–2016

Institutional site (adjacent authoritarian features (1980s–2014)	Monarchy	Military	Bureaucracy	Law	Executive power and parliamentary power
Un-responsible power	Unscrutinized exercise of power. Council of Elders (Privy Council) acts on its behalf. Subject to social acceptance.	High in operational fields, martial law, opaque economic interests.	Increasingly administered by process; neopatrimonial elements permeate the system; sub-parliament regulations govern functions; technocratic expertise legitimates in some domains.	Self-governing elements in judiciary, but largely act by legal dictate, in a context of poorly established rule of law. Police: rampantly corrupt and unaccountable. Pliable to political and veto powers.	If derived from parliamentary form, tendency to capture regulatory institutions. In dictatorial, decisionist regimes, self-referencing power.
Universal claims	Embodiment of Thainess, mythic social contract with the people. Quasi-religious infallibility.	Security and development.	Security and development claims; development liberalism/guardian bureaucracy.	Weak claims to rule of law norms as form of procedural legitimacy through 1997 instruments gradually established relations between state and subjects (Administrative Court/ NACC etc.); under military regime elements of rule by legal dictate.	In parliamentary form will of the people through electoral expression. In decisionist forms—general will, nationalism, monarchism, guardian savior of country.

Hierarchy of linkages	Sits at the top of a national power bloc. "Network monarchy" of different hues activates its interests, but it is also articulated to liberal interests engaged in a graduated democratic transition even as succumbs to states of exception.	Works with networks of politicians, bureaucracy, and palace.	Split allegiance to regime framers.	Across the social spectrum.	Extensive web of interests across state, regime, and capital actors.
Propensity to coercion	Ideological structural coercive power, legal support, economic and political interests backed by state actor. Social base among varied populations.	High, legal amnesty and indifference, corporate interests safeguarded by opaque state support.		Politically derived or bribed judgments are a form of coercion: power in law. Police at center of coercive practice.	Rule of Law Power of emergency legislation or decisionist interventions. Apparatuses of security normally at disposal unless parliamentary executive and decisionist state clash.

continued on next page

Table 5.2. Continued.

Institutional site (adjacent) authoritarian features (1980s–2014)	Monarchy	Military	Bureaucracy	Law	Executive power and parliamentary power
Corruption and anticorruption observations	Untouchable power and thus open to abuse (pretenders extorting, privy councilors on the make). Opaque impact on policy. Moral discourse on corruption in part emanates from the monarch's teachings on "good people."	Opaque/secret budgets support neopatrimonial factional relations. Coercive power creates barrier to exposure. Select corruption examined by accountability agencies but shielded from extensive scrutiny.	Subject to stringent mechanisms of accountability, but power resources enable evasion or aversion of auditors. Administrative Court, National Anticorruption Commission, State Audit Commission, and other agencies conduct surveillance. Corruption by power of budget, illegal use of budget, and buying and selling of office.	Police through extortive corruption; highly corrupt through position, licensing, power to enforce. Coercive powers deliver goods. Judiciary considered the cleaner arm of the Thai state, but anecdotal evidence of major bribery for decisions. Also, political interference as a form of corruption may be considered pervasive.	The 1997 Constitution set up a range of instruments to combat money politics—buying votes, buying MPs, buying cabinet positions, etc. Major political figures seek control over ministries, interventions in budget allocations for projects, connections to construction industry.

Big-capital control of the state meant policy expressly for the benefit of companies (claims of policy corruption's benefiting connected families).

In decisionist form, corruption likely to be grand as mechanisms of accountability are decimated.

Table 5.3. Regime configurations

Regime features and regime type	Predominating center	Authoritarian matrix at the center 1. Un-responsible power 2. Universal claims 3. Hierarchy of linkages 4. Propensity to coercion	Anticorruption politics
1. Liberalizing bureaucratic authoritarian regime 1978–1988.	Bureaucratic-military centers of power, business groupings, and palace.	1. Medium-high exercise of arbitrary power. 2. Medium-high nationalism. 3. Highly centralist/securitizing. 4. Medium-high.	*Weak institutional means to combat routine corruption. *Beginning of money politics and rise of "corrupt politician discourse."
2. Emergent liberal conservative regime 1992–2001 (liberal regime).	Parliament and executive, legal centers of the state, palace, business groupings.	1. Low-medium exercise of arbitrary power. 2. Low-medium—development of rights and citizenship framework within conservative democracy with king-as-head-of-state ideology. 3. Liberal decentralizing/security imperatives on borders. 4. Low-medium on specific issues.	*Rise of institutional reform movements seeking good governance, electoral accountability, and liberal divisions of power. *Anticorruption networks and linkage of regime change with clean politics. *No-go areas (military/palace).

3. Consolidating electoral populist/ (2001–2006, 2008) (illiberal populist regime). The pro-Thaksin government of 2011–2014, constrained by the military, does not conform to this regime pattern—the state/regime hybridity was a function of coercive compromise.	Political executive, party executive, electoral support base.	1. Medium-high exercise of arbitrary power (in context of liberal political framework). 2. Medium nationalist and populist idiom. 3. Managerialism of the state, securitization of the border, pockets of liberalism in ministries/economy. 4. Medium-high in specific domains.	*Clash of new institutional structures with strong capture of state by Thaksin. *Rise of discourse of policy corruption. *Thaksin wages war on "influentials" in name of open economy. *Democracy as court of justice. *Rise of anti-anticorruption politics.
4. Military decisionist regime 1991–1992, 2006–2007, 2014–present (decisionist regime).	State apparatus held by junta and supported by social base accepting the state of exception, palace.	1. High exercise of arbitrary power. 2. High nationalist/royalist idiom. 3. Highly centralist. 4. High propensity to coercion across a range of domains.	*Highly selective prosecution, invoking of hyper-pitch moralism. *Antipolitician rhetoric. *Suppression of news on state corruption.

politics. This chapter considers anticorruption politics across regime forms to illustrate the structures of power that shaped anticorruption politics and countermovements. But first, something needs to be said on anticorruption instrumentalities in the context of regime battles.

Despite the fluctuating regime types across Thailand's recent past, the specific institutional and legislative framework for anticorruption measures (Counter Corruption Commission, state auditor, parliamentary ombudsman, etc.) largely holds good across regimes 2, 3, and 4 listed in table 5.3 (liberal, illiberal populist, and decisionist regimes). Any of these regimes formally audit the public objective of suppressing corruption. What changes across regimes is the political form of anticorruption. Those changes have to do with both ideological mobilization in the contest of regime framers seeking to embed patterns of political power within state apparatuses that will serve their respective social bases and hegemonic projects *and* the particularities of the existing power structure. The moment anticorruption politics are no longer solely an administrative enforcement of a political settlement (the liberal-conservative regime period), or a tit-for-tat political scandal, but become engulfed in sovereignty wars (contests between regime framers over who has the legitimate right to possess the state), it hardly matters that corruption might have happened, for evidence against one side is made redundant by evidence against another. A politics of "whataboutism" then prevails. Thus analysis requires a distance from the cacophony of claims and counterclaims to show how anticorruption politics in the Thai case occurred as part of regime battles, which is to say that the salience of anticorruption efforts lies in attempts by particular forces or regime framers to impose on the state liberal-conservative, pluto-populist, democratic, or statist arrangements of power. Seen in this context, anticorruption politics are multivalent and need not be collapsed into a single interpretation.

If we follow Rodan and Hughes's (2014) previously discussed analysis of what they call "ideologies of accountability," we may plot a trajectory of anticorruption politics against the regime types in table 5.3. In the late 1990s and early 2000s, anticorruption politics are first regime-affirming as the fragile constitutional liberal regime is defended against the emerging illiberal populist regime. These regime battles are precisely about the ultimate source of authority—and in their irresolution (2005 onward) the different positions transform. Anticorruption politics move from the administration of policing routines by a posited neutral liberal state to *the political*, taking form in a decisionist regime; the illiberal populist transforms to a formal democratic position. This plot will be elaborated later, but some general features may be observed first. Within the liberal regime, anticorruption politics raised the question of political legitimacy, since no corruption, even that which is expedient, is legitimate by liberal procedural definition. After 2006 and the return of pro-Thaksin governments in 2008 and 2011–2014, and during the Aphisit government's tenure (2008–2011), populist-democratic discourse tended to downplay corruption, even as it eagerly highlighted that of its enemies through a strategy of whataboutism. Rather, focus shifted from the legitimacy of the 1997 Constitution and the routine question of institutionalization to the more fundamental question of the source of sovereignty, opening up from left and right the question of the purpose of the state. This contest played a role in the process whereby anticorruption politics as regime institutionalization morphed into a weaponized instrument to establish new forms of politics and to deny legitimacy to the sovereign claims of an elected government (2006, 2008, 2014). This is reflected in the history of the National Anticorruption Commission (NACC), which will now be briefly examined, after which some flesh will be placed on the skeleton bones of the argument so far.[4]

The NACC was a major element of the new accountability mechanisms of the 1997 Constitution. It began its work properly in 2000, inheriting over two thousand cases from a paper-tiger predecessor that had sat in the prime minister's office. The NACC's major focus was not solely on politicians but rather corruption across all public sectors. Although critics often depicted the independent agencies of the state that work on corruption, including the NACC, as mere instruments of the dominant regime in power, they offered space for some independence—indeed, such independence was a mandated feature of the liberal regime. Moreover, while the NACC might receive an average of two thousand cases a year and must verify tens of thousands of asset declarations by civil servants and politicians, it is dependent on other agencies to then deliver verdicts and issue punishment. This means its work intersects with the authoritarian features of the dominant regime form. Across the liberal and illiberal populist regimes, the NACC's efforts were primary, making the case that corruption had occurred and referring the matter on; success then depended on the entire enterprise of state reform.

Of the thousands of cases that have passed through the NACC, the majority have involved civil servants, mostly within the Interior Ministry, and police. The NACC often referred such cases to disciplinary boards, lower-level anticorruption bodies, the administrative court, or the attorney general, while politicians' cases were sent to the attorney general, the Supreme Court (for political officeholders, in cases of criminal corruption), or the Constitutional Court. Across the entire period the NACC sought to establish new norms on clean public service. It sponsored thousands of events on ethics and anticorruption mechanisms, its offices spread to the provinces, and it became a major research house. Its annual reports show massive scrutiny of corrupt civil servants, more so than of politicians, but it was the latter cases that were deemed media-worthy and so were highlighted in the press. One area in which political scrutiny outstripped civil servant scrutiny was in asset declaration, as decentralization created thousands of elected municipal and provincial political positions. The military was also subject to scrutiny, with the NACC's taking on some prominent cases that it then forwarded to relevant agencies, but this was greatly limited (see Ukrist and Connors forthcoming).

The NACC, as the premier institution of the 1997 Constitution charged with shaping public practice by a demonstration effect, was not always subject to political interference; it sought to address corruption in line with the intentions of the 1997 reforms and embed the new system. It operated through an approach to sovereignty in the 1997 Constitution that permanently delayed "the people's" sovereign power through the liberal transmission belt of a division of powers. No doubt it played a part in promoting a politics of virtue, but this was as much aimed at the civil service as the political class. Such pieties are likely to accompany any anticorruption campaign where corruption is rife and where public office by appointment or election is practiced as a fiefdom. The NACC's fragile independence was compromised on particular cases; after the 2006 coup it was increasingly subject to manipulation and control. For example, the 2007 Constitution reduced the role of the Senate (which in any case, was now only half-elected) in the selection process for the appointment of boards of independent agencies of the state (including the NACC). This further distanced the agencies from parliamentary legitimacy.

In its early period, and despite countervailing pressures, the NACC was dedicated to constitutional mandates, and its officials and allied consultant researchers aimed to advance good governance by developing the capacity to arrest corruption across all spheres. The exceptional moments of political bias and intervention in the early period of its operations did not substantially shift it from this task. However, its subsequent integration into regime battles in the post-2006 period meant that while it continued to deal with mundane matters of corruption, its pursuit of grand corruption was no longer in the service of the 1997 settlement. Its failure was not so much of its own making as due to the larger regime structures to which it had to relate. This may account for the low level of success in major cases of corruption by the NACC. Thus, if the NACC in its administrative form was conceived as a support for the institutionalization of the 1997 settlement, it may be said that the earlier focus on significant corruption during the Thaksin period was in service to that objective. Anticorruption politics in this period, despite the coexistence of moralistic and conservative rhetoric, saw a general alignment of NGOs, foundations, and public intellectuals fighting corruption in support of the independent agencies of the state. This would lead to a countermovement in the rhetorical form of democratic sovereignty against which a decisionist regime would arise.

How did authoritarian power across institutions affect anticorruption politics of this period? For purposes of this discussion we have begun with the liberal regime form, which saw reduced barriers to dealing with corruption and, indeed, in which the political institutions mandated by the 1997 Constitution were in effect a founding super-accountability coalition formed by the independent agencies of the state and their support base in civil society. This was a period, then, when ideological mobilization of a rights framework, liberal ideologies of a limited state, and the maturing of a civil society infrastructure that had emerged in the bureaucratic-authoritarian period of the 1980s and grew in the 1990s mitigated the acute power of state institutions. This context reduced un-responsible power in the whole regime, although some institutions retained it. Thus, mechanisms for scrutiny of power expanded in bureaucratic, legal, and parliamentary arenas under the universal claims of a rights framework that presented the state as the servant of the morally able citizen, understood both from a mixed liberal-republican position of civic virtue and political participation and from a conservative sense of living up to the moral strictures of the monarchy and religion. Decentralization also forced a drawdown of the bureaucratic security state, which retreated to border areas and the insurgency in the South. Yet if this was the general line, in their own quarters, the military and palace networks retained high levels of un-responsible power in relation to formal mechanisms of accountability and were not fully subject to the new accountability mechanisms (as the double-standards discourse deployed by the red-shirt movement would later highlight).[5] Moreover, while the relative political opening meant that the propensity to coercion diminished in this period, the pacted nature of

Thailand's transition also meant that legal and opaque coercion surrounded the monarchy and military, respectively, enabling a consolidation of royal nationalism in this period, because the resources for its contestation were meagre. Also, ideologically, the space for moving from the monarchy toward a more egalitarian form of liberalism was limited because elite Thai liberalism had articulated with the monarchy as a super-ombudsman that, through its elevated position above politics and its assumed virtue, would act as a power-above-power, a Thai reprisal of Constant's hope for the French monarchy in the nineteenth century. These were the power conditions that determined the mobilization of moralism and royalism against the Thaksin government.

When the elite form of the liberal regime confronted the emergence of illiberal populism, instead of deepening its democratic politics, it first sought the application of the posited liberal state. But in the face of assaults on that state, it migrated to a conservative moralistic politics in some instances, and in others, sought resolution in a strike from above (Connors 2017). Thus liberal regime framers split three ways—first, with quiet but satisfied resignation in the face of the 2006 coup and to holding out for new opportunities to reprise liberal politics (Connors 2019); second, with a restrictive liberalism expressed in containing electoral politics represented in the 2007 Constitution and a shift to bureaucratic authoritarianism with a liberal ideological makeover; and third, with the politics of exceptionalism, or regime 4 in table 5.3.

The countermovement to liberal institutional anticorruption politics took two forms. One strategy entailed avoidance of capture and escaping institutionalization's net. The prospects for this were greatly enhanced when the work of the NACC was delayed for several years when the commissioners provided themselves with a hefty pay raise and were subject to suspension, then removal, leading to thousands of cases being held up and fading from view. The other strategy was to do battle with these same institutions by controlling, discrediting, or working against them, while at the same time waging populist-logic society-level battles against "dark influences" and drugs and other social ailments so as to create an alternative politics that could, by force of popular support, effectively discount accountability surveillance. This strategy characterized the emergence of Thaksin's challenger illiberal populist regime within the 1997 settlement—and this framed the politics of the first phase of the movement against Thaksin (see Connors 2009). Thaksin's challenge created the conditions for the expansion of the moralistic politics of monarchy and nation outlined by Aim earlier. Thaksin's countermove to institutionalization was of a piece with his emerging illiberal populism, first glimpsed when Thaksin mobilized popular support in 2001 to pressure the Constitution Court to strike down the NACC's finding that he had deliberately concealed assets, enabling him to remain as prime minister. Present, too, during this period was an argument against the independent agencies of the state that touched on their lack of democratic legitimacy and their bias (see Connors 2008). Finally, the Thaksin government proved willing to use accountability agencies to suppress dissent. For example, it appeared that the Anti-Money Laundering Agency had been instructed to probe the affairs of critical journalists and NGO activists in an effort to intimidate them into silence (see Pasuk and Baker 2009). Another challenge came against key personnel of the independent agencies of the state. For example, the auditor general, who, having been scrutinized by the elected Senate and then appointed by the king, Thaksin removed. She had challenged several of the Thaksin government's budgetary practices. After the government removed her, the royal bureau did not return a royally signed appointment for her successor—which was read as royal displeasure. It was as if the different regime framers were now seeking to occupy the same state domains. Here we see pockets of authoritarian power dueling with each other in the space the liberal 1997 Constitution provided (Connors 2008).

This countermovement of delegitimating the liberal settlement as antidemocratic continued into the post 2006 coup period, with pre-red-shirt political activists beginning the intellectual work of reorienting political discourse away from virtue and morality to the question of democracy and double standards. When a pro-Thaksin party won elections in late 2007 this countermovement to anticorruption politics assumed the status of a policy, expressed in a nationally broadcast television show called *Truth Today* (after a pro-Thaksin newspaper and fronted by three activist-politicians who would come to play major roles in the red-shirt movement). The program was unashamedly pro-government. It declared itself against the People's Alliance for Democracy that had played the coordinating role in the major February and March 2006 demonstrations against Thaksin and assailed the Democrat Party as a party that worked with dictators; it also waged a relentless attack on the Constitution Court, NACC, 2007 Constitution, and auditor general. *Truth Today*'s basic premise was that the 2006 coup was illegitimate and therefore everything that had flowed from the coup was illegitimate, including the corruption cases against Thaksin. It considered the 2007 Constitution, moreover, the child of a dictatorship.[6]

In 2008, transformative anticorruption politics took full form. This was essentially a matter of two sides' meeting at the borders of sovereignty, from which one repelled the other. This was the year of PAD's "uprising" against the pro-Thaksin government, when it shifted its protests from central Bangkok to occupation of Suvarnabhumi airport, a move that impacted the Constitutional Court's removal of the government that had been in office for less than one year. If we consider the matrix of power in table 5.3, we note that anticorruption politics as it took shape on the streets of Bangkok in 2008 moved from favoring a liberal regime (type 2 in the table) to favoring a decisionist one (type 4): arbitrary, unaccountable, coercive, and highly hierarchical, with the military at the pinnacle of execution in the name of rescuing the nation and the monarchy from a corrupt regime. This was a politics to be repeated with greater effect in 2014. But this was a discursive transition; it did not run along a predetermined line. It is notable that the military junta of 2006 moved the corruption cases against Thaksin into an ad hoc Asset Scrutiny Committee. It established a constitutional tribunal and abolished the Constitutional Court, with the former voting to disband Thaksin's party, for example, in 2007. The extant literature refers to this period as the judicialization of politics, but in some senses this characterization underestimates what happened, for it conflates the original Constitutional Court decision to declare invalid the outcome of the elections (2006) with subsequent quasi-judicial attempts under a military regime to disband Thaksin's party, Thai Rak Thai, and expedite cases against Thaksin. Such features accompanied the post 2014 regime, only by this time, the junta used existing agencies to carry out its mission, assured that they had been transformed to fit their purpose.

Conclusion

This chapter has shown that the legal issue of corruption and the sanctioned institutions for its mitigation in the period of liberal embedding was subject to two transformative dynamics. One dynamic saw the legal administrative anticorruption project align with militantly liberal and conservative anti-Thaksin social mobilization, which in its failure then elevated to its core the moralism analyzed earlier. The second transformative dynamic was that of the countermovement against the first, which took the shape of democratic sovereign politics, in which corruption was displaced and made mundane, then attributed across the political spectrum so that obsessive focus on one side came to seem a form of "double standards." (There is a dialectic here, for the ousted corrupt politicians the burden of proof soon falls on the decisionist regime once it looms over politics; should a decisionist anticorruption politics and a democratic anticorruption politics quickly succeed each other mirroring a broader political conflict, a condition of mutual exhaustion may lead to a deepening of institutional accountability in the long run based on expanded political legitimacy).

To return to the question Chen and Weiss ask regarding the interests and motives of anticorruption politics, a first observation is that in the period of transition from the liberal-conservative to the electoral-populist regime anticorruption politics were conducted predominantly in the register of institutionalization and the development of civic norms to give spirit to those institutions. In the second period, with the uncertainty accompanying a sequence of momentary regimes (2006 onward) the operation of active private, political party, and movement mobilization of corruption discourses to delegitimate others became dominant (*you are corrupt; no you are*). And within this conflict emerged what I have termed sovereignty wars (Connors 2017), whereby clean government for one side was exemplified by virtue politics centered on the monarchy (McCargo 2015), while the other side made corruption a second-order question (an *anti-anticorruption politics*), rather prioritizing democratic sovereignty as the source of accountability against the divided sovereignty of the 1997 Constitution (1997–2006) or the decisionist sovereignty of "monarchized military" (2006–2007, 2014 onward), as Chambers and Napisa (2016) term it. In this second period, anticorruption politics and their countermovement become intelligible when viewed as a form of sovereignty wars in which there is a hyper-politics of maneuver in the Gramscian sense to impose a line on the state by frontal assault rather than working within state ambivalence to advance a regime frame through a politics of position.[7] As such, the authoritarian attributes of un-responsible power, universal claims, hierarchy, and coercion acutely marked both the illiberal populist and decisionist regime periods and their accompanying anticorruption and countermovement politics.

Notes

1. Decisionist regimes that have emerged across Thailand's political history are not so much identifiable by their continuity of identity as their respective

projects. Each decisionist occurrence marks a critical breakdown and recomposition of the ruling strata and its social base, a process overdetermined by both structural and agential factors at multiple levels, including geopolitics, corporate interests, internal conflicts, and pressures from below. If the faces and institutions look familiar, the projects do not. The events of 1976, 1991, 2006, and 2014 reflect acutely different decisionist moments and projects. This approach differs to the application of the concept of a "deep state" in Thailand (see Mérieau 2016).

2. Linz's definition is regime-focused and centered on a distinction between democratic and authoritarian regimes, whereas my definition seeks to identify authoritarianism trans-regime: "Authoritarian regimes are political systems with limited, not responsible, political pluralism; without elaborate and guiding ideology (but with distinctive mentalities); without intensive nor extensive political mobilization (except some points in their developments); and in which a leader (or occasionally a small group) exercises power within formally ill-defined limits but actually quite predictable ones" (Linz 1975, 255).

3. This section and the tables that follow draw upon Connors 2008 and 2009.

4. Other agencies played important roles including the highly politicized State Audit Commission—see Connors 2008, 152–153.

5. The military was unevenly subject to NACC investigations and at times some senior figures were referred to relevant judicial, institutional, or review boards (see Ukrist and Connors forthcoming).

6. For more details on this framing, see http://sovereignmyth.blogspot.com.au/2008/08/thailands-media-and-law-wars-hijacking.html. This section draws on this blog post from 2008.

7. Use of the term "hyper-politics of maneuver" and "hyper-politics of position" (rather than war) is meant to indicate that while Gramscian ideas are being invoked, they are done so analogously. These strategies are not particular to any one class configuration.

Bibliography

Aim Sinpeng. "Corruption, Morality, and the Politics of Reform in Thailand." *Asian Politics and Policy* 6, no. 4 (2014): 523–538.

Bencharat Sae Chua. "When Democracy Is Questioned: Competing Democratic Principles and Struggles for Democracy in Thailand." In *Political Participation in Asia*, edited by Eva Hansson and Meredith L. Weiss. London: Routledge, 2018.

Chambers, P. W., and Napisa Waitoolkiat. "The Resilience of Monarchised Military in Thailand." *Journal of Contemporary Asia* 46, no. 3 (2016): 425–444.

Connors, M. K. "Sovereignty Wars: Patterns of Constituent Power in Thailand." Paper presented to Consortium of Southeast Asian Studies Conference, December 16–17, Chulalongkorn University, 2017.

Connors, M. K. "Political Reform and the State in Thailand." *Journal of Contemporary Asia* 29 no. 2 (1999): 202–226.

Connors, M. K. "Liberalism, Civil Society and New Projects of Subjection." In M. K. Connors, *Democracy and National Identity in Thailand*, revised edition. Copenhagen: NIAS Press. 2007.

Connors, M. K. "State Ambivalence and the Struggle between Liberal and Authoritarian Regime Framers." Paper presented to Workshop on Contemporary Authoritarianism in Southeast Asia: Structures, Institutions, and Agency, City University, Hong Kong, May 9–10, 2008.

Connors, M. K. "Liberalism, Authoritarianism and the Politics of Decisionism in Thailand." *The Pacific Review* 22, no. 3 (2009): 355–373.

Connors M. K. "Liberalism Against the People: Learning to Live with Coups d'État." *Journal of Political Ideologies* 24, no. 1 (2019): 11–31.

Jessop, B. *The State.* Cambridge: Polity, 2016.

Linz, J. *Totalitarian and Authoritarian Regimes.* Boulder: Lynne Rienner, 2000.

Malloy, J. "Contemporary Authoritarian Regimes." In *Encyclopedia of Government and Politics, Volume 1*, edited by Mary Hawkesworth and Maurice Kogan, 229–248. London: Routledge, 1992.

McCargo, D., ed. *Reforming Thai Politics.* Copenhagen: Nordic Institute of Asian Studies, 2002.

McCargo, D., and Ukrist Pathamand. *The Thaksinization of Thailand.* Copenhagen: NIAS Press, 2005.

McCargo, D. "Peopling Thailand's 2015 Draft Constitution." *Contemporary Southeast Asia* 37, no. 3 (2015): 329–354.

Mérieau, E. "Thailand's Deep State, Royal Power and the Constitutional Court (1997–2015)." *Journal of Contemporary Asia* 46, no. 3 (2016): 445–466.

National Anticorruption Commission. Raignan Prajam Pi 2014 [Annual report 2014]. Bangkok: Office of the National Anticorruption Commission, 2014.

National Anticorruption Commission. Kanpatirup rabob ngoppraman khong thai pheu to tan kantujarit [Thai budgetary reform to counter corruption]. Bangkok: Office of the National Anticorruption Commission, 2012.

Pasuk Phongpaichit. ja do su kap khorapchan yangrai di [How to battle corruption]. Address to the 100 years of Puey Seminar, August 17, 2015. Retrieved from https://thaipublica.org/2015/08/puey-100-pasuk-3/.

Pasuk Phongpaichit and Chris Baker. "Jao Sua, Jao Poh, Jao Tii: Lords of Thailand's Transition." Paper presented at the Fifth International Conference in Thai Studies, School of Oriental and African Studies, University of London, 1993.

Pasuk Phongpaichit and Chris Baker. *Thaksin*, second edition. Bangkok: Silkworm Books, 2009.

Pasuk Phongpaichit and Sungsidh Piriyarangsan. *Corruption and Democracy in Thailand.* Chiang Mai: Silkworm Books, 1994.

Poulantzas, Nicos. *State, Power and Socialism.* Translated by Patrick Cammiler. London: Verso. 2000.

Quah, J. S. T. "Chapter 8 Thailand." In *Curbing Corruption in Asian Countries: An Impossible Dream*, 269–306. Bingley, UK: Emerald Books, 2011.

Race, J. "Restructuring, Renorming, Rethinking: Inferences from Canonical Thai Corruption Cases." *NACC Journal* (2010): 113–126.

Research Institute for National Development. ประเมินองค์กรอิสระตามรัฐธรรมนูญว่าด้วยการต่อต้านคอร์รัปชั่น [Evaluating independent agencies in the struggle against corruption]. Bangkok: Research Report of TDRI, 2015.

Rodan, G., and Caroline Hughes. *The Politics of Accountability in Southeast Asia: The Dominance of Moral Ideologies*. Oxford: Oxford University Press, 2014.

Schmitter, P. C. "The Consolidation of Political Democracies: Processes, Rhythms, Sequences, and Types." In *Transitions to Democracy: Comparative Perspectives from Southern Europe, Latin America and Eastern Europe*, edited by Geoffrey Pridham, 556–558. Brookfield: Dartmouth, 1995.

Thitinan Pongsudhirak. "After a Decade of Polarisation, a New Balance in Thailand." *Straits Times*, August 30, 2016. Retrieved from http://www.straitstimes.com/opinion/after-a-decade-of-polarisation-a-new-balance-in-thailand.

Transparency International. Global Corruption Barometer (various years). n.d. Retrieved from https://www.transparency.org/.

Transparency International. Corruption Perceptions Index (various years). n.d. Retrieved from https://www.transparency.org/.

Ukrist Pathmanand and Michael K. Connors. "Thailand's Public Secret: Wealthy Generals and the Thai State." *Journal of Contemporary Asia*, forthcoming.

World Bank. "Worldwide Governance Indicators World Bank Country Data Report for Thailand, 1996–2014." 2015. Retrieved from http://documents.worldbank.org/curated/en/336381468197105853/pdf/105585-WP-PUBLIC-Thailand.pdf.

6

Korea's Anticorruption Struggles

Fighting against Networks

RAY DONGRYUL KIM

The strictest anticorruption law in Korea's history recently came into effect. In 2015, the Korean National Assembly passed the Improper Solicitation and Graft Act after extensive deliberations and review. The act adopted provocative measures to prevent corruption, such as prohibiting civil servants from taking gifts worth more than the equivalent of fifty US dollars, or threatening prison sentences for accepting more than the equivalent of a thousand US dollars from anybody regardless of their government position or whether a policy favor is expected in return. The act also radically expanded the reach of anticorruption regulations to the relatives of government officials and certain nonpublic workers, private school teachers, and journalists, holding them all accountable under the law for graft or improper solicitation.

Though the severity of this new law might suggest otherwise, Korea is not notoriously corrupt. The country was well regarded for its professional governance and its economic performance during the 1970s and 1980s (World Bank 1993; Wan 2007). Even after the political and economic reforms of the 1990s, Korea did not experience a rise in corruption,[1] although the Corruption Perceptions Index has ranked Korea consistently at around fiftieth of over 150 countries since the index's inception in 1996. In 2016, when the new law went into effect, Korea scored 53/100, placing it fifty-second out of 176 countries.[2] It is not obvious, therefore,

why Korea needed such a drastic new anticorruption law. It is also puzzling that the legislation was passed after Korea had become a successful
liberal democracy. The act's passage suggests that, despite all the reforms
to decentralize political power and promote democracy, Koreans generally
believe it is necessary to tackle public corruption with an aggressive law.[3]
That said, the timing of the law, so long after democratic transition, leaves
open the question, why this renewed zeal, at this moment?

This chapter examines the political logic behind the Improper
Solicitation and Graft Act, informally known as the Kim Young-ran
Act. The analysis traces the impetus for the anticorruption law back to
institutionalized corruption built into informal networks spread across
the Korean bureaucracy and the private sector. The historical context
shows why Korea ran the risk of violating its constitutional principles to
pass the Improper Solicitation and Graft Act. Corruption, especially by
high-ranking bureaucrats, is difficult to detect and even harder to punish
due to its hidden nature under the thick policy networks ranging across
the government, public organizations, and private corporations. Seeds of
corruption germinated in these networks through common practice of
personal exchanges of graft, bribes, and policy favors. Such corruption
becomes resistant to regulations because these networks collectively protect their interests. The Kim Young-ran Act reflects social demands that
network-based corruption should be weeded out before it strangles the
country's hard-earned economic success, once society finally perceived the
costs entailed, thanks to such incidents as the 2011 prosecutor scandal
and the 2014 Sewol ferry disaster, and responded.

In light of social demands that networked corruption be eliminated,
this chapter will focus on how Korea has addressed corruption and upon
the role of bureaucratic policy networks. The first section defines the
bureaucratic character of Korea's corruption. The historical survey that
follows shows the incremental but transformative advancement of Korea's
anticorruption efforts.[4] Democratization represented the critical point in
Korean development when networked corruption was exposed for the
threat it posed to economic prosperity and liberalization, building support
over the years after transition for stronger laws to combat this corruption.
The last section examines the Kim Young-ran Act and the political and
societal factors that either hindered or facilitated the passage of the law.
The chapter concludes with a discussion of new trends in Korean political
economy as suggested by the revolutionary Kim Young-ran Act.

Characterization of Korea's Corruption

Public corruption in Korea is hard to define if one relies on studies found in the literature to comprehend its causes, contexts, and effects.[5] Corruption in Korea could be classified as either personal or structural.[6] Corruption has also played different roles at different levels of political and economic development in Korea.[7] Sometimes corruption is fully understandable in economic terms, when its expected benefits are higher than its costs,[8] but not at other times, unless with reference to Korea's social and cultural norms.[9] A single definition or theory cannot fully capture Korean corruption, given its distinctiveness. Moreover, as the historical review to come shows, Korean corruption has transformed, adapted, and changed from one kind to another at critical times. As anywhere else, individuals in Korea may make unethical choices to engage in one-time corruption, but at other times, corruption appears more systematic, as when actors repeatedly commit corrupt acts.[10] What most clearly defines corruption in South Korea is a particular, systematic networked variant that transcends the individual level.

Despite the multifaceted characteristics of corruption in Korea, the Kim Young-ran Act specifically targets this network-based corruption.[11] A structural definition of corruption following Korea's political economic framework might be suitable for understanding network-based corruption,[12] but it would not be able to address historic functional changes in the networks as they shifted from serving the public good to rent-seeking upon the advent of democratization. In order to fully comprehend corruption in Korea, this chapter presents the focal point as the bureaucracy, whose self-interest was implanted in policy networks, thereby blending personal and structural causes of corruption within Korea's political life.

BUREAUCRATIC CORRUPTION

The developmental characteristics of the Korean state have deeply entrenched the state's influence over the economy. Bureaucrats have been among key state economic actors, along with politicians (Johnson 1982). The roots of bureaucratic corruption stem from the state's prerogative and reflect the country's political-economic structure.[13] The bureaucracy wields a heavy influence over the market due to policy specialization and information advantages.[14] In essence, Korean bureaucrats are technocrats playing significant roles in the country's economy, giving them plenty of opportunity for corruption.

The Korean bureaucracy consists of economic and noneconomic services, with the former having more policy autonomy than the latter. The bifurcated bureaucracy played an important role in the Korean developmental state (Kang 2002, 63–64). The political leadership protected economic agencies from political intervention, ensuring that the bureaucracy in economic affairs was immune to political corruption like financing the governing party or presidential elections. The control of political corruption unrelated to Korea's economic performance depended on the will of the country's political leadership. As a consequence, the state gave the bureaucracy almost free rein to exploit the market for personal gains with its empowered status and policy discretion.[15] Despite Korean bureaucrats' high vulnerability to corruption, historical records show that corruption in Korea remained manageable. The bureaucracy's success in minimizing corruption owes a lot to policy networks that provide alternative sources of income to make up for potential corruption. The preventive benefits, however, are not available for all bureaucrats. Most low-level bureaucrats are excluded.[16] As a matter of fact, official records indicate that moderate bureaucratic corruption has persisted all along but has been overwhelmingly committed by low-ranked bureaucrats.[17]

The lopsided corruption by low-rankers presents another identifiable division within Korea's bureaucracy. Upper and lower ranks of Korean bureaucrats have separate recruitment and promotion processes. In the current system, the division between the ranks is set at the fifth rank out of nine in total. The fifth and above have to take a special high-ranking official exam before they can follow the promotion ladder up to the first level. Lower-level officials are hired through exams for entry at the seventh or ninth grade, usually rising up to the sixth level. Promotion to higher positions is legally possible but rare due to the high wall separating the two groups, such as in job specializations or evaluation standards (Park 2001, 174–179). In this dual ranking system, corruption has been pervasive among low-level officials, with a much higher number of indicted officials from the sixth to ninth than the first to fifth levels. The larger share of the indicted among low-rankers might simply reflect their sheer numbers vis-à-vis the higher echelons, but the proportion of incidents among high-ranking officials still is unusually low, given the vulnerability to corruption their absolute policy power over the economy confers.[18]

As suggested earlier, policy networks play a critical role in deterring high-ranking officials from corruption, but the compensation part is

Table 6.1. Rank distribution of corruption-related crimes (1981)

Rank (High)	Number	Ratio (%)	Rank (Low)	Number	Ratio
1st	1	0.17	6th	101	17.50
2nd	2	0.34	7th	97	16.89
3rd	7	1.2	8th	118	20.5
4th	25	4.5	9th	177	30.8
5th	46	8.0	Total	574	100

Source: Yoon (1984, 198).

necessary to the network mechanism that keeps corruption at bay. Concerns with insufficient compensation drive bureaucrats to corruption, but policy networks lessen those concerns by providing opportunities for extra compensation. Depending on how the two parts interact, bureaucrats may look either self-restrained from corruption or smart enough to conceal their corruption. History indicates that both aspects have appeared as typical behaviors at certain points in time, covering the stages of these networks' positive and negative contributions to Korea's political economy.[19]

COMPENSATORY CORRUPTION

Generally, low salaries for civil servants, despite expectations of high-quality service, are associated with bureaucratic corruption.[20] It is not low compensation per se but the high competitiveness of some civil servants that makes Korea's compensation-related corruption distinctive. High-ranking officials in Korea go through an extremely tough recruitment process and are widely considered by Korean society as the corps of certified elites. It is held that those bureaucrats would reasonably have chosen different careers unless they lacked interest in material comfort or knew they would be somehow compensated with extra income, not from corrupt sources, to augment their low government salaries (Evans 1995).

Korean bureaucrats are paid less than their counterparts in the private sector.[21] This income disparity is wider between high-ranking officials and their private-sector counterparts and might be assumed to drive upper-level bureaucrats to corruption, given the ample opportunity to take bribes, embezzle state funds, or secure other sources of income.

However, a unique system of deferred compensation developed in Korea that has historically effectively kept corruption levels low among highly qualified, high-ranking bureaucrats.[22] The system, if it works as planned, enables bureaucrats to endure their low salaries until after they retire from government, when they are paid much more by their new nongovernment and private-sector corporate employers.[23] The premise is that private employers will value those retired high-ranking bureaucrats' expertise and skill sufficiently to pay them above-market salaries.

The same opportunities for deferred compensation, however, are not available to low-ranking officials. Private-sector demands for former bureaucrats seeking reemployment depend on the information and connections that the bureaucrats take with them when they retire. Since low-

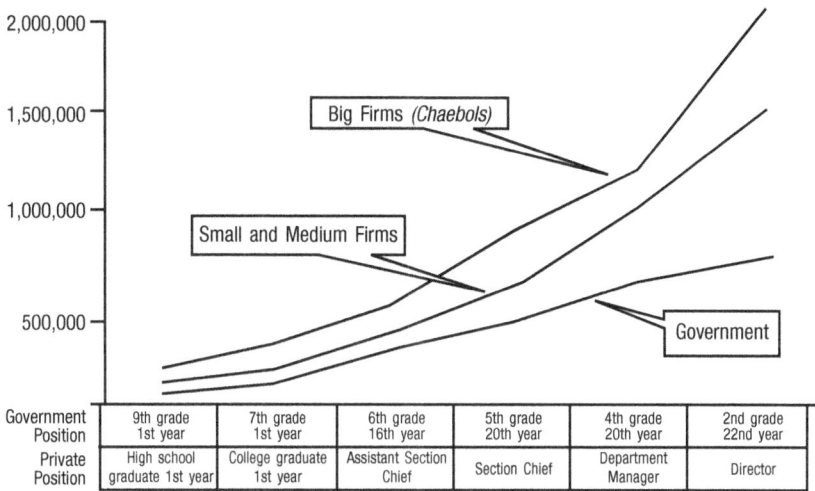

Government Position	9th grade 1st year	7th grade 1st year	6th grade 16th year	5th grade 20th year	4th grade 20th year	2nd grade 22nd year
Private Position	High school graduate 1st year	College graduate 1st year	Assistant Section Chief	Section Chief	Department Manager	Director

Figure 6.1. Public–private sector salary gap. **Source:** Ministry of Government Administration (1981, 184).

level officials have much less experience in major policy decision-making than high-ranking officials, they are given much fewer opportunities for deferred compensation. At the same time, low-ranking bureaucrats have more direct contact with ordinary people than high-ranked civil servants due to the nature of their positions in general civil service or community affairs. The combination of the lack of opportunities for deferred compensation and proximity to public complaints therefore underlies the usual compensatory corruption for low-level bureaucrats.

While the framework for bureaucratic compensation has consistently followed these dual paths for high- versus low-ranked officials, the deferred compensation system has varied over time. Before the 1990s, or until Korea's political and economic liberalization, the system worked well to discourage high-ranking officials from outright corruption. Unfortunately, since the political and economic liberalization of the 1990s, the system has performed less well. Compensation-driven corruption is no longer limited to low-ranking bureaucrats, as rising numbers of corruption cases against high-ranking officials attest (see figure 6.2). The reason for this trend, however, is found in qualitative changes in policy networks rather than in any change within the bureaucracy, including its approach to compensation.

NETWORKED CORRUPTION

Deferred compensation has typically fallen outside of the legal definition of corruption in Korea because it was hidden within the policy networks linking the government and the private sector. Bureaucrats pursuing deferred compensation used their personal connections across the web of organizations anchored in the government to make up for their low salaries as government bureaucrats. Public awareness of the practice increased, however, during Korea's period of democratization as a distinctive feature of Korean public corruption. This increased attention is why the Kim Young-ran Act targeted the mechanism of policy networks.

Until recently, the practice of personnel transfers across policy networks occurred without causing serious problems. The system of informal connections provided incentives for both bureaucrats and private firms to participate, while at the same time curbing the pursuit of deferred compensation so that it did not impair the primary goals of the government. It was not easy to manage the system in such a way as to achieve both objectives. Nevertheless, the deferred and complementary compensation supported by informal networks has managed to avoid being formally considered as corruption in practice, even if such activities probably qualify as corruption in theory because they effectively blur the line between official and private interests.

The internal mechanism of deferred compensation demonstrates how the difficult task is executed within thickly webbed policy networks. As the Korean economy grew rapidly under government leadership, bureaucratic policy networks spread throughout the economy and objects of exchange grew between the government and private business. Retiring bureaucrats worked the system best because they were familiar with both the government and the market. They moved on demand across networks with the help of an old-boy community that acted both to funnel transferring bureaucrats to public or private firms and to arrange their assignments to secure the greatest advantages.[24] One positive effect of the collective management of these networks was that it limited the kind of overexploitation of deferred compensation that could happen when individual bureaucrats privately sought chances to secure a better income. As such, Korea's bureaucratic corruption is a collective enterprise built on policy networks that both promote the opportunities for corruption and prevent corruption from growing out of control.

Network-based corruption has been both praised and blamed over time. When the government guided the economy, as during the period of rapid industrialization in the 1960s–1980s, Korean society accepted corruption-laced policy networks as necessary because they secured the key policy goals the government established.[25] When the economy grew beyond the government's control, however, this kind of corruption became unacceptable, regardless of the government's performance, because private firms by this time could proceed independently and needed government officials' intervention only to secure improper benefits, like illegal purchases of government assets. Worse still, the networks lost their

Crimes in 1981-1984

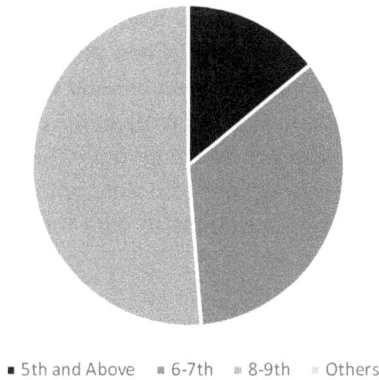

■ 5th and Above   ■ 6-7th   ■ 8-9th   ▫ Others

Crimes in 2002-2012

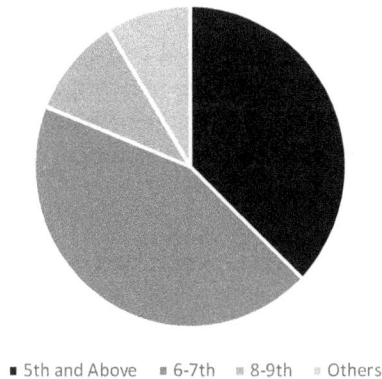

■ 5th and Above   ■ 6-7th   ■ 8-9th   ▫ Others

Figure 6.2. Increasing corruption-related crimes by high-ranking officials. *Source:* Reconstructed from Yoon (1984, table 7.1) and Kim et al. (2013, 26).

managerial "wisdom," such as self-control among bureaucrats, when outsiders, including politicians, rushed into the networks to take the spoils.
The old bifurcated government, with a clear division of labor between
bureaucrats and politicians under the authoritarian regime, disappeared
with democratization. The once-restrained deferred compensation system
turned into full-blown corruption.

As a consequence, high-level officials' corruption-related crimes
have increased rapidly since the democratic transition compared to those
committed by low-ranking officials, as illustrated by figure 6.2. We can
now better understand Korea's struggles to fight against corruption. Today,
the network character of corruption in Korea is its most salient attribute,
leading the new law, the Kim Young-ran Act, to target network-based
corruption in the interest of political institutionalization (per Chen and
Weiss's introduction to this volume). Corruption in Korea, however, has
always also included both political or individual malfeasance. In response,
Korea has addressed corruption incrementally over time, by trial and
error resulting in the Improper Solicitation and Graft Act. The following
historical review, therefore, explores the different causes of corruption in
Korea and the proposed prescriptions to cure the malady.

History of Korea's Anticorruption Efforts

The history of Korea's anticorruption efforts can be divided into three stages,
characterized by political campaigns, regulatory embodiment, and tailored
execution.[26] These anticorruption efforts have targeted politicians, low-level
public servants, and high-ranking officials, respectively. In other words,
the history of Korea's efforts to combat corruption reflects the sequential
adoption of anticorruption strategies, reflecting in sequence the political
use of anticorruption campaigns, institutionalization of anticorruption laws
and regulations to control individual corruption, and strategic design to
fight against corrupt networks.

ANTICORRUPTION CAMPAIGNS UNDER AUTHORITARIAN GOVERNMENTS

Korea's anticorruption history until the 1980s consists of several rounds
of the same cycle, from all-out prosecution of corrupt politicians under
the previous regime, to selective punishments for political distraction,

and finally to huge political scandals involving top political leaders. Such political campaign–type anticorruption practices left Korea without any substantial institutionalization of anticorruption strategies until the end of the 1980s.

Korea spent a decade or so embroiled in political commotion and the Korean War immediately after its independence from Japan. The first government after independence from Japan in 1945 was simply too busy to be concerned with corruption because, on the one hand, it had to lay the foundation for a new country, while on the other, it had to defend the country from the threat of communism. President Syngman Rhee promised in his inauguration that one of his primary missions was to clean Korean society of the corrupt policy practices inherited from the Japanese colonial government. Policies reflected his promise, as when the government and leading party together launched the Special Committee on Punishment of Treason. These government initiatives soon faded, though, once President Rhee's supporters were revealed to be involved with treason. Even if the president earned some credit for guiding the country through the turmoil of nation building after the Korean War, the first modern Korean government ended up tarnished by political scandals involving the highest-ranked political figures.[27]

In the 1960s, Korea set its sights on industrialization and economic growth. While three consecutive governments, led by ex-military generals, prioritized economic growth over other agendas, corruption was under control by policy networks or benignly neglected by the authoritarian political leaders. At the beginning of their rule, the former generals tended to embark on nationwide anticorruption campaigns to make up for their weak political legitimacy. The campaigns were only temporary and dissipated once the generals consolidated political power. To make matters worse, the leaders themselves could not avoid the seduction of corruption toward the end of their regimes, when they amassed huge wealth, either for their political parties' or personal benefit.

The military coup in 1961 established military rule in Korea for the next three decades. The first military-government leader, General Park Chung-hee, inaugurated the strategy of using anticorruption campaigns for political purposes, complementing national concern for economic development. His successors, Chun Doo-hwan and Roh Tae-woo, followed his example. President Park recalled in his biography that Korea's corruption under the Rhee government was actually one of his motives for military action to seize control of the government (Cho 2006, 48–54). When the coup was successfully executed, President Park included anticorruption in his six proclaimed missions along with strengthening national defense, promoting economic development, and transferring political power to a civilian government. In 1961, he launched the "Law against Illegal Wealth Accumulation" to punish those who had used public policy for personal profit during the previous administration, 1953 to 1961. This enactment was the first retroactive law in Korea.

President Park next built an independent agency within the government to monitor the public service for corruption. In 1963, he combined two loosely connected bureaus in the Interior Department with the Board of Audit and Inspection to manage corruption issues. He also set up a few complementary organizations to help monitor agencies and deal with politically sensitive cases requiring resolution through compromise or negotiation among government departments. With both the anticorruption law and the inspection board, President Park could have established an effective anticorruption regime, as the name of his campaign, *seo-jung-shae-sin* (renewal of governance), implied.

Soon, however, political interests overtook President Park's policy agenda. To defend himself against emboldened critics of his unjustified political power, he began to use his anticorruption policies to win popular support by launching occasional anticorruption campaigns. He preferred to stage symbolic punishments to randomly victimize government officials rather than to pursue a consistent program against corruption. Moreover, President Park's economic growth-oriented political strategy encouraged him to be lenient toward public corruption, because he feared any aggressive attempts to punish corruption would interfere with his economic program. Most corruption cases involving prominent government figures were therefore left uninvestigated or prosecuted behind closed doors, with only a few conspicuous cases made public.

Both President Chun and President Roh T. W. mimicked Park's strategy of rooting out corruption in the beginning of their regimes and then launching nationwide anticorruption campaigns opportunistically whenever they were in political trouble. For the twelve years under their rule, history repeated itself: largely driven by private or partisan interests as outlined in the introduction to this volume, Chun and Roh first punished their political opponents in the name of illegal wealth accumulation,[28] made a show of ridding the government of corruption with highly publicized campaigns, and finally lowered their guard against corruption when they themselves had to resort to corruption in pursuit of their political interests.[29]

Nevertheless, the two military regimes made two significant steps against political corruption, the enactment of a public service law and preparation for a government-wide review system. Korea's first Public Service Law (PSL), originally the Public Service Ethics Act (1981), was passed under President Chun. The law's impact was limited since it allowed the government to keep civil servants' personal financial information out of public auditors' hands. The PSL aimed at building an effective corruption-control system, to include both punishments and preventive measures, through such means as publishing annual reports on the personal wealth of high-level officials and prohibiting reemployment of retired bureaucrats in private-sector areas related to their previous positions, thus prohibiting them from taking advantage of their friends in the bureaucracy. Arguably, the real significance of the law was that it helped to change public opinion, to encourage an understanding of corruption as not just an ethical matter but a criminal one. Along with a presidential order to set up a multiagency committee to review Korea's public service to improve transparency, the PSL was Korea's first step toward catching up with the anticorruption systems of advanced Western democracies.

To sum up the history of the Korean approach to corruption up to the 1980s, the anticorruption systems implemented during Korea's three military regimes were limited due to the private and partisan use of anticorruption measures. The primary targets of the anticorruption campaigns during this period were political figures, mostly opponents of the president. The few cases of effective enforcement were limited to lower-ranked bureaucrats. Anticorruption laws and regulations began to have a real effect only after Korea began the process of democratization.

Political versus Bureaucratic Corruption during Democratization

Korea's first civilian president after democratization, Kim Young-sam, was a radical reformer in every respect. His main object was political reform. His anticorruption initiatives targeted dishonest or underground financial transactions that he believed had substantially contributed to the political power of the previous authoritarian regimes. The president wanted to eradicate the flow of "black money" surrounding political parties and elections. The first ambitious step he took to lay the foundation for clean politics was to implement real-name bank accounts for all financial transactions. The idea had been around since the beginning of the 1980s, but implementation was delayed until democratization. President Kim believed that transparent financial transactions would discourage graft and bribery in politics.

The Kim government pushed for many legal initiatives against corruption under his "New Korea" initiative. He revised the PSL to increase its transparency, and launched laws like the Private Information Act, the Public Administration Procedure Regulations, a Special Act on Confiscation of Illegal Wealth to strengthen the PSL, the Comprehensive Election Law, and the Political Finance Law to purify the political process (Park 1999, 108–111). Initially the Kim administration sought transparency in both politics and the bureaucracy. President Kim was as resolute to build a clean government as he was to clean up the National Assembly. A committee was established on his order to address administrative reform, as well as a special bureau on bureaucratic corruption within the supreme prosecutor's office.

As time went on, however, these administrative reforms proved not to be as successful as Kim's political reforms. While its progress in political cleanup was impressive, the Kim administration made less headway in reforming the bureaucracy because it could not sever the well-established and profitable links between the bureaucracy and the private sector.[30] Toward the middle of his presidency, President Kim met with substantial resistance from the bureaucracy against his anticorruption efforts. Bureaucrats responded to the presidential demand for clean administration with policy nonchalance and direct sabotage. President Kim increased the pressure with more inspections and severe punishments, which produced a vicious cycle of retaliation. The more the president moved against corruption, the less cooperative the bureaucracy became.

The unsatisfactory results of public administration reforms gave rise to heated debates in both academia and policy circles in Korea. The debates focused on the cause of the unsuccessful administrative reform in comparison with the success in political reform under the same pressure of democratization. Some argued for an early adoption of stricter ethical codes for civil servants, similar to standards recommended under the New Public Management (NPM) model in Europe. NPM approaches present individual-based moral prescriptions as equally likely to work in Korea as Europe, given the political leadership's weakening control of the bureaucracy (Yoon 2013). Others suggested further strengthening of the existing regulatory system, including expanding the scope of anticorruption initiatives (Lee 2013).

The two sides eventually converged in the Kim Act in 2015, but the road was bumpy. During the 1990s, while the Kim government was pushing for transparency in the policy process, against bureaucratic resistance, a new kind of political scandal broke out in Korea.[31] The distinction between political and bureaucratic responsibility had become blurred because bureaucrats had begun to seek personal profits through cooperation with politicians. Such opportunities arose as politicians took advantage of the policy networks that bureaucrats controlled. A new collaborative and rent-seeking type of corruption suddenly became rampant in the Korean economy leading up to the 1997 financial crisis and eventually weakened the impetus for Korea's administrative reforms (Pempel 1999; Choi 2002).

TOWARD A COMPREHENSIVE ANTICORRUPTION LAW AFTER DEMOCRATIZATION

The first decade of the twenty-first century saw Korea mature as a democracy by electing its first president from an opposition party.[32] Democratization brought on a new age of anticorruption initiatives. President Kim Dae-jung initiated plans to crack down on the web of corrupt networks; Roh Moo-hyun, who moved Korean politics further away from old practices, later continued with these plans. Both progressive[33] presidents had few connections with the old bureaucracy entrenched in the political establishment, so they could launch bold initiatives to uproot the structural corruption of bureaucrats. The public also supported these initiatives, having begun to develop a negative perception of bureaucrats and demand change. The 2007 financial crisis triggered such changes, which significantly helped President Kim win election and then respond to societal demands. The progressive governments at the turn of the century secured two meaningful anticorruption achievements, namely, the enactment of Korea's Anticorruption Act and the establishment of Korea's Corruption Prevention Committee.

In September 2000, the Civilian Federation of Anticorruption and thirty-eight NGOs submitted a proposal for an anticorruption law to the National Assembly. Both the majority and minority parties, the Millennium Democratic Party and the Grand National Party, accepted the proposal. Together the parties passed the Anticorruption Act of 2001.[34] This enactment was Korea's first comprehensive law on anticorruption in the sense that it included both punitive and preventive measures. Most importantly, the act adopted such precautions against corruption as a code of conduct and conflict-of-interest guidelines for public servants. These standards borrowed from OECD and US standards for ethical conduct and detailed best practices, such as reporting potential conflicts of interests in financial transactions, declining an official position that would lead to personal gain at the expense of the public interest, and monitoring paid lectures and the reemployment of bureaucrats.[35]

The Corruption Prevention Committee was created in 2001. In 2005, the committee was renamed the Korea Independent Commission against Corruption; then in 2008, it merged with the Ombudsman of Korea to form Korea's Anticorruption and Civil Rights Commission (ACRC). When the committee was first created, its partisan character was reduced by distributing the membership equally among those recommended by the president, the National Assembly, and the Supreme Court.[36] To fight against corruption, the committee pursued three key missions: basic planning for anticorruption, annual anticorruption reviews of government agencies, and evaluation of each agency for its progress in ensuring transparency. The results were required to be published for both public accountability and an interdepartmental competition within the Korean government.

Despite the initial success of this ambitious anticorruption project, tangible outcomes, including full enactment of the law, were not achieved until the end of the decade. Two factors hindered reforms. First, there was a political backlash in Korea's nascent democracy. Many NGO activists who had first led the anticorruption movement were elected to political office by leveraging their NGO credentials.[37] Once in politics, their fervor for reform surrendered to parochial political interests. Korean society began to doubt the intentions of NGO-led anticorruption movements. Many Koreans perceived NGOs' activities as cynical political campaigns similar to the anticorruption initiatives of the military regimes. The initial energy for transparency dissipated.

Second, the bureaucrats the anticorruption law targeted outsmarted the political activists seeking to deprive them of privileges from their policy networks, especially their deferred compensation. The resources and tools that bureaucrats used to protect their interests proved more effective than the strategies the ACRC and political leadership adopted. Rent-seeking bureaucrats mobilized policy networks to nullify the political pressures they faced. For instance, they invited influential political figures into their corruption networks and later manipulated these individuals to bear the brunt of blame when the network got in trouble.[38] The bureaucrats themselves avoided any charges by exploiting loopholes in the law, with the help of the networks.

When large-scale scandals broke out again,[39] despite the radical steps taken by the democratic governments, Korea's political leadership and the Korean society together had no choice but to look for another way to address public corruption. Korea, it appeared, was ready to adopt a more radical law: the Improper Solicitation and Graft Act, or the Kim Young-ran Act.

Improper Solicitation and Graft Act (Kim Young-ran Act)

In 2015, the National Assembly passed the Improper Solicitation and Graft Act, the strongest anticorruption law in Korea, after years of legislative deliberation. In 2011, ACRC chair Kim Young-ran submitted the first draft of the bill with a preliminary title, Prohibition of Illegal Solicitation and Prevention of Conflict of Interests in the Public Service. Since then, the act has been called the Kim Young-ran Act.

The Kim Young-ran Act represents a two-pronged effort to prevent corruption. It prohibits any deals outside the regular policy process as well as financial favors to public servants over limits specified in the law. The first prong is to insulate government from the influence of policy brokers who are either ex-bureaucrats or maintain personal relations with civil servants. These hidden lobbyists are presumed to be the cause of corruption when connected to the government through informal relationships, connections, and associations. The second part resembles a typical legislative effort to eliminate bribery. However, it is more severe and strict than the typical law, because the financial regulations stipulated are unconditional, regardless of public servants' duties. Gifts or special treatment valued over a certain amount are punishable regardless of whether the receiving official has policy discretion over the business of the donor.[40]

The new anticorruption law is an outcome of the struggle to create a tailored system for present-day Korea. The law thus differs from all previous attempts to combat corruption in Korea. Underscoring the differences are the distinct background leading up to the law, the debates that flared up during the enactment of the law, and post-promulgation controversies.

BACKDROP TO AND TIMING OF THE LEGISLATION

The 1990s saw many debates on the paradigm shift in Korea's anticorruption initiatives. When President Kim Dae-jung was elected in 1998, Korea appeared readier to tackle public corruption, as the country was forced to consider political and public administration reform following the financial crisis and accelerated democratization. The ground for the new anticorruption legislation was therefore laid at the turn of the millennium. The political trigger for the legislation was the conservative-to-progressive shift in the regime. When a second progressive president was elected in 2003, the movement to renovate old systems, including the bureaucracy, became even more active, foreshadowing stronger anticorruption legislation such as the Kim Young-ran Act.

However, delivery of the first draft to the National Assembly had to wait until 2011. The political and bureaucratic causes of the delay were discussed in the previous section, but there was also a social reason. Over the preceding decade, Korea had witnessed intense debates over the future of the country in the context of the global rise of neoliberalism. As the pros and cons of neoliberalism were discussed in every corner of Korean society, bureaucrats also joined the debate over whether Korea had to adopt the new trend of New Public Administration that emphasized market efficiency or stay with the old developmentalist administration, characterized by government leadership of the economy (Ahn and Han 2006). At that time within the Korean bureaucracy, the conservative view was pervasive, even though personnel in top positions, mostly political appointees, were progressive. The conservative bureaucracy blocked the speedy application of the new approach to public corruption the Kim Young-ran Act expected. Furthermore, the progressive camp lost the 2007 presidential election to the conservative candidate, Lee Myung-bak. The only progress in the battle against corruption under the Lee government, which wanted to negate the achievements of the previous progressive regimes, was the addition of a few complementary measures to existing anticorruption laws, such as a Code of Conduct for Public Officials that went into effect in 2003.

A major political scandal in 2011, however, provided a significant push toward adoption of the Kim Young-ran Act. The so-called sponsored-prosecutor scandal involved a businessman who went to jail for minor financial crimes. It was leaked to the media that he had long supported a prosecutor financially, with the expectation of some return down the road. But the prosecutor refused to save the businessman from jail. Rage spread throughout Korean society, bringing into focus the corrupt policy networks that facilitated unethical trades of favors between government officials and private businesses.[41] ACRC chairperson Kim Young-ran, one of the few progressives within President Lee's conservative administration, seized the opportunity to present her ideas of how to free Korea from decades-old network-based corruption.

The legislation again dragged on in the National Assembly, where it met with opposition from a conservative coalition comprised of political and bureaucratic elites. Their opposition revealed that their primary concern was their own interests embedded in the old system, such as electoral support for politicians and reemployment opportunities for bureaucrats. Only after it was agreed that the new regulations would exclude lawmakers did the National Assembly hurry to proceed to enactment. In passing the law, politicians thus distanced themselves from the bureaucracy, leaving bureaucrats as the new law's main targets.

Another push for the Kim Young-ran Act emerged out of the tragic 2014 Sewol ferry accident, in which more than three hundred high school students and teachers lost their lives. It was later revealed that the accident was caused by a violation of safety regulations. Former bureaucrats who used to administer Korean maritime affairs had colluded with safety inspectors on behalf of their new employer, Chonghaejin Marine. These former bureaucrats protected the company's interests from government regulations and inspections by influencing the inspectors, even though the latter came from another company; retired bureaucrats also held key positions in that company. In the end, the former bureaucrats were all informally connected and known to each other through a network linking the government, the cruise company, and the inspection company. The accident revealed the exorbitant price the Korean society had to pay for bureaucratic corruption. As the facts of the tragedy came to light, the conservative coalition of politicians and bureaucrats could no longer defend the status quo. The news media, which once benefited from such networks under the authoritarian regime, also lost ground from which to obstruct stricter controls on corruption. As quickly as circumstances permitted, the National Assembly ratified the act.[42]

CONCERNS ABOUT UNCONSTITUTIONALITY

Kim Ki-shik, a member of the legislative subcommittee for the Kim Young-ran Act, said in a National Affairs Committee general meeting on the revised and resubmitted bill, "The reason that other countries do not enact such a comprehensive law as ours to proscribe improper solicitation is because they are concerned about the law's potential encroachment on the rights of individuals, including freedom of speech and national petition."[43] He was not opposed to the act; rather, he was more intent on warning the committee that the act should be refined and revised against the charge of unconstitutionality. The vulnerable parts of the bill included excessive criminalization, curtailed civil rights, and collective punishment. The proposed Kim Young-ran Act addressed both violations of codes of conduct and attempted crimes subject to criminal punishment, insofar as they were related to graft or improper solicitation.[44] Several parts of the Kim Young-ran Act overlapped with Korea's criminal law, such as the prohibitions against accepting or soliciting bribes, which required stricter burdens of proof under criminal law than under the new act. The act might not only come into conflict with the criminal law's burden of proof, but it might also jeopardize the constitutional right to appeal to the government, since it discouraged public appeals for policy correction. The solution lawmakers proposed was to divide jurisdiction, to allow for separate rules for punishment. Legislators set a threshold for criminal punishment for graft, below which graft was subject to civil penalty or exempt, if not relevant to the perpetrator's duties. As for solicitation, any favor that a public servant provided in return for improper solicitation or third-party brokerage would fall under the criminal law, while neglect in not reporting an attempted improper solicitation or a potential violation would be subject to civil penalty.

Second, critics—legislators against the act, bureaucrats, and mass media—thought the act would curb civil rights if it included members of the National Assembly, members of the media, and private schools. They were concerned that the act would make certain kinds of legislative activities criminal offenses and therefore undermine the deliberative nature of the National Assembly. Similarly, critics felt that private schools, as private entities with private employees, should not be subject to the law, even if they were engaged in public education. Moreover, there were concerns that the law would undermine the independence of the press and the public good it serves. Revisions of the draft narrowed the definition of private schools to include curriculum-management and government-aided projects only. The provisions concerning the media were left almost untouched, however, as lawmakers could count on public resentment toward the media for its collaboration with political or bureaucratic elites over the years. The most radical of all the revisions, though, was to drop the National Assembly from being covered under the new law. The decision was justified on the grounds of protecting the constitutional right of the public to have their interests fully represented in the National Assembly.

Finally, the Kim Young-ran Act was controversial because of its design for collective punishment. Family members of public servants were subject to the same rules and regulations governing solicitation, graft, and conflict of interest. Family members were prohibited from taking money beyond a threshold or accepting gifts of equivalent value, acting on solicitations, or applying for any job or government position that may influence policy execution by public servants within the family. Of the three areas included in the original bill, critics found the provisions regarding conflicts of interest entailed outdated collective punishments based on familial association. The compromise was to drop the provision in the final draft and instead strengthen the code of conduct for civil servants. The first two areas, namely, solicitation and graft, were also toned down by limiting the scope of "family" from the broader one defined in Korea's civil law to immediate relatives.

The Department of Justice took the lead in opposing the law by raising legal issues with it.[45] The ACRC delivered the department's reservations to the National Assembly in keeping with the procedural requirement of prior legal consultation on draft legislation. Other government agencies allegedly supported the Department of Justice, agreeing that the new anticorruption law called for too radical a change.[46] Although the assembly passed the Act, these controversies surrounding its provisions foreshadowed difficulties in putting the new law into effect.

POST-LEGISLATION UNCERTAINTIES

In addition to these constitutional concerns, other points of contention appeared after the law's passage. The first concerned the esprit de corps of the Korean bureaucracy. The public has typically held public officials in Korea in high esteem for their success in modernizing the Korean economy but, at the same time, has blamed them for widespread corruption. Once economic growth declined, the bureaucracy previously heralded for its economic acumen came to be viewed under a cloud of suspicion, as if it were a criminal enterprise. These different perceptions of the Korean bureaucracy derived not so much from the sector's changing qualities and abilities as from the changing conditions surrounding policy networks. The Kim Yong-ran Act, however, seemed to assume that the quality of Korean bureaucrats was declining, which, in turn, drove their networks to corruption. Such a perception at the heart of the act was thought likely to discourage bureaucrats from working actively for the public good and instead to hold them back, such that they would only passively respond to political needs.

Other critics worried about an economic downturn as a result of cramping the service industries with the new anticorruption law. The presidential decree to enforce the Kim Yong-ran Act prohibits public servants from accepting a dinner worth over thirty US dollars, gifts worth more than fifty dollars, or donations worth more than one hundred dollars for either a wedding or funeral from anyone who might potentially benefit from a change in policy. The fear was that these limits would affect the economy by discouraging consumption and would lead to an economic downturn. As of August 2017, the economic consequences of the act have been hotly debated in the media, the National Assembly, and academia. An economic concern of this kind would have blocked a similar law from being enacted during the 1970s or 1980s, when economic growth of the Korean economy was prioritized over all other policy goals. Today, it appears that fighting corruption overrules economic concerns.

The anticorruption act nevertheless enjoys wide public support. Lawmakers in the subcommittee charged with reviewing the act agreed that the act did not merely aim to build an effective legal system to control corruption but also attempted to change the Korean society to eradicate the corrupt practice of trading policy favors for financial benefits.[47] In this sense, the recent anticorruption efforts in Korea are clearly part and parcel of the systematic institutionalization of a new political economy. As radical as the Kim Young-ran Act is, it is necessary to address the roots of corruption in the form of far-reaching networks of personal relations built on geographical, educational, and familial bonds.

Conclusion: Toward a New Society

The Improper Solicitation and Graft Act (2016) represents a seismic shift in Korea's efforts to root out public corruption. The act is an outcome of long struggles by successive Korean governments and civil society that wrongfully targeted private corruption while the true sources of the problem were in policy networks. Korea's political and economic liberalization, as well as recent scandals and a tragic accident, provided the means finally to address institutionalized corruption properly.

The act changes how the Korean people perceive corruption as well as presenting an aggressive solution to the problem. By attempting to break down the networks surrounding the public policy process, the law offers a fresh approach to countering corruption in Korea. Bureaucrats at the center of policy networks were the primary beneficiaries of the old system. They have been able to sustain their administrative power over the market and to earn material compensation through the exchange of favors. The act directly tackles this uniquely Korean form of corruption with correspondingly unique means of delinking personal relations built throughout these policy networks. The act criminalizes the tools used to build private relations within these networks such as gifts, bribes, or excessive social activities.

At the same time, the new law heralds a new era for Korea's political economy. As previously described, corruption in Korea is tightly intertwined with Korea's political and economic development. For decades, Korean public policy has been shaped by the primary goal of economic growth, but today the country is trying to shake off its decades-old developmental state. Policy networks represent part of the developmental state that prioritized economic growth over other policy goals. Today these same networks are considered burdensome for Korea because the country is working to build a transparent and accountable modern democracy. In addition, the negative effects of the networks are beginning to outweigh their previous benefits, namely, policy coordination between the government and the private sector. With the passage of the Kim Young-ran Act, Koreans are preparing for life without these networks.

In the broader context of culture, the Improper Solicitation and Graft Act (2016)[48] points to a new Korean society. By cutting loose the interpersonal relations within policy networks, the law ultimately cuts the link between official government business and private relations in Korean society. In the past, policy networks were strengthened by the interconnections between public administration and the private sector, which were largely overlooked because they supported the country's primary goal of economic growth. Today, the costs of such networks have become exorbitant and these networks have turned counterproductive. Moreover, once network-based corruption became dominant, the usefulness of the networks eroded, providing the impetus for new anticorruption efforts that directly target the bureaucracy. From a legal point of view, the act targets the behavior of government officials, but in practice, it encourages Korean society to look at governmental corruption with new eyes. The act both represents and calls for a cultural sea change.

We have yet to see how effective the Kim Young-ran Act will be against the entrenched, interconnected interests of the bureaucracy and private sector in the long run. But the fact that Korea initiated such an unprecedented measure to directly address corruption highlights its renewed determination to bring about systematic change, beyond narrow private and partisan considerations. In this sense, Korea has moved further along than many other Asian countries presented in this volume in its protracted yet sustained fight against corruption.

Notes

1. There are few studies of Korean political corruption that rely upon an independent theory depicting the unique character of Korean corruption. Moon and Mo (1999) and Kim (1985) are rare attempts to build a Korean model.

2. Transparency International, Corruption Perceptions Index https://www.transparency.org/country/KOR (accessed August 17, 2017).

3. A 2002 survey conducted of almost 1,500 adults by the Korea Corruption Prevention Commission (KCPC) shows that more than two-thirds of respondents felt their public officials were corrupted. A similar survey done in 2011 by the Anticorruption and Civil Rights Commission (ACRC, previously KCPC) shows little to no progress in anticorruption efforts. Of those surveyed 65.4 percent responded negatively about Korea's transparency.

See http://www.acrc.go.kr/acrc/file/file.do?command=downFile&encoded-Key=MTY5NDdfMg%3D%3D (accessed November 30, 2017).

4. The configuration confirms the classification of corruption and anticorruption efforts presented in the introduction to this book by Chen and Weiss. The Korean case demonstrates its move from private-driven to institution-driven anticorruption struggles.

5. It does not, however, deny the commonly held definition of corruption as "the abuse of entrusted power for private gain." See Transparency International, https://www.transparency.org/what-is-corruption#define (accessed November 30, 2017).

6. For a general comparison between the two kinds of corruption, see Caiden and Caiden (1987, 306–308).

7. See Leff (1970), Bayley (1966), and Tilman (1970) for the potential economic benefits of corruption. See Huntington (1989) for political benefits. See Nye (1967) and Werner (1983) for the negative effects.

8. Such economic explanations of corruption have a long history. Klitgaard (1991) believes that public servants always measure the expected benefits and costs of engaging in corruption before their actions, and Tanzi (1998) analyzes corruption from the analogy of the market by figuring out the demand for and supply of corruption.

9. For example, Khan (1998) emphasizes cultural effects based on strong patron–client bonds in Asian countries.

10. The transformation is well-developed in the theory of crony capitalism. For instance, Kang (2002) explains the escalation of corruption in Korea with the breakdown of the mutual hostage situation between political and business elites against excessive corruption in the 1990s when the country was democratizing.

11. The goal was clearly announced by many lawmakers, including Sung-tae Kim, chair of the Subcommittee for Legislation under the Plenary Committee of the National Assembly. He repeatedly pointed out that the new legislation would primarily aim at delinking corruption networks.

12. A few Korean studies have argued for structural causes of Korea's corruption, but their focus is limited either in terms of time period or the scope of corruption considered. For example, Kim (1985) defines Korea's corruption as a product of Korea's developmental state and tests the theory with government data on crimes and punishment. The study does not consider the corruption of high-ranking officials during the postreform era. For a general structural explanation, see Johnston (1997, 61–82) or Rose-Ackerman (1978, 60–73).

13. Yoo (2016) summarizes the political economic nature of Korea's corruption from a different perspective by tracing corruption to the wealth inequality that has prevailed in Korea throughout history.

14. Studies on Korea's public administration have developed an overarching definition of "developmental administration" to characterize a system where the state prioritizes economic growth over any other public policy (for example, Park 2001). The minister of economic planning, for instance, holds the position of vice prime minister, and only economic agencies are fully specialized within the government to meet the requirements of economic development. At the same time, the system empowers bureaucrats over politicians in key policy decisions, including both legislation and policy execution.

15. Cultural factors increase this vulnerability, especially public tolerance of bureaucratic corruption, so long as the sums involved are not excessive or methods of extraction inhumane. The Confucian tradition of the public's respecting the government gives more discretionary power to Korean bureaucrats in comparison with those in other cultures, leaving the public service more vulnerable to corruption (Rocca 1992).

16. In contrast to cultural accounts, the "Weberian state" literature describes the Korean bureaucracy as armed with genuine professionalism, suggesting bureaucrats have been immune to corruption as they benefit from meritocracy and lifetime employment (Evans 1995; Wade 1990; Amsden 1989).

17. Rose-Ackerman (1978, 60–73) also divides public corruption between acts by upper- and lower-level officials but does not look to different dynamics that explain these differences.

18. It is hard to obtain exact data on the number of government officials at each level every year due to the several rounds of government restructuring during the time under consideration. The Korean system started with nine levels in the beginning, changed to five, and then reverted to nine later. But the group comparison between high- and low-level officials is manageable and confirms these temporal changes. Park and colleagues (1999, 32) measure the corruption rate of high-ranking officials during 1983–1998 as less than 10 percent on average, whereas Hong and colleagues (2010, 90) raise it to 20 percent by applying the same process for the period 1999–2009.

19. By the 1990s, the public became well aware of corruption committed by high-ranking officials. In a 1999 survey conducted by *Donga Ilbo*, one of the leading daily newspapers in Korea, the respondents perceived low-ranked

bureaucrats to be cleaner than those in the higher ranks (Donga Ilbo, June 8, 1999).

20. Tanzi and Wickham (1997) find a positive relationship between income level and corruption. Nadeen and Sahay (1996) trace the reason for this connection to bureaucrats' insufficient income for minimum living expenses. Lindbeck (1998) also concludes that low corruption in Sweden is due to the fact that civil servants' wages are twelve to fifteen times higher than those of factory workers.

21. The gap may need recalibration if we consider the much higher fringe benefits, including a generous pension, for civil servants, but officially the gap is still wide.

22. The system is similar to the US type of revolving door in the sense that people move between the government and private firms, but deferred compensation is different from the revolving door as the former is only a one-way move from the government to private firms.

23. The amount of deferred payment is usually determined by performance while in service, reflecting final rank in the government; bureaucrats are incentivized to work hard for the policy goals set by the political leadership. The same restraint does not work during democratization, which turns the restrained corruption to full rent-seeking. Under democratization, the Korean political system is unable to keep deferred compensation under control (Kim 2006, 37–48).

24. The prototype of the system is found in Japan under *amakudari*, literally meaning "descent from heaven." Korea similarly calls the practice *nak-ha-san*, meaning "parachute." For the case of Japan, refer to Calder (1989), Shaede (1995), and Colignon and Usui (2003).

25. This aligns with the functionalist interpretation of corruption. In many developing countries corruption works positively for the problems that the given countries have to deal with, such as economic development (Mauro 1995).

26. Most historical reviews of Korea's anticorruption efforts have covered the first two stages. This chapter newly adds the third one, the better to explain the history behind the Kim Young-ran Act.

27. The scandals were as follows: the National Defense Army scandal, the Korea Tungsten Co. incident, the Defense Department Embezzlement of Military Clothes, and the military soap-supplier scandal (Kang 2012, 3).

28. Presidents Park and Chun's slogans differed—"rebuilding the nation" and "social purification," respectively—but both campaigns were to eliminate political competitors at the beginning of their regimes.

29. The presidents accumulated up to two billion US dollars each for their party and for personal use toward the end of their regimes.

30. Bardhan (2005) also discusses the differences between political and bureaucratic corruption, suggesting the higher culpability of politicians than bureaucrats for corruption in most developing countries, but finding the ratio may be reversed with the advent of democratization.

31. The exemplary cases were the Hanbo Corporation and Yuwon Construction scandals. These two rising companies bribed influential politicians to press government agencies to permit their business expansion and also illegally solicited bailouts when they were in trouble financially (Yoon 1999, 124–169).

32. Kim Yong-sam, Kim Dae-jung's predecessor, was also originally an opposition leader. His party joined in coalition with the then leading party, which enabled him to run as the leading party's presidential candidate.

33. It is common for Koreans to differentiate between "progressive" and "conservative" parties and regimes, even though these popular identifications do not exactly track academic usage. Since democratization, the Kim Dae-jung and Roh Moo-hyun governments have been counted among progressives, whereas the Kim Young-sam, Lee Myung-bak, and Park Geun-hye administrations belong to the conservative camp. For academic debates on political ideologies in Korea, see, among others, Choi (2012, 60–65) or Lee (2012, 31–53) for the identification and history of Korea's conservative political groups.

34. Korea's financial crisis of 1997, which produced widespread economic hardship, encouraged cooperation between the parties. Since Korean society perceived the crisis as an outgrowth of Korea's corrupt politics, including the scandals discussed earlier, the opposition party could not stand up against President Kim Dae-jung's push for a radical approach to corruption.

35. For a comparison of Korea's anticorruption efforts with those of the United States and the OECD, see Yoon (2013).

36. The committee includes fifteen members in total. The president appoints the chairperson, three vice chairs, and three standing members on the prime minister's recommendation; three are recommended by the Supreme Court; and three by the National Assembly. See http://www.law.go.kr/법령/부패방지및국민 권익위원회의설치와운영에관한법률 (accessed November 30, 2017).

37. Kim (2003) explains that the number of the ex-NGO leaders running for political positions decreased during the Roh government because President Roh did not welcome them to politics as eagerly as President Kim had, but the number was still considerable.

38. Two big financial sandals during the Kim government, Jin Seung-hyun Gate and Lee Yong-ho Gate, both involved illegal loans from secondary financial intermediaries, secured with the help of government officials in charge of financial monitoring. The cases resulted in the arrest of two sons of the president for accepting bribes, but most bureaucrats were absolved or incurred only minor civil punishments.

39. The mutual savings bank scandal in 2011 is a good example: more than fifteen second-tier financial intermediaries had been involved with illegal or imprudent project-financing loans to unqualified businesses for a decade. See Kim (2012).

40. Originally there was a third part to the act, to prevent conflicts of interest, but it was dropped at the last moment in the National Assembly. That

prong would have regulated employment of or financial trade with those who share any interest with government employees. Instead, the National Assembly reinforced the Public Service Act along these lines.

41. Koreans have looked up to prosecutors as among the very best of government officials; the Department of Justice appoints fewer than 15 percent of those who pass the Korean bar exam to these positions.

42. History makes a good case for a "garbage can model" of the public policy process, which sees policy as emerging out of several favorable conditions rather than from a systemized process (for instance, Kingdon 2010). Chung and colleagues (2017) actually applied the theory to the case of the Kim Young-ran Act.

43. "전 세계에서 부정청탁 관련하여 이런 포괄적인 금지 입법을 하지 않는 것은 국민의 표현의 자유나 참정권을 침해할 수 있다라고 생각하기 때문에 안하는 겁니다." These remarks and other historical facts introduced in this chapter draw upon the minutes from the National Assembly. For this speech, see National Policy Committee, Subcommittee for Deliberation, Minutes, January 8, 2015, 25. Author's translation.

44. "Improper" has two meanings under the Kim Young-ran Act. The first is the injunction against soliciting improper duties from civil servants, and the second is against accepting improper solicitation or remaining silent about solicitation by a public servant. Anybody who intervenes in a solicitation or works as a broker is culpable. In case a person directly solicits help, the recipient of the solicitation (i.e., a public official) should decide whether the request is proper and immediately report it to the agency head if it is deemed improper. Agency heads are directed to seek solutions to discourage improper solicitations. See Improper Solicitation and Graft Act, No. 13278. http://www.law.go.kr/법령/부정청탁및금품수수의금지에관한법률/(13278,20150327) (assessed April 22, 2019).

45. The Justice Department could be expected to be sensitive to the new law since it maintains the most active professional networks in Korea, within which deferred compensation has been highly activated. In the Korean court system, the Justice Department appoints prosecutors and judges immediately after they graduate from a training institute following the bar exam. Those the department selects later move to private law firms after having served the government for an average of about three decades. It would be extremely difficult, though, to find hard evidence that private concerns about losing the privilege to build second careers motivated opposition to the law, because no one would readily concede that premise, even if true. The public in general, however, accepts that retiring judges or prosecutors enjoy such benefits, as represented in the notion of *jun-kwan-yae-woo*, or "respecting ex-government officials."

46. Bureaucrats could not openly oppose the new anticorruption act, given popular rage over corrupt bureaucratic networks and pressure to break them down with a new law if necessary. Bureaucrats indirectly expressed concerns about the radicalness of the proposed law, however, through media channels, including major newspapers. *Chosun Ilbo*, the biggest newspaper in Korea, for example,

introduced many bureaucrats' complaints in surveys of Korea's bureaucracy in January, March, and August 2015. The story included several cases of promising bureaucrats' leaving the government due to their dissatisfaction and worries about their future under the Kim Young-ran Act. Other newspapers, like *Hankyoreh* (August 16, 2012) and *Joongang Ilbo* (August 1, 2013), reported similar stories around the same time.

47. ACRC chief Sung-bo Lee said that the proposed law aimed practically at overhauling Korean society when he presented it to the National Assembly National Policy Committee, Subcommittee for Deliberation, on May 27, 2014.

48. The law was passed in 2015 and went into effect on September 28, 2016.

Bibliography

Ahn, Byeong Chul, and Chong Hee Han. "New Public Management Oriented Administrative Reform and Its Appropriateness for Korea: Focusing on Open Position System and Executive Agency System." *Korean Public Administration Quarterly* 18, no. 3 (2006): 765–792.

Amsden, Alice. *Asia's Next Giant: South Korea and Late Industrialization.* New York: Oxford University Press, 1989.

Bardhan, P. "Institutions Matter, but Which Ones?" *Economics of Transition* 13, no. 3 (2005): 449–532.

Bayley, David H. "The Effects of Corruption in a Developing Nation." *Western Political Studies* 19 (December 1966): 719–732.

Caiden, Gerald E., and Naomi J. Caiden. "Administrative Corruption." *Public Administration Review* 37, no. 3 (May/June 1977): 301–309.

Calder, Kent. "Elites in an Equalizing Role: Ex-Bureaucrats as Coordinators and Intermediaries in the Japanese Government-Business Relationship." *Comparative Politics* 21 (July 1989): 379–403.

Cho, Gap-je. *Park Chung-hee.* Seoul: Chogapjedotcom, 2006.

Choi, Jin-Wook. "Regulatory Forbearance and Financial Crisis in South Korea." *Asian Survey* 42, no. 2 (March 2002): 251–275.

Choi, Kwang. "Big Government vs. Small Government: Controversies on the Size and Role of Government" (in Korean). *Institutions and Economy* 6, no. 2 (2012): 57–96.

Chung, Ki-duk, Ju-ho Chung, Min-jung Kim, and Min-hyo Cho. "Examining the Policymaking Process of the Kim Yong-ran Act: Using the Combined Model of ACF and MS" (in Korean). *Korean Society and Public Administration* 28, no. 2 (2017): 217–245.

Colignon, Richard A., and Chikako Usui. *Amakudari: The Hidden Fabric of Japan's Economy.* Ithaca: Cornell University Press, 2003.

Evans, Peter. *Embedded Autonomy: States and Industrial Transformation.* Princeton: Princeton University Press, 1995.

Hong, Young-o, Bum-jun Kim, and Hyun-a Koo. *Corruption among Public Officials and Its Control (II)* (in Korean). Korean Institute of Criminology Research Series 10-01 (2010).

Huntington, Samuel P. "Modernization and Corruption." In *Political Corruption: A Handbook*, edited by Arnold J. Heidenheimer et al., 253–264. New Brunswick: Transaction, 1989.

Johnson, Chalmers. *MITI and the Japanese Miracle: The Growth of Industrial Policy 1925–1975*. Stanford: Stanford University Press, 1982.

Johnston, Michael. "Public Officials, Private Interests, and Sustainable Democracy: When Politics and Corruption Meet." In *Corruption and the Global Economy*, edited by Kimberly Ann Elliot, 459–477. Washington, DC: Institute for International Economics. 1997.

Kahn, Mushtaq. "Patron-Client Networks and the Economic Effects of Corruption in Asia." *European Journal of Development Research* 10, no. 1 (1998): 15–39.

Kang, David. *Crony Capitalism: Corruption and Development in South Korea and the Philippines*. New York: Cambridge University Press, 2002.

Kang, Sungnam. "Anti-corruption Tasks for Next Administration" (in Korean). In *Proceedings of KAPA International Conference*, June 27–29, 2012, 1–17. Seoul: Korean Association for Public Administration, 2012.

Kim, Byung-sup, and Soon-ae Park, eds. *Corruption in Korea: Diagnoses and Prescriptions* (in Korean). Seoul: Park Young Sa, 2013.

Kim, Dongryul. Bureaucratic Institutions and Economic Reforms: The Effects of Disrupted Post-Retirement Incentive Structures on the Performance of Korean Officials. Unpublished dissertation, University of Virginia, Charlottesville, 2006.

Kim, Dongryul. "The Legacy of Deferred Compensation in Korea's Administrative Reforms." *Korean Journal of Political Studies* 27, no. 2 (2012): 203–218.

Kim, Young-jong. A Model Building of Bureaucratic Corruption in Developing Countries: The Case of Korea. Unpublished dissertation, Florida State University, Tallahasee, 1985.

Kim, Young-rae. "Civil Society in Korea: Achievements and Future Projects" (in Korean). *NGO Studies* 1, no. 1 (2003): 5–34.

"Kim Young-ran Act to Expect Eradication of Bureaucratic Corruptions" (in Korean). *Hankyoreh*, August 16, 2012.

Kingdon, J. W. *Agendas, Alternatives and Public Policies*. London: Longman, 2010.

Klitgaard, Robert. *Controlling Corruption*. Berkeley: University of California Press, 1991.

Korea Independent Commission against Corruption. *Guidebook for Building a Transparent Government* (in Korean). KICAC, 2004.

Lee, Hyo-won. "Suggested Solutions to the Corruption-Related Crimes by High-Ranking Government Officials" (in Korean). In *Corruption in Korea:*

Diagnoses and Prescriptions, edited by Byung-sup Kim and Soon-ae Park, 197–227. Seoul: Park Young Sa, 2013.

Lee, Wan-bum. "The Lineage and Thoughts of Korean Conservatism: Traditional Conservatism and Neo-Conservatism" (in Korean). *Peach Research* 13, no. 1 (2012): 31–53.

Leff, Nathaniel H. "Economic Development through Bureaucratic Corruption." In *Political Corruption: Readings in Comparative Analysis*, edited by Arnold J. Heidenheimer, 510–520. New York: Holt, Rinehart, and Winston, 1970.

Lindbeck, Assar. "Swedish Lessons for Post-Socialist Countries." Working Paper Institute for International Economic Studies, no. 6, Stockholm University, 1998.

Mauro, Paolo. "Corruption and Growth." *Quarterly Journal of Economics* 110, no. 3 (August 1995): 681–712.

Ministry of Government Administration. *Annual Report on Welfare of Government Officials* (in Korean). 1981.

Moon, Jung-in, and Jongryn Mo, eds. *Korea's Corruption: Cost and Contents* (in Korean). Seoul: Orum, 1999.

Nadeen, Ul Haque, and Ratna Sahay. "Do Government Wage Cuts Close Budget Deficits? The Cost of Corruption." *IMF Staff Papers* 43, no. 4 (December 1996): 754–778.

National Assembly. *Minutes*. National Policy Committee. Subcommittee for Deliberation. May 27, 2014.

National Assembly. *Minutes*. National Policy Committee. Subcommittee for Deliberation. January 8, 2015.

Nye, Joseph S. "Corruption and Political Development: A Cost-Benefit Analysis." *American Political Science Review* 63, no. 2 (June 1967): 417–427.

Park, Dong-suh. *Korean Public Administration* (in Korean). Seoul: Bummunsa, 2001.

Park, Joong-hoon. "Anticorruption Reform Policies under Kim Dae-jung" (in Korean). *Korean Journal of Public Administration* 8, no. 4 (January 1999): 99–130.

Park, Joong-hoon, Ji-yoon Yoo, Ji-won Chang, Sung-guk Yoon, and Jong-suk Hahm. "Current Status of Korea's Corruption and Analysis of Its Causes" (in Korean). Korea Institute of Public Administration Research Service Report to the Office for Government Policy Coordination under Prime Minister 7, 1999.

Park, Soon-ae. "Public Corruption: Diagnoses and Prescriptions" (in Korean). In *Corruption in Korea: Diagnoses and Prescriptions*, edited by Byung-sup Kim and Soon-ae Park, 3–33. Seoul: Park Young Sa, 2013.

Pempel, T. J., ed. *The Politics of the Asian Economic Crisis*. Ithaca: Cornell University Press, 1999.

Rocca, Jean-Louise. "Corruption and Its Shadows: An Anthropological View of Corruption in China." *The China Quarterly* 130 (June 1992): 402–416.

Rose-Ackerman, Susan. "The Political Economy of Corruption." In *Corruption and the Global Economy*, edited by K. Elliot, 31–60. Washington, DC: Peterson Institute for International Economics, 1997.

Rose-Ackerman, Susan. *Corruption: A Study in Political Economy*. New York: Academic Press. 1978.

Shaede, Ulrike. "The 'Old Boy' Network and Government-Business Relationships in Japan." *Journal of Japanese Studies* 21, no. 2 (Summer 1995): 293–317.

Tanzi, Vito. "Corruption, Government Activities and Markets." IMF Working Paper 94/99. Washington, DC: International Monetary Fund, 1994.

Tanzi, Vito. "Corruption Around the World: Causes, Consequences, Scope, and Cures." IMF Working Paper 98/63. Washington, DC: International Monetary Fund, 1998.

Tanzi, Vito, and Peter Wickham. "Corruption and the Rate of Temptation: Do Low Wages in the Civil Service Cause Corruption?" IMF Working Paper 97/73. Washington, DC: International Monetary Fund, 1997.

Tilman, Robert O. "Black Market Bureaucracy." In *Political Corruption: Readings in Comparative Analysis*, edited by Arnold J. Heidenheimer, 62–66. New York: Holt, Rinehart, and Winston, 1970.

Wade, Robert. *Governing the Market: Economic Theory and the Role of Government in East Asian Industrialization*. Princeton: Princeton University Press, 1990.

Wan, Ming. *The Political Economy of East Asia: Striving for Wealth and Power*. Washington, DC: CQ Press, 2007.

Werner, Simcha. "New Directions in the Study of Administrative Corruption." *Public Administration Review* 43 (March/April 1983): 146–154.

"What Is the Justice Department Worrying about by Cutting Down the Kim Young-ran Act by Half?" (in Korean). *Joongang Ilbo*, August 1, 2013.

World Bank. *The East Asian Miracle: Economic Growth and Public Policy* (World Bank Policy Research Report). Oxford: Oxford University Press, 1993.

Yoo, Jong-sung. *Democracy, Inequality and Corruption: Korea, Taiwan and the Philippines Compared*. Cambridge: Cambridge University Press, 2016.

Yoon, Duk-jung. *Criminal Sociology*. Seoul: Park Young Sa, 1984.

Yoon, Tae-bum. "Public Ethics and Conflicts of Interest" (in Korean). In *Corruption in Korea: Diagnoses and Prescriptions*, edited by Byung-sup Kim and Soon-ae Park, 103–129. Seoul: Park Young Sa, 2013.

Yoon, Young-kwan. *Korea's Political Economy in the 21st Century: Beyond the Leftist, Rightist, and Centrist* (in Korean). Seoul: Sinho, 1999.

7

The Evolution of China's Anticorruption Strategy

Andrew Wedeman

The crackdown on corruption Chinese president Xi Jinping initiated in 2013 was not only more intense than earlier anticorruption drives, it also continued a major shift in China's anticorruption strategy. While China had a long history of anticorruption campaigns, Xi's diverged in several significant ways. First, while popularly characterized as a "campaign," Xi's anticorruption drive was not a mass movement of the sort launched during the Maoist era. During the 1950s, the "masses" played a role in anticorruption campaigns, albeit a supporting role rather than a leading role, in what were essentially top-down campaigns initiated, directed, and controlled by the party and formal state institutions. The masses moved to the forefront of the mass-campaign strategy during the 1960s, after Mao called for a revolution from below and formal institutions of power were pulverized and paralyzed. In the late 1970s, the leadership rebuilt the formal institutions vested with responsibility for combating corruption and sidelined the public, transforming it into an essentially passive audience rather than an active participant. Faced with rising corruption, post-Mao leaders launched a series of intense anticorruption drives during the 1980s. These drives were, however, short-lived and sought to use sharp bursts of scattershot hyper-enforcement to root out and punish corrupt cadres and officials while also hoping that swift, hard-hitting crackdowns would deter other cadres and officials from giving in to the temptation to usurp the authority vested in them by the state and party to seek self-enrichment. In these drives, the public was not mobilized en masse, but individuals were asked to mail in tips and provide evidence to party investigators.

Although these campaigns, combined with a stepped-up drive against corruption among midlevel leadership in 1993, may have prevented corruption from spiraling out of control, as Xi moved toward assuming the paramount leadership in 2010–2012, evidence surfaced that, while the aggregate level of corruption might have remained constant, corruption had "deepened" and had infected even the senior ranks of the party-state. In response, in early 2013, Xi launched a drive that was unprecedented in the intensity of its assault on high-level corruption and its duration. Whereas the drives of the 1980s lasted months, Xi's campaign proved to be a multiyear effort. The duration of Xi's drive, in fact, may well render the term "campaign," with its connotations of a drive of finite duration, a misnomer; as discussed later, it is better understood as a "new normal," or open-ended struggle. It may ebb and flow but have no defined end point.

In the pages that follow, I trace the evolution of China's anticorruption strategy from the 1950s to the 2010s to elucidate how Xi's anticorruption strategy departs from past precedent. Tracing structures of China's anticorruption strategy suggests that over time, there has been a shift from a strategy that combined elements of what Chen and Weiss (in the introduction to this volume) define as institutionalized anticorruption efforts motivated by private and partisan interests of powerful actors to efforts that were motivated by a desire to strengthen the organizational capability of the regime to combat corruption. Thus, whereas Mao relied on "mass campaigns" in which corruption was viewed as a manifestation of ideological degeneracy and the public was mobilized to attack corruption, under Deng Xiaoping, corruption was redefined as a legal offense and the public was marginalized as party and state institutions assumed control over anticorruption efforts. Like Deng, Xi Jinping has relied on party and state institutions to attack official corruption and has relegated the public to the role of passive onlookers. Xi's shift from attacking corruption among the rank and file to attacking high-level corruption, however, has allowed him to use corruption as a weapon to attack potential political rivals and to consolidate his grip on power. As such, although Xi has pursued what Chen and Weiss describe as private political goals, he has also been motivated by a perceived need to strengthen the institutions of power.

The Evolution of China's Anticorruption Strategy

Corruption is not a new phenomenon in China. To combat official corruption and malfeasance, as far back as the Qin dynasty (221–209 BCE), imperial governments relied on what became known as the "Censorate." In theory, the Censorate was independent of the regular bureaucracy and responsible for investigating officials. Censors could impeach those they found to be corrupt, incompetent, or disloyal (Hucker 1951; Hucker 1966; Herson 1957; Walker 1947).

The Censorate did not, however, appear to have been an effective hedge against official corruption. Prosecutions were rare. Indeed, during the sixty-year reign of Emperor Qianlong (1711–1799), only four hundred officials were impeached for corruption. Few of these ended up facing criminal prosecution.

THE MAOIST PERIOD

Faced with rampant corruption within the bureaucracy it inherited from the defeated Guomindang-led (Nationalist) government in 1949, the Chinese Communist Party (CCP) launched a series of attacks on corruption after it came to power (Andreas 2007).[1] In August 1951, the party launched the "Three Antis Campaign" against the "three vices": corruption, waste, and bureaucratism (Barnett 1952). That campaign was followed in January 1952 by the "Five Antis Campaign" targeting the "five poisons": bribe-paying, tax-evasion, stealing state property, cheating on government contracts, and using state secrets to engage in speculation.[2] A year later, the party launched the "New Three Antis Campaign" against bureaucratism, authoritarianism, and indiscipline. In April 1957, a party rectification campaign attacked bureaucratism, as well as subjectivism and factionalism. Three years later, in March 1960, the "Rural Three Antis Campaign" targeted graft, waste, and bureaucratism. Two years later, President Liu Shaoqi and Vice Premier Deng Xiaoping used Mao's call for a "Socialist Education Movement" in the countryside to launch the "Four Cleans" campaign to attack the serious corruption among local cadres and officials that had spread during the 1959–1961 famine that followed the failure of the Great Leap Forward (Unger 1998; Baum 1969; Yang 1969). Contemporaneously, the New Five Antis Campaign focused on graft and pilferage, speculation and profiteering, extravagance and waste, and bureaucratism in the cities (MacFarquhar 1997). Although Mao's primary purpose in launching the

Cultural Revolution was to eradicate the "revisionist" political line being pushed by "capitalist roaders" within the party, in key respects the Cultural Revolution targeted corruption in that one of the overt manifestations of this alleged revisionism was officials' and cadres' use of their authority to seek material privileges (Lee 1966). Yet another campaign, the "One Attack Three Antis" targeting corruption, waste, and most importantly, speculation, was launched in 1970 (Woodward 1981).[3]

During the Maoist era, anticorruption campaigns generally took the form of "mass campaigns" in which the public was mobilized to expose and attack corruption (Ginsberg and Stahnke 1968).[4] Mass campaigns were not, however, necessarily spontaneous, bottom-up movements initiated and led by the masses. On the contrary, during the 1950s, the masses were mobilized by work teams composed of party cadres (Kelkar 1978). The teams conducted investigations, gathered information from the masses, identified suspects, and then orchestrated "accusation meetings" during which the masses were called on to bear witness against the accused and the accused were called on to publicly confess their crimes (叶曙明 1995; Strauss 2006). After this drama, some of the accused were turned over to the procuratorate for a formal legal investigation and prosecution (Xie 1988). Others were tried by ad hoc "People's Tribunals" set up independently of the people's court system for the duration of the campaign and empowered to hand down sentences ranging from fines to prison sentences of up to ten years. The regular people's court system continued to play a role and meted out more severe punishments, including death (Barnett 1952).

The Three Antis, Five Antis, and other campaigns were thus largely top-down, organization-based campaigns in which the masses played a supporting role. During the 1953 New Three Antis Campaign, for example, the procuratorate, public security apparatus, and people's courts first culled through letters from the masses exposing bureaucratism, authoritarianism, and indiscipline to identify malfeasant cadres. Teams of party cadres then mobilized the masses to attack the miscreants (刘义生 and 周永学 1997). The pattern of top-down campaigns in which the masses were relegated to a secondary role was similar to that of other mass campaigns during the 1940s and early 1950s, including the 1942–1943 Counterespionage Campaign, the 1950–1953 Land Reform; the 1950–1951 Suppression of Counterrevolutionaries Campaign, and the 1950–1953 Anti-Cult Campaign (Vogel 1969; Seybolt 1986; Yang 2008; Hung 2010). Thus, Strauss argues, the mass campaigns of the 1950s were actually campaigns orchestrated by the party to "stir up the masses" in which the masses were relegated "to vicariously participate" in "heavily staged political theater" (Strauss 2006; Strauss 2002). Although the masses did not initiate or direct the mass campaigns during the 1950s, they nevertheless often played an active role in denouncing and even physically assaulting those selected by the party activists for attack. The masses were thus an integral part of the Maoist "political theater" (Perry 2002).

In some instances, movements initiated from above gave rise to "spontaneous" action by the masses. During the land reform movement in the liberated areas of North China, according to Li, after President Liu Shaoqi called for a party rectification campaign to root out "rotten" grass-roots cadres who had abused their power, become corrupt, and allied with the landlords and local bullies, in some areas the poor peasants actually rose up independently and attacked cadres and even beat them to death (Li 2012). Although the general pattern was one of top-down direction, during the early 1950s, given the lack of an established legal framework, the formal institutions that directed these campaigns relied on ad hoc notions of justice based on politics rather than the law (Tao 1974). In the mid-1950s, Tao explains, as a more formal legal system emerged and policing institutions were consolidated, the role of the masses was reduced as the police, procuratorate, and court assumed roles that stressed "pro-tecting" the masses without necessarily involving them in the prosecution of corruption and other crimes. Cohen also argues that up to 1953, the "revolutionary justice" meted out during the mass campaigns was handed down by informal, "thinly veiled kangaroo courts" (Cohen 1966, 478).

Top-down "mass movements" were gradually replaced by bottom-up movements, first in the later 1950s and then more dramatically in the mid-1960s. Mao first experimented with a bottom-up anticorruption strategy in 1956, when he called on the masses to criticize abuse of power and corruption by cadres and officials in what became known as the Hundred Flowers Movement. After a tentative start in which individuals generally leveled mild criticisms about official arrogance and bureaucratism, the Hundred Flowers mushroomed into bitter attacks on "systemic corruption of power." In essence, critics charged that while the party rode to power amid promises of a "new democracy," once in power, cadres and officials had used the party's monopoly on political power to enrich themselves and transform the official class into a de facto hereditary aristocracy. Faced with unwanted attacks on the communist system itself, Mao, with the support of Deng Xiaoping and other members of the leadership, launched a vicious top-down counterattack in the form of the Anti-Rightist Campaign, in which both active critics and innocent bystanders were branded as rightists and purged.

The Great Leap Forward and the "three hard years" that followed its collapse spawned increased corruption and abuse of power as cadres used their power to grab food for themselves and their families, as well as extorting bribes from others seeking food. The leadership thus initiated a new anticorruption campaign in 1963. Initially, Liu Shaoqi and Deng Xiaoping sought to conduct the Socialist Education Movement and the subsidiary Four Clean Campaign as top-down campaigns controlled and directed by the party apparatus, using ad hoc "work teams" composed of cadres and officials dispatched from higher-level party organizations to first investigate allegations of corruption and other malfeasance by local cadres (Teiwes 1993; Baum 1975; Young 1984).[5] During their investigations, the work teams were to consult with the masses and draw them out. Once the team had concluded its investigation, they would then reeducate errant cadres or, in extreme cases, sack them (Baum and Teiwes 1968; Baum 1969). To the extent that the masses were brought into the movement at this stage, they were organized "under the watchful eye" of the county and brigade party committees to struggle against "corrupt cadres and bad elements" who were "paraded through the streets and forced to confess" (Dikotter 2016, 21). Many were beaten and some were killed by the "enraged masses." The masses were thus active participants in the campaign. The targets of their activism were, however, selected by the work team.

At first, directives from the center suggested that the primary problem at the grassroots level was petty corruption, which mild measures would be sufficient to address. In 1964, however, a new central directive called for the mobilization of the masses and the formation of peasant groups to actively "supervise" the cadres. As a result, local cadres found themselves "besieged" from below and many of the work teams began to lose control over the cleanup (Baum and Teiwes 1968).

In response, in 1965, yet another directive called for an end to attacks on local cadres by the masses. The masses, it declared, had "gone too far" and had used improper methods, included beatings, physical punishment, and forced confessions. The directive also called for a shift in focus to more senior cadres who were accused of "taking the capitalist road." Despite what appeared to be a call for scaling back of attacks on local cadres by the masses, during the summer of 1965, peasants in some localities began to intensify verbal attacks against cadres whom they began calling "freaks and monsters" (Baum 1969, 99). Cadres who had been criticized and punished during the earlier Small Four Cleans (小四清), moreover, now took advantage of the apparent "immobilization" of the work teams that accompanied the Big Four Cleans to seek revenge against the cadres who had attacked them earlier. Thus, what began as an orthodox top-down anticorruption campaign had begun to morph into a bottom-up mass movement by the spring of 1966.

That spring, even as the party was apparently losing control over the Socialist Education Movement in parts of the countryside, Mao launched a frontal assault on the party itself. Convinced that the petty corruption, abuse of power, and arrogance of rural cadres targeted by the Socialist Education Movement were merely the visible manifestations of the reemergence of a new ruling class, in May 1966, under intense pressure from Mao, the Central Committee issued a circular calling for a "Great Proletarian Cultural Revolution" in the cities (Walder and Su 2003).[6] Seeking to placate Mao, the leadership dispatched work teams to schools and universities to organize a campaign against "revisionists" "taking the capitalist road." The plan was for the teams to mobilize "revolutionary" faculty and students, expose "class enemies," and remove them from power. Mao and more radical students, however, saw the work teams as a ploy to stifle the Cultural Revolution by hauling out a few scapegoats and throwing them to the wolves while protecting other revisionists and opposing Mao's repeated calls for an intensification of the class struggle. As defined by Mao and the radicals within the party leadership, the Cultural Revolution was thus a struggle to overthrow a party establishment that had been consolidating itself as a new ruling class.

As such, on a broad level the Cultural Revolution was an attack on corruption. Having entrenched themselves in power, members of the party-state establishment had usurped the authority delegated to them by the "people" and the party-state apparatus to seek material benefits and privileges for themselves and their families, as well as the ability to make their claims to power and privilege heritable by their children. What Mao denounced as revisionism was in fact a form of "grand corruption" in that a broad stratum of those vested with public authority sought to enrich themselves by institutionalizing and entrenching their claims to political power.[7]

Therefore, when the party leadership moved to launch a controlled, top-down, and likely superficial attack on "class enemies" using work teams, Mao responded by exhorting the masses to rebel. In August 1966, he called for a "Sweeping Away of All Monsters and Demons" and the destruction of the "Four Olds." For complex reasons that are outside the scope of this work, students poured out of China's high schools and universities after the work teams were hastily withdrawn and launched into an anarchic frenzy of attack on "four olds" (old thinking, old culture, old customs, and old habits) and the "seven black categories" (landlords, rich peasants, counterrevolutionaries, rightists, capitalists, reactionaries, and "evildoers") (Lu 1994–1995; Dikotter 2016; MacFarquhar and Schoenhals 2006). Radical students began to form a myriad of largely autonomous "Red Guards" to fight Mao's alleged enemies and wage "revolution." In early 1967, at the behest of Mao, Red Guards moved to overthrow local authorities and seize power, leading to an increasingly intense battle for power among rival Red Guards, extending to warfare using automatic weapons, machine guns, flame throwers, and artillery in some localities.

In the process, the fragmented and chaotic bottom-up Red Guard mass movement immobilized and even pulverized formal control institutions. In many localities, the procuratorate and the Discipline Inspection Commission effectively ceased to exist or were taken over by the People's Liberation Army (PLA) (Xie 1988; Wedeman 2012). To the extent they continued to function, the people's courts were transformed into revolutionary tribunals that handed down sentences based on politics, not law (Chang 1978; Guo 2012). Many of those "dragged out" by the Red Guard were imprisoned in informal "cowsheds" before being sent to "May 7 Schools" for indefinite "reeducation." Ultimately, in 1968, faced with a looming threat of uncontrollable chaos, Mao allowed the PLA to seize power. The Red Guards were rounded up and "sent down to the countryside and up to the mountains" along with young Chinese who had sought to sit out the Cultural Revolution to "learn from the peasants."

In the latter years of the Cultural Revolution, the party reverted to a top-down approach to mass campaigns against corruption. In late 1969, for example, Jiangxi Province launched a new Four Antis Campaign (四反) against speculation, manipulation, corruption, and theft. "Mao Zedong Thought Propaganda Teams" were dispatched to localities to mobilize the masses to engage in "face-to-face struggles" with those cadres who "had carried out activities of corruption, theft, and speculation" (Woodward 1981, 103 and 107). Other localities launched similar crackdowns. In 1970, these local Four Antis campaigns morphed into the nationwide One Strike Three Antis Campaign targeting counterrevolutionaries, "corruption and theft, speculation and profiteering, and extravagance and waste" (Woodward 1981, 111).

Once again, the party relied on a work team-led approach in which the masses played a supporting role. How successful the teams were in evoking enthusiastic participation is, however, unclear and there is some evidence from memoires by ex–Red Guards and other "sent-down youth" that by the early 1970s, participation in mass campaigns had become stylized and ritualized, with the masses' mouthing slogans given to them by the work teams and simply "going through the motions." These same accounts also reveal the presence of extensive petty corruption, much of it involving the payment of small, in-kind bribes as a sort of toll for "going in the back door" to obtain "privileges." By 1972, the One Strike Three Antis campaign had apparently faded, thus bringing an end to active anticorruption campaigns during the Maoist period (Woodward 1972).

Mao's anticorruption strategy clearly approximates what Chen and Weiss describe as being "privately" motivated. In Mao's case, however, his private political interest in holding on to power was cloaked in ideology. Hence, in attacking corruption, Mao also saw himself as attacking revisionism within the party and defending the revolution. The result was that Mao's anticorruption strategy combined elements of private and partisan motivations, even though the mass campaign strategy was based on temporary and ad hoc organizations.

THE POST-MAO PERIOD

After Mao's death, the leadership moved to further reassert the institutional power of the party and state. In the late 1970s, the procuratorate and Central Discipline Inspection Commission (CDIC) were reconstituted and a new Criminal Code was promulgated, thus laying the foundation for a formal institution-based approach to fighting corruption (Leng 1982; Chiu 1980; Dutton 2000).[8] The adoption of a criminal code signaled an important shift from what Forster describes as the loose, moralistic, and subjective definition of corruption that prevailed during the Maoist era to a more legally delineated set of criminal offenses, with defined penalties (Forster 1985).[9] As a result, corruption was largely depoliticized and rendered a crime rather than an ideological deviation. Corruption nevertheless remained under the purview of the party, and even as the system became more firmly institutionalized, the convention emerged that the party's CDIC and its subnational agencies had prior jurisdiction over cases involving party members (Gong 2008; Sullivan 1984; Sapio 2005).

The CDIC, however, lacked judicial authority and only could mete out punishments that ranged from warnings, demotions, and probation to expulsion from the party. Hence, if party investigators found evidence of criminality, they had to remand the case to the procuratorate, which was part of the judicial system and had the authority to indict individuals and hand them over to the people's court for trial and possible conviction. In 1987, a third actor was added when the State Council reestablished the Ministry of Supervision. Originally set up as the People's Supervisory Commission in 1949, reconstituted as the Ministry of Supervision in 1954, then disbanded in 1959, the reestablished ministry was tasked with administrative oversight of state agencies and public servants. Like the CDIC, the ministry lacked judicial authority and could only impose sanctions such as warnings, demerits, demotions, and dismissal from office (China Factfile 2016). Thus it, too, had to remand cases involving possible criminal acts to the procuratorate for prosecution. The jurisdiction of the ministry quickly proved problematic because the public servants over whom it had supervisory responsibility were apt to be party members. As a result, the ministry and the CDIC were effectively merged in 1992, and a system of joint investigations replaced parallel party and administrative investigations (He 2000; Chang 1998).

Even though the formal institutions tasked with rooting out and fighting corruption were still in relatively nascent form, faced with evidence that corruption was not simply a legacy of the anarchic Cultural Revolution era, could not be controlled merely by the promulgation and enforcement of new regulations, and was instead mounting in the transitional economic conditions created by early market reforms, the leadership warned in early 1982 that corruption had become of "vital importance to the Party's life and death" and initiated a series of anticorruption reforms (Forster 1985, 8). In March 1982, the National People's Congress (NPC) Standing Committee increased the severity of penalties for economic crimes including graft, bribery, and embezzlement by raising their maximum sentences to include life in prison and the death penalty. The reconstruction of the party and state institutions tasked with combating corruption and adoption of laws codifying what constituted corruption and stipulating the penalties for engaging in corruption thus shifted China's anticorruption strategy away from the private and partisan orientations of the Maoist period and toward a new institution-defending focus.

The leadership also ordered a new crackdown on corruption. The new regulations were to go into force as of April 1, 1982, and corrupt officials were offered a month to surrender and receive a possible amnesty. Few apparently took advantage of the offer. That spring, a new campaign unfolded. Fearful that the campaign might degenerate into "an outpouring of personal vindictiveness and forced confession," party leaders strictly limited public participation (Forster 1985). As a result, unlike the mass campaigns of the 1950s, the 1982 campaign, known as the Strike against Economic Crime, largely sidelined the public. Instead of being mobilized as a supporting actor, as had been the case during the Maoist mass campaigns, the public was called on to serve as individual informants, while the CDIC took the lead.

By February, less than a year after it began, the party declared the campaign complete. According to Chen Yun, the secretary of the CDIC, the party had investigated 164,000 cases, 30,000 individuals had been sent to prison, and 5,500 party members had been expelled from the party. Despite these numbers, the campaign was not deemed a rousing success.[10] To begin with, the party establishment was ambivalent about severe punishments for party members and even Deng Xiaoping seemed to believe that some offenders should be granted leniency. Regardless of the actual results, the 1982 campaign marked a sharp departure from the top-down mass campaigns of the 1950s. The public had clearly been relegated to the role of a passive audience whose primary involvement was either as individual informants or as consumers of official media, and hence, the party's narrative on both corruption and anticorruption.

A new anticorruption campaign took place in 1986. Officially, the campaign was part of a larger party rectification drive that began in 1982 and ran until 1987, but the main anticorruption crackdown began in January 1986 and continued through the end of that year (Lee 1986). Like in 1982, because party leaders feared that an "open door" rectification would lead to turmoil, the new campaign was organized as a "closed door," intraparty affair (Dickson 1990). The public was thus once again relegated to the role of passive audience. An ad hoc Central Commission for Guiding Party Rectification was organized and it, in turn, dispatched work teams to guide specific party organs in setting up local party rectification committees. These committees took the lead in investigating "unhealthy" tendencies that included, on the one hand, leftist political radicalism and, on the other hand, corruption, including nepotism, bribery, improper use of public funds, irregularities in the allocation of housing, using "back door" connections to obtain access and privileges, and embezzlement (Dickson 1990). Although the party proclaimed that investigators would "beat tigers" and punish high-level officials, in the end, few senior cadres or officials were taken down. On the contrary, in March 1986, just months after the crackdown was unveiled, fears that relatives of the senior leadership might be implicated in questionable activities and that too intense a crackdown could hamper economic reform led the leadership to back off from attacking high-level corruption. As a result, the 1986 campaign, like its 1982 predecessor, ended up concentrating on the party rank and file, or what has come to be known as the "flies" (Rosen 1987).

The next massive anticorruption crackdown, officially known simply as the 1989 Anticorruption Struggle, was launched in the wake of nationwide antigovernment demonstrations in 1989 and followed a new pattern. In July 1989, the regime signaled the commencement of the campaign with a media blitz. It announced an amnesty period during which corrupt officials and cadres who turned themselves in, confessed, and informed on others would receive leniency. After the amnesty period, those who failed to confess, the official media warned, would be punished to the maximal extent provided by the law. The investigatory organs, meanwhile, were mobilized for hyper-enforcement after the end of the amnesty period. The media, finally, exhorted the public to send in tips exposing corrupt officials (Quade 2007; Wedeman 2005).

Each of the three anticorruption crackdowns launched during the 1980s produced distinct "spikes" in the total number of indictments handed down by the procuratorate (see figure 7.1).[11] Most of those indicted and punished during the 1982, 1986, and 1989 campaigns were, however, rank-and-file officials. Only a few big tigers were "bagged."

The 1993 campaign, known, echoing the 1989 drive, simply as the 1993 Anticorruption Struggle, by contrast, targeted junior administrators: cases involving leading cadres and officials at the county and department level, and midlevel cadres and officials at the prefectural and bureau levels. The 1993 crackdown led to significant increases in the number of senior officials indicted and the number of death sentences and suspended death sentences handed down for corruption-related offenses (see figure 7.2).

Despite the continuity with the crackdowns of the 1980s in terms of a sudden escalation in the intensity of enforcement, the 1993 crackdown, Sapio argues, witnessed a major shift in the regime's anticorruption strategy. Unlike its post-Mao predecessors, the 1993 crackdown was not a short-lived burst of hyper-enforcement but rather the start of a sustained

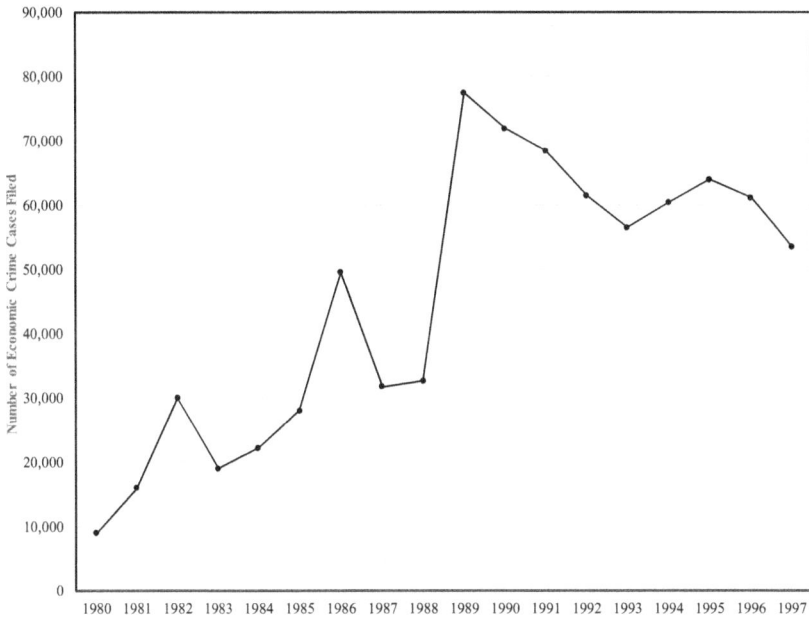

Figure 7.1. Impact of the 1982, 1986, and 1989 crackdowns. *Source:* 中国检察年鉴 [Procuratorial yearbook of China] (Beijing: Zhongguo Jiancha Chubanshe, various years) and 中国年鉴 [China yearbook], 最高人民检察公报 and [Work report of the Supreme People's Procuratorate], various years, available at http://www.spp. gov.cn/gzbg/. Data for the procuratorate include the number of economic crime cases (bribery, graft, embezzlement, and misappropriation).

drive that essentially morphed into a new heightened intensity of routine enforcement (Sapio 2005; Manion 1998; Cho 2001).[12] Thus, having sidelined the public and replaced the top-down Maoist mass campaign approach to combating corruption with a top-down, institutionally based approach in the 1980s, in the 1990s, the leadership replaced episodic anticorruption campaigns with what Sapio terms a sustained and routinized anticorruption struggle (Sapio 2005).

To the extent the public played a role in this new strategy, it was relegated to that of an atomized audience. This is not to suggest that the public was irrelevant. On the contrary, public opinion and the regime's need to protect its legitimacy by at least appearing to be determined to fight the highly unpopular "scourge" of official corruption remained

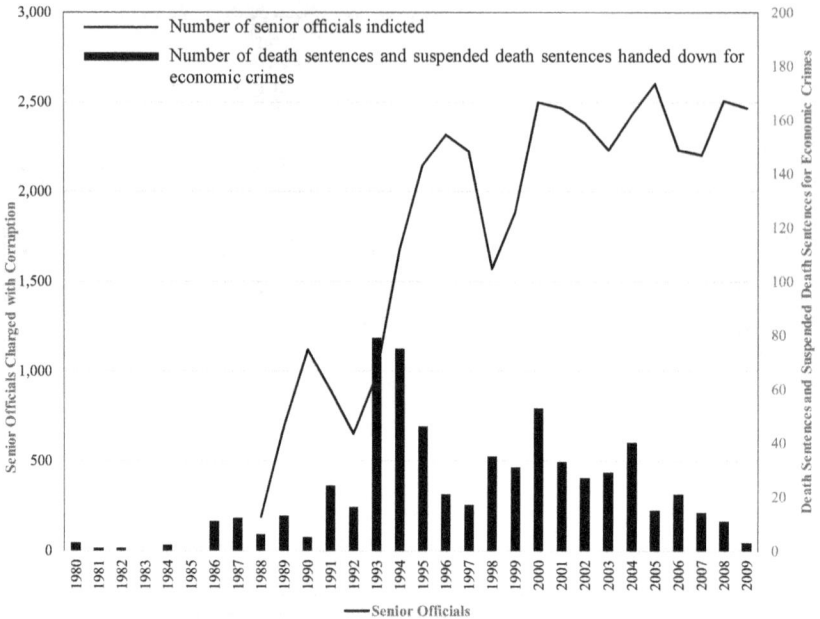

Figure 7.2. Impact of the 1993 crackdown. *Source:* Senior officials indicted: see figure 7.1. Death sentences: based on Amnesty International, "Death Penalty Log," various years and media reports, http://www.amnesty.org/en/documents. *Note:* An individual receiving a suspended death sentence, also known as a death sentence with two-year reprieve, is eligible to have their sentence commuted to life in prison if they cooperate with authorities. In corruption cases, it appears that almost all those given a suspended death sentence had their sentence commuted to life.

a major driver of the regime's anticorruption struggle. The regime also continued to call on the public to send in tips exposing corruption. The actual mechanics of investigating, prosecuting, and punishing corruption, however, were almost completely internalized and institutionalized by the mid-1990s (Trevaskes 2007; Trevaskes 2002; Trevaskes 2003; Tanner 1989).[13]

THE XI JINPING ERA

Xi Jinping's anticorruption campaign further sidelined the public. With the spread of the internet and social media, citizen-activists and investigative journalists turned to the internet not only to accuse officials of corruption but also to root out evidence of corruption. During the early days of the crackdown, a number of high-profile cases involving official corruption went viral on social media. Citizen activism was, however, soon crushed. In September 2013, ten months into the crackdown, a judicial notice jointly issued by the Supreme Court and the Supreme People's Procuratorate announced that any individual who posted on the internet unfounded rumors that were accessed by five thousand or more individuals would be charged with defamation and could face three years in prison (Xinhua 9/9/2013; Kaiman 9/10/2013). The *Xinhua* announcement specifically focused on "fabricated rumors" that might trigger "mass incidents" (collective protests). Clearly, however, the ruling also applied to the spreading of rumors about official corruption. Thus, the masses were again marginalized from anticorruption efforts under Xi.

The second difference between Xi's crackdown and the crackdowns that preceded it is that Xi has gone after high-level corruption much more vigorously and systematically than his processors. Prior to Xi's crackdown, only two members of the Politburo had been charged and convicted of corruption: Beijing party secretary and Politburo member Chen Xitong in 1995, in connection with a collapsed Ponzi scheme that revealed that he had been siphoning "commissions" paid by developers seeking prime Beijing real estate into a personal slush fund,[14] and Shanghai party secretary and Politburo member Chen Liangyu (no relation to Chen Xitong) in 2006, when an audit revealed that he and his lieutenants had been diverting funds from the Shanghai municipal pension fund to lend to crony developers (Wedeman 2000; Wedeman 1996). Both Chen Xitong and Chen Liangyu were thus exposed not as a result of intensive investigation by the CDIC or the procuratorate, but rather by exogenous events. Similarly, the investigation into a Xiamen smuggling ring was triggered when a "disgruntled" former employee sent a lengthy letter spelling out details of the operation, enclosing bills of sale for smuggled goods (Menshausen 2007).

In the past, therefore, major corruption cases were triggered by essentially stochastic events and were centered on a specific individual or group of individuals. They were thus limited in scope and tended to be "short" in the sense that once the triggering case was resolved, that was the end. Moreover, these high-level cases were not connected to the major crackdowns in 1982, 1986, and 1989 that focused primarily on the rank and file. Even the 1993 crackdown did not target high-level corruption but instead focused on officials and cadres at the county and departmental levels.

Xi's crackdown, by contrast, has been not only sustained but systematic; it has targeted corruption not only at the lower and middle levels but also at high levels. As of June 2016, over 120 officials ranked at the vice-ministerial and vice-gubernatorial levels had been convicted, indicted, and placed under investigation. More than ninety senior (major general and above) PLA and People's Armed Police (PAP) officers had been taken down. Four members of the Politburo (three of them retired), two of whom were also vice chairs of the Central Military Commission, had been taken down. Investigators have moved systematically to identify corrupt officials, then have "followed the money," rolling up those who paid bribes and other senior officials linked to the focus of their first target. Spouses, children, relatives, and mistresses who collected bribes on behalf of corrupt senior officials have been indicted and convicted. Xi's crackdown has thus attacked corruption at the very top in ways unlike any previous crackdown (Wedeman 2017). In fact, the most significant increases in the number of indictments by the procuratorate have been at the senior level (see figure 7.3).

Finally, whereas the 1982, 1986, and 1989 crackdowns were essentially short-lived bursts of hyper-enforcement, measured in months, Xi's crackdown has seen a sustained increase in enforcement, lasting years. The 1993 crackdown against midlevel corruption could also be said to have been a sustained drive, in that after a jump in the number of midlevel

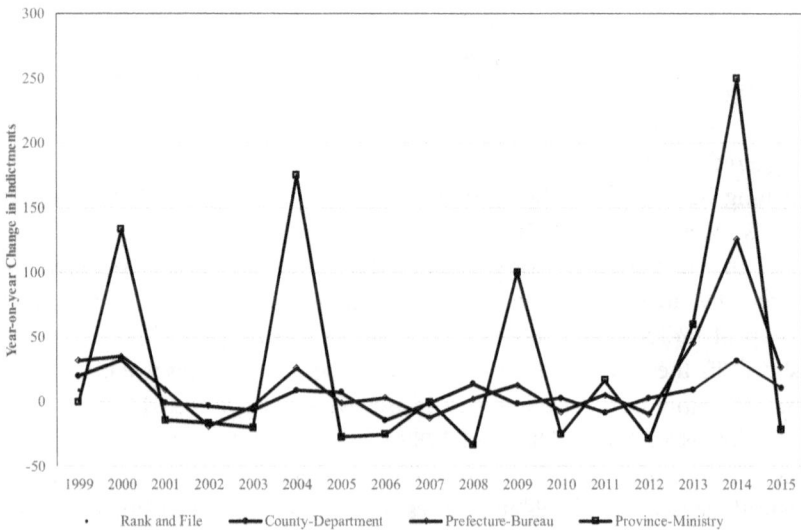

Figure 7.3. Impact of Xi Jinping crackdown. *Source:* See figure 7.1.

officials and cadres in 1993, the number of such officials indicted by the procuratorate remained at heightened levels. But after an initial burst of publicity, the crackdown on midlevel corruption became routinized and, while the leadership would occasionally speak out about the need to fight corruption more intensely, it tended to do so in boilerplate fashion, using the same set of stock phrases over and over again.[15]

Xi and the CDIC head, Wang Qishan, by contrast, have made the fight against corruption a much more central part of regime rhetoric. The media have kept the anticorruption drive in the headlines. The CDIC has maintained a website on which it posts reports of new investigations and decisions to expel party members and hand them over the procuratorate for criminal investigation, an obvious effort to publicize its ongoing attack on corruption. Thus, not only has Xi's drive against corruption been sustained over a period of years in terms of intensified enforcement, it has been sustained on an unprecedented rhetorical level. Moreover, the prolonged nature of the drive means that it is not a campaign in the sense that it has an identifiable beginning and end. Rather it is perhaps better thought of as a shift from one level of intensity to a new, higher level of intensity, with the result that it has become the "new normal" and as such is essentially an open-ended, slow-moving war of attrition that will grind on for years to come.

Xi and Wang did not, however, completely abandon the older campaign model. As discussed previously, prior to the Cultural Revolution, during a mass campaign, the party deployed work teams composed of cadres from one level to guide and orchestrate the campaign at subordinate levels. Xi and Wang have also dispatched teams made up of inspectors from the CDIC to the provinces, ministries, and major state-owned enterprises. In this respect, they have partially adopted what some have informally characterized as the work team model employed by President Liu Shaoqi in the early days of the Cultural Revolution, albeit with the important caveat that while the inspection teams dispatched by Xi and Wang have been tasked with rooting out corruption and stimulating greater vigor by subordinate levels, neither they nor local investigatory teams have been tasked with mobilizing the public to participate directly in the prosecution of corrupt officials and cadres.

In sum, Xi's crackdown is actually just one more offensive in a war against corruption that the party has been fighting since long before it seized power in 1949. Time and time again, the leadership has declared that corruption is a cancer on the party that will kill the party if it is not fought. Time and time again, campaigns have been launched with great fanfare. Although intensified enforcement during the height of each campaign may have spread new fear among official ranks, with the result that those with dirty hands may have decided to lay low and those with as-yet-unstained hands might have been persuaded to keep them clean, after the Sturm und Drang died down, corruption endured and over time worsened, thus necessitating new vows to fight corruption to the death and another campaign.

It is not clear that the long-term results of Xi's intensification of the war against corruption will be any different from those of these early initiatives. Regardless, Xi's approach to fighting corruption is obviously different in terms of structure. Like Deng Xiaoping, as discussed earlier (and also like Jiang Zemin and Hu Jintao), Xi has eschewed Mao's mass campaign approach and has pushed the public to the sidelines, thereby reducing their role to that of passive bystanders. Primary investigatory authority has been given largely to the party's disciplinary organ and the state's supervisory agency. Cases have been developed through a defined organizational process, wherein the disciplinary and supervisory agencies have the authority to indefinitely detain suspects under what is known as *shuanggui*, which translates literally, awkwardly, as "double regulation" (Sapio 2008).

In essence, *shuanggui*, which is based not on legal statute but instead derives from party rules, allows party investigators to order a suspect to present themselves at a specific time and in a specific place for questioning.[16] Unlike in the judicial system, where suspects are assumed to be innocent until proven guilty, under *shuanggui*, because party members agreed to submit to party disciplinary rule when they joined the party, the burden of proof falls on their shoulders. Suspects must, in other words, convince investigators that they are innocent. Proving innocence may be difficult. The accused are often not allowed to see the allegations leveled against them or even know who made the allegations. They cannot cross-examine their accusers. Nor do they have the right to legal or other council. Moreover, there is no right of habeas corpus under party rules. Suspects may be held indefinitely and incommunicado.[17] Once detained, suspects are pressured to confess. Those who refuse may face unauthorized coercive measures, ranging from sleep deprivation to outright torture.

Despite having powerful investigatory authority, neither the CDIC nor the ministry has judicial authority. If they conclude a suspect has committed a crime, the case must be remanded to the procuratorate for a formal criminal investigation and possible indictment.[18] After an indictment is handed down, the procuratorate takes the case to the peoples' court, which reviews the evidence and determines if the case warrants a trial. Trials are generally short and may consist of little more than a recitation of the charges followed by a guilty plea. Even in cases in which the accused refuses to confess, most trials are quick and if a case goes to a "full" trial, guilty verdicts are generally handed down after only a few hours of deliberation. Sentences may, however, not be handed down at the time of the trial but may instead be announced weeks or even months later. It appears that in many instances, sentencing is delayed because the severity of the sentence depends on whether the accused cooperates with investigators in recovering dirty monies and identifying other parties to their corrupt activities or others who may have engaged in corruption.

Although many observers question the justness of the process—there is some evidence that investigators rely heavily on forced confessions[19] and defendants have little if any access to the evidence or means to prove their innocence—the process through which corruption cases have been prosecuted under Xi clearly conforms to a formal set of institutionally based regulations and is at least technically grounded in law. As such, the process is distinct from the ad hoc "processes" used during the Maoist era. Nor does Xi's approach resemble the mass "revolutionary justice" that characterized the mass campaigns of the Maoist period.

Conclusion

As Xi Jinping's anticorruption crackdown unfolded and intensified, a number of observers described it in terms that seemed to draw parallels with the political purges of the 1950s and 1960s, including Mao's massive assault on the party during the Cultural Revolution (Wedeman 2017). Various commentators have in fact branded Xi's crackdown as a purge or political witch hunt. There is unquestionably a political element to Xi's crackdown, and the removal of figures such as Bo Xilai, Zhou Yongkang, Ling Jihua, General Guo Boxiong, and General Xu Caihou has certainly enabled Xi to consolidate his grip on the Chinese political system and presumably reduced the leverage of retired CCP general secretaries Jiang Zemin and Hu Jintao. Nevertheless, as argued herein, Xi's anticorruption crackdown is structurally distinct from the old Maoist mass campaign. Whereas the Maoist campaign combined top-down direction by the party with bottom-up mobilization of the public, Xi's crackdown is for all intents and purposes a purely top-down, institutionally grounded approach to fighting corruption. The main actors are party investigators, prosecutors from the procuratorate, and members of the people's court. The public's role has been limited to feeding potential evidence of corruption to the formal institutions and the consumption of the party-state's narratives on corruption and anticorruption as publicized in the official media. Independent grassroots activism has been discouraged and largely curtailed. As such the crackdown has not spilled over into the public sphere in the ways that the old Maoist mass campaigns did. Nor has the crackdown created the sorts of political turmoil and strife triggered by the campaigns of the 1950s and 1960s.

More critically, whereas Mao's mass campaigns sought to concurrently purge the party-state of those who were corrupt in a legal sense and those who were corrupt in an ideological sense, the primary focus of Xi's crackdown has been to cleanse the ranks of those who have committed the legally defined crime of corruption. During the Anti-Rightist Campaign and the Cultural Revolution, for instance, Mao's primary targets were either active "counterrevolutionaries" (e.g., hidden Guomindang agents and sympathizers) or empowered individuals who had succumbed to the insidious "silver bullets" of a form of grand corruption, wherein those delegated public authority fell victim to the human weakness of privilege-seeking and the temptation to use their authority to restore elite-class status. For Mao, corruption was not a simple matter of greed but an overt manifestation of deeper ideological degeneration. Hence, his attacks on corruption sought to defend the party as an institution.

To an extent, Xi, too, appears to view corruption as a political threat to the party-state and its fundamental integrity. Like Mao, he sees cleansing of the party-state ranks as a means to restore the political health of the party and officialdom. But whereas Mao seems to have often been "hunting witches," looking for "hidden" political enemies, Xi's crackdown has primarily concentrated on those who have committed tangible crimes and used their delegated authority to seek personal enrichment. That some of these miscreants also happen to be real or potential political rivals is unquestionably true. It is quite reasonable to assume that the crackdown has been selective and that malfeasance—and other seemingly untoward behavior—by others may have been tacitly ignored or that such individuals have been afforded the opportunity to quietly "clean their acts up" and cease and desist from overt and visible forms of corruption. It is also likely true that Xi's campaign has unleashed a wave of fear and apprehension within the party-state ranks that is perhaps much greater than any of the other post-Mao anticorruption crackdowns. Yet this campaign remains guided overall by an institutional logic, not by Xi's pursuit of private political interest. But that line between institutional motives and private motives becomes blurred because in defending the party-state against corruption, Xi is also consolidating his own power.

The means employed by Xi to cleanse the party-state ranks are nevertheless markedly different from those employed by Mao and, for that matter, other leaders in the post-Mao era. Xi has relied on a systematic, sustained, legally grounded, and institutionally based strategy rather than the ad hoc means associated with the Maoist mass campaign or the short-term bursts of hyper-enforcement employed during the 1980s and 1990s. Xi thus appears to have not only a short-term goal of attacking the deep-seated corruption that has developed in China during the reform period, but he also seems to be trying to establish a much greater institutional capability to combat, deter, and control corruption over the long run.

Notes

1. Even before the founding of the PRC, work teams dispatched to implement the land reform program begun in 1946 were told to investigate possible corruption among local cadres.

2. The distinction between the Three Antis and the Five Antis campaigns is blurred. In theory, the Three Antis Campaign focused on officials and cadres and the Five Antis Campaign focused on private businesses. In the case of offenses such as bribery, a nexus exists in that the business side presumably pays bribes to corrupt officials and cadres. Similarly, in the case of extortion, the political side presumably extracts funds from the business side. Moreover, neither campaign focused purely on criminal offenses and instead mixed cracking down on corruption, waste, and so on, with attacks on politically suspect members of the bourgeoisie and hidden counterrevolutionaries.

3. According to Dikotter, black marketeering flourished amid the political turmoil of the Cultural Revolution, as individuals abandoned collectives and units to seek profits. Because corruption, waste, and speculation were not defined by the center, local units were left to decide what they meant; definitions varied widely. A farmer could, therefore, be accused of speculation if he sold produce from his private plot. Dikotter thus describes the One Strike Three Antis campaign as among the largest and speculates that as many as sixteen million might have been

accused, the vast majority of whom were likely not state officials (Dikotter 2016, 236–241). Also see "One Strike-Three Anti Campaign," http://america.pink/one-strike-three-anti-campaign_3328165.html. In addition to these national campaigns were campaigns initiated by provincial and possibly lower-level governments.

4. In the mid-1950s, the People's Procuratorate, which was the formal judicial body charged with investigating and prosecuting corrupt officials, relied on a network of informal "correspondents" to ferret out corruption.

5. According to Young, Liu Shaoqi barred the party's formal control organs from participating in the Socialist Education Movement and instead vested full authority in the ad hoc work teams.

6. The Cultural Revolution would spread to the countryside in late 1966/ early 1967.

7. The definition of "corruption" has been the subject of protracted debate. Much of the debate has been over the varying cultural notions of what is and what is not corruption. Most specialists, however, accept definitions that boil down to variations on "the misuse of delegated authority for the purpose of personal gain." Note that my definition is broader than most in that it not only applies to the usurpation of delegated authority by officials but also encompasses the usurpation of a much wider range of fiduciary authority. An executive of a private corporation who accepts a kickback from an executive of another private corporation is therefore corrupt in the same way as an official who accepts bribes from private citizens.

8. This is not to imply that China lacked any sort of legal code prior to 1979. China had a patchwork of legal statutes, which included the 1952 "Act for the Punishment of Corruption." But the code was opaque and punishments were heavily affected by a defendant's class background. Moreover, the "reform through labor" (劳改) system evolved parallel to the formal criminal justice system. A draft code was circulated between 1954 and 1957 but was never formally ratified.

9. Morality did not, however, disappear from the Chinese discourse on corruption, and even today corruption is not simply seen as a crime but as moral degeneracy and failing. Officials charged with accepting bribes and embezzlement are frequently also alleged to have engaged in "degenerate lifestyles" that include drunkenness, debauchery, whoring, and womanizing. Even so, corrupt officials are almost always sent to prison for defined criminal offenses, not moral or political deviance. This does not mean, of course, that factional politics does not lurk behind the prosecution of corruption. If present, political motives are apt to be cloaked in legal charges when a case moves out of the party disciplinary system and into the formal judicial system for criminal prosecution.

10. Exactly how many of these reported cases involved corruption is unclear because the 1982 campaign also targeted smuggling and profiteering, offenses that need not necessarily involve officials or the misuse of delegated public authority.

11. Functionally, there are three separate stages in a corruption case involving a party member or state official. In the first stage suspects are investigated by teams consisting of cadres from the Discipline Inspection Commission and officials of the Ministry of Supervision. If evidence of an indictable crime is found, the case is remanded to the procuratorate, which conducts a second-stage criminal investigation. If the charges meet the threshold for formal judicial prosecution, the procuratorate "files" (立案) the case with the people's court. After a review of the case, the court may then try and sentence the accused or return the case to the procuratorate for further investigation or administrative adjudication. Given these multiple layers, cases often move slowly through the system and there is considerable "leakage" in that a considerable percentage of cases end in administrative punishments rather than prison sentences. Some of the guilty also presumably manage to escape prosecution either because they prove to be innocent or they and their "protectors" are able to improperly quash the investigation.

12. Cho, however, argues that the 1993 campaign continued through 1997, a view that accords with Sapio's argument that the drive against low-level leading cadres and officials was sustained.

13. The public continued to have a more active role in the series of Strike Hard (严打) anticrime campaigns. In these anticrime blitzes, groups of criminals convicted by the courts were often hauled en masse to public rallies where thousands of spectators cheered as their sentences were read out. Such rallies have become increasingly rare.

14. Public agencies, including state-owned enterprises, state agencies, and party organizations, often had such funds, which were used to pay bonuses and finance the construction of facilities for the use of the organization and its employees. Monies collected from nonbudgetary sources, such as rental income from properties, various fees, and "commissions" paid by individuals and other organizations were deposited in these funds. In Chen Xitong's case, he had been collecting commissions from real estate developers seeking land-use rights in downtown Beijing. When he was caught, his defense was reportedly that he had been engaged in a "normal" and widely accepted practice and was not pocketing the money but using it for the common benefit of the Beijing party apparatus. Clearly some of the money was being pocketed. When the Wuxi Ponzi scheme collapsed, Deputy Mayor Wang Baosen killed himself at his "luxury villa" in suburban Huairou County. It is hard to imagine how Wang could have afforded a luxury villa on his official salary.

15. The available evidence suggests that anticorruption efforts were far from lackluster between 2002 and 2013. On the contrary, a series of senior officials were taken down during the Hu era and a number of extensive networks of corrupt officials were broken up. What seems to distinguish the Hu decade from the Xi crackdown is that few of the high-level cases prosecuted under Hu

involved senior officials of the central government or, with the exception of Chen Liangyu, members of the inner leadership. That said, it appears that some of the major cases pursued under Xi had their roots in investigations begun under Hu.

16. Abstractly, because *shuanggui* has its foundation in party regulations, it ought to apply only to party members. In practice, because the CDIC and the Ministry of Supervision merged their investigatory teams in 1993, civil servants (some of whom are also party members) suspected of disciplinary transgressions may be detained under *shuanggui*. Some investigators have further broadened their interpretation to include the ability to detain anyone suspected of being involved in corruption or other forms of official malfeasance.

17. Under Xi, the CDIC has, however, become somewhat more transparent. In cases involving senior party members, a short notice is generally posted on the CDIC's website (http://www.ccdi.gov.cn/jlsc/). Less important officials and cadres might have their cases posted on provincial or local DIC websites. At best, only a fraction of the total case load is reported.

18. The most severe punishment that can be imposed, according the CCP Constitution, is expulsion from the party. Lesser sanctions such as reprimands, demotions, and probationary membership can also be imposed. Constitution of the Chinese Communist Party, amended and adopted at the sixteenth Party Congress, November 14, 2002: chapter 7, available at www.chinadaily.com/CPP%20 Constitution.htm (accessed August 4, 2016).

19. According to legal experts, confessions made to nonjudicial party investigators cannot be used in court as evidence. It is said, however, that some suspects confess to party investigators in order to get their cases moved from the CDIC system, where they have no procedural rights and face indefinite detention, to the judicial system, where they are supposed to have rights, including the right to a trial. They then discover when they get to trial that many courts improperly accept extralegal confessions as evidence of guilt.

Bibliography

程大方. "从'三反' 运动看新中国建立初期反腐败斗争的历史特点和深远影响." 中共党史研
    究 no. 1 (1995): 22–26.
刘义生 and 周永学. "'新三反'运动论析." 北京党史论坛 107, no. 6 (1997): 14–19.
叶曙明. "在 '三反五反' 风暴中." 广东史志 no. 1 (2003): 9–15.
Andreas, Joel. "The Structure of Charismatic Mobilization: A Case Study of
    Rebellion during the Chinese Cultural Revolution." *American Sociological
    Review* 72, no. 3 (2007): 434–458.
Barnett, A. Doak. "Five Anti Campaign I: Nationwide Campaign: Letter to Mr.
    Walter S. Rogers." *Institute of Current World Affairs* (July 29, 1952). Retrieved
    from http://www.icwa.org/wp-content/uploads/2015/08/ADB-ADB-44.pdf.

Baum, Richard. *Ssu-ching: The Socialist Education Movement of 1962–1966.* Berkeley: Center for Chinese Studies, University of California, 1968.

Baum, Richard. "Revolution and Reaction in the Chinese Countryside: The Socialist Education Movement in Cultural Revolutionary Perspective." *China Quarterly* 38 (1969): 92–119.

Baum, Richard. *Prelude to Revolution: Mao, the Party, and the Peasant Question, 1962–66.* New York: Columbia University Press, 1975.

Baum, Richard, and Frederick C. Teiwes. "Liu Shao-ch'i and the Cadres Question." *Asian Survey* 8, no. 4 (April 1968): 323–345.

Chang, I-huai. "An Analysis of the CCP's Role in Mainland China's State Supervisory Systems." *Issues and Studies* 34, no. 1 (January 1998): 38–78.

Chang, Parris H. "The Rise of Wang Tung-hsing: Head of China's Security Apparatus." *The China Quarterly* 73 (March 1978): 122–137.

China Factfile. "Ministry of Supervision." Retrieved from www.gov.cn/english/200510/03/content_74320.html.

Chiu, Hangdah. "China's New Criminal and Criminal Procedure Law." School of Law, University of Maryland, Occasional Paper/Reprint Series in Contemporary Asian Studies, 1980.

Cho, Young Nam. "Implementation of Anticorruption Politics in Reform-Era China: The Case of the 1993–97 'Anticorruption Struggle.'" *Issues and Studies* 37, no. 1 (January 2001): 49–72.

Cohen, Jerome Alan. "The Criminal Process in the People's Republic of China: An Introduction." *Harvard Law Review* 79, no. 3 (January 1966): 469–533.

Dickson, Bruce J. "Conflict and Non-Compliance in Chinese Politics: Party Rectification, 1983–87." *Pacific Affairs* 63, no. 2 (Summer 1990): 170–190.

Dikotter, Frank. *Mao's Great Famine: The History of China's Most Devastating Catastrophe, 1958–1962.* New York: Walker Books, 2010.

Dikotter, Frank. *The Cultural Revolution: A People's History, 1962–1976.* New York: Bloomsbury Press, 2016.

Dutton, Michael. "The End of the (Mass) Line? Chinese Policing in the Era of the Contract." *Social Justice* 27, no. 2 (2000): 188–192.

Forster, Keith. "The 1982 Campaign against Economic Crime in China." *The Australian Journal of Chinese Affairs* 14 (July 1985): 1–19.

Ginsberg, George, and Arthur Stahnke. "The People's Procuratorate in Communist China: The Institutional Ascent, 1954–1957." *China Quarterly* 34 (April 1968): 82–132.

Gong, Ting. "The Party Discipline Inspection in China: Its Evolving Trajectory and Embedded Dilemmas." *Crime, Law and Social Change* 49, no. 2 (March 2008): 139–152.

Guo, Xueshi. *China's Security State: Philosophy, Evolution, and Politics.* New York: Cambridge University Press, 2012.

He, Zengke. "Corruption and Anti-Corruption in Reform China." *Communist and Post-Communist Studies* 33 (2000): 243–270.

Herson, Lawrence J. R. "China's Imperial Bureaucracy: Its Direction and Control." *Public Administration Review* 17, no. 1 (Winter 1957): 44–53.

Hucker, Charles O. "The Traditional Chinese Censorate and the New Peking Regime." *American Political Science Review* 45, no. 4 (December 1951): 1041–1057.

Hucker, Charles O. *The Censorial System of Ming China.* Stanford: Stanford University Press, 1966.

Hung, Chang-tai. "The Anti-Unity Sect Campaign and Mass Mobilization in the Early People's Republic of China." *China Quarterly* 202 (June 2010): 400–420.

Kaiman, Jonathan. "China Cracks Down on Social Media with Threat of Jail for 'Online Rumours.'" *The Guardian,* September 10, 2013.

Kelkar, Govind S. "The Chinese Experience of Political Campaigns and Mass Mobilization." *Social Scientist* 7, no. 5 (December 1978): 45–63.

Lee, Mary. "Chinese Launch Campaign against Corruption among Senior Officials." *The Times,* London, 1/11/1986.

Lee, Rensselaer W., III. "The Hsia Fang System: Marxism and Modernization." *China Quarterly* 28 (October 1966): 40–62.

Leng, Shao-chuan. "Criminal Justice in Post-Mao China: Some Preliminary Observations." *Journal of Criminal Law and Criminology* 73, no. 1 (1982): 204–237.

Li, Fangchun. "Mass Democracy, Class Struggle, and Remolding the Party and Government during the Land Reform Movement in North China." *Modern China* 38, no. 4 (2012): 411–445.

Lu, Xiuyuan. "A Step Toward Understanding Popular Violence in China's Cultural Revolution." *Pacific Affairs* 67, no. 4 (Winter 1994–1995): 533–563.

Manion, Melanie. "Issues in Corruption Control in Post-Mao China." *Issues and Studies* 39, no. 4 (1998): 1–21.

MacFarquhar, Roderick. *The Origins of the Cultural Revolution, Volume 3: The Coming of the Cataclysm, 1961–1966.* New York: Oxford University Press, 1997.

MacFarquhar, Roderick, and Michael Schoenhals. *Mao's Last Revolution.* Cambridge: Harvard University Press, 2006.

Menshausen, Simone. "Corruption, Smuggling and Guanxi in Xiamen, China." Internet Center for Corruption Research, 2007. Retrieved from www.iegg. org/downloads/contributor14_menshausen.pdf.

Perry, Elizabeth J. "Moving the Masses: Emotional Work in the Chinese Revolution." *Mobilization* 7, no. 2 (2002): 111–128.

Quade, Elizabeth A. "The Logic of Anticorruption Enforcement Campaigns in Contemporary China." *Journal of Contemporary China* 16, no. 40 (February 2007): 65–77.

Rosen, Stanley. "China in 1986: A Year of Consolidation." *Asian Survey* 27, no. 1 (1987): 35–55.

Sapio, Flora. "Implementing Anticorruption in the PRC: Patterns of Selectivity." Lund University, Centre for East and South-East Asian Studies, Working Paper 10, 2005.

Sapio, Flora. "*Shuanggui* and Extralegal Detention in China." *China Information* 22, no. 7 (March 2008): 7–37.

Seybolt, Peter J. "Terror and Conformity: Counterespionage Campaigns, Rectification, and Mass Movements, 1943–1943." *Modern China* 12, no. 1 (January 1986): 39–73.

Strauss, Julia. "Paternalistic Terror: The Campaign to Suppress Counterrevolutionaries and Regime Consolidation in the People's Republic of China, 1950–1953." *Comparative Studies in Society and History* 44, no. 1 (January 2002): 80–105.

Strauss, Julia. "Morality, Coercion and State Building by Campaign in the Early PRC: Regime Consolidation and After, 1949–1956." *China Quarterly* 188 (December 2006): 891–912.

Sullivan, Lawrence R. "The Role of the Control Organs in the Chinese Communist Party, 1977–83." *Asian Survey* 24, no. 6 (June 1984): 597–617.

Tanner, Harold M. *Strike Hard! Anti-Crime Campaigns and Chinese Criminal Justice, 1979–1985*. Ithaca: East Asia Program–Cornell University.

Tao, Lung-Sheng. "Politics and Law Enforcement in China: 1949–1970." *The American Journal of Comparative Law* 22, no. 4 (1974): 713–756.

Teiwes, Frederick C. *Politics and Purges in China*. East Armonk: Westgate Books, 1993.

Thaxton, Ralph. *Catastrophe and Contention in Rural China: Mao's Great Leap Forward, Famine, and the Origins of Righteous Resistance in Da Fo Village*. New York: Cambridge University Press, 2008.

Trevaskes, Susan. "Courts of the Campaign Path in China: Criminal Court Work in the 'Yanda 2001' Anti-Crime Campaign." *Asian Survey* 42, no. 5 (September–October 2002): 673–693.

Trevaskes, Susan. "Public Sentencing Rallies in China: The Symbolizing of Punishment and Justice in a Socialist State." *Crime, Law, and Social Change* 39, no. 4 (June 2003): 359–382.

Trevaskes, Susan. "Severe and Swift Justice in China." *British Journal of Criminology* 47 (2007): 23–41.

Unger, Jonathan. "Cultural Revolution Conflict in the Villages." *China Quarterly* 153 (March 1998): 82–106.

Vogel, Ezra. "Land Reform in Kwangtung 1951–1953: Central Control and Localism." *China Quarterly* 38 (April 1969): 27–62.

Walder, Andrew G., and Yang Su. "The Cultural Revolution in the Countryside: Timing and Human Impact." *China Quarterly* 173 (March 2003): 74–99.

Walker, Richard L. "The Control System of the Chinese Government." *The Far Eastern Quarterly* 7, no. 1 (1947): 2–21.

Wedeman, Andrew. "Corruption and Politics." In *China Review 1996*, edited by Kuan Hsin-chi, 61–94. Hong Kong: Chinese University of Hong Kong Press, 1996.

Wedeman, Andrew. "Budgets, Extra-Budgets, and Small Treasuries: The Utility of Illegal Monies." *Journal of Contemporary China* 9, no. 25 (2000): 489–511.

Wedeman, Andrew. "Anticorruption Campaigns and the Intensification of Corruption in China." *Journal of Contemporary China* 14, no. 42 (February 2005): 93–116.

Wedeman, Andrew. *Double Paradox: Rapid Growth and Rising Corruption in China*. Ithaca: Cornell University Press, 2012.

Wedeman, Andrew. "Xi Jinping's Tiger Hunt: Anti-Corruption Campaign or Political Purge?" *Modern China* 24, no. 2 (2017): 35–82.

Woodward, Dennis. "Rural Campaigns: Continuity and Change in the Chinese Countryside—the Early Post-Cultural Revolution Experience (1969–1972)." *The Australian Journal of Chinese Affairs* 6 (July 1981): 97–124.

Xie, Baogue. "The Function of the Chinese Procuratorate Organ in Combat Against Corruption." *Police Studies* 38 (1988): 38–43.

Yang, Jisheng. *Tombstone: The Great Chinese Famine, 1958–1962*. New York: Farrar, Straus and Giroux, 2012.

Yang, Kuisong. "Reconsidering the Campaign to Suppress Counterrevolutionaries." *China Quarterly* 193 (March 2008): 102–121.

Young, Graham. "Control and Style: Discipline Inspection Commissions since the 11th Congress." *China Quarterly* 97 (March 1984): 24–52.

Conclusion

The Comparative Study
of Anticorruption Campaigns

Where Do We Go from Here?

RUDRA SIL

This concluding essay takes stock of what this volume has added to the existing literature on corruption in comparative politics and lays out some ways in which the study of anticorruption campaigns can advance further in the future. The contributions assembled here add to the rapidly growing body of work that has moved away from the treatment of corruption as a concomitant of—or obstacle to—political and economic development in order to elaborate on the origins and effects of anticorruption practices in various countries or regions. Yet, in contrast to studies that view anticorruption efforts from the perspective of policy-oriented agendas—such as improving governance, maximizing productivity, or improving the climate for foreign investment—the chapters in this volume seek to better understand how particular political contexts shape the specific forms of prevalent corrupt practices and the specific dynamics of anticorruption campaigns in a given setting.

For this purpose, the editors have brought together a group of country experts to examine the pathways taken by anticorruption campaigns across seven countries within a single region, specifically within Northeast and Southeast Asia. This regional focus serves two purposes. First, in empirical terms, it serves to deepen our knowledge of anticorruption efforts that have sprung up across one of the most dynamic and high-growth areas within the global economy. Second, the focus on Northeast and Southeast Asia provides at least a degree of control for broad cultural, historical, and geographic aspects that shape the regional arena within which political elites in any given country frame the problem of corruption and configure anticorruption programs. Certainly, within a specific country, the policies developed to curtail corruption are worth analyzing in their own right. There are also payoffs from systematically comparing anticorruption battles across different regions and historical epochs (e.g., Kroeze, Vitoria, and Geltner 2018). But, in between these two poles there is a distinctive set of insights attached to what we might call, following Robert Merton (1968, 39–72), "middle-range" analyses that are designed not to generate universal laws or test axiomatically derived formal propositions but to uncover mechanisms that account for the specific content and impact of policies given some set of common background conditions. In this volume, the regional focus on Northeast and Southeast Asia serves to capture a number of shared contextual attributes within which it is possible to recognize and understand the distinctive dynamics of anticorruption campaigns within a set of countries facing similar kinds of challenges. That is, the essays in this volume, taken as a whole, allow us to differentiate between the approaches within a regional "neighborhood" in roughly the same time period, while also illuminating how an anticorruption campaign within a particular country tends to be conditioned by particular constellations of motivations and political contexts.

What keeps such an effort from devolving into a series of idiosyncratic observations is a systematically designed template the editors have developed for tracking the emergence and evolution of anticorruption campaigns in relation to the motivations of differently situated groups of actors. Each of the chapters has sought to identify the main political dynamics and individual or group interests evident in the initiation and implementation of an anticorruption program. And each offers an assessment of the impact of a given campaign, both intended and unintended, on different types of corrupt practices. The studies combine to show why the analysis of anticorruption campaigns cannot be limited to an examination of general policies aimed at improving corporate governance or advancing the climate for foreign investment. Careful attention must be paid to the specific political contexts—and not just regime types—within which different types of corrupt practices have emerged and within which specific actors choose to target some of these practices (and not others). The motivation-centered framework set up by Chen and Weiss nicely balances the attention to context with the building of a portable analytic framework that facilitates comparable narratives. Thus, while each of the chapters certainly represents a stand-alone contribution to our empirical stock of knowledge, it is also possible to compare the narratives in many of these chapters to each other while envisioning how any subset of these cases might be situated within a still broader comparative context. This is no small accomplishment.

Looking ahead, there are at least four avenues along which scholars interested in corruption and anticorruption campaigns may be able to build on the work presented here to expand and deepen our understanding of the subject. The first would be to further explore a more complex, eclectic approach to the *interactions* of discrete political motivations in classify-ing—and partially explaining—the forms of anticorruption movements. A second concerns a more deliberate and focused examination of what may be the most novel aspects of contemporary anticorruption movements, which is a greater awareness (and even mobilization) of domestic and international audiences in bringing pressure to bear on specific targets. A third path points to the generation of more portable hypotheses about anticorruption practices through direct cross-case comparisons, not only of the countries covered in this volume but also of carefully selected cases from different geographic regions. And, a final issue for further exploration concerns the time horizons for the study of anticorruption campaigns, with due attention to the question of whether campaigns aimed at reining in certain kinds of corrupt practices, even if successful, unintentionally sow the seeds for new forms of corruption over a longer time frame.

First, there is the question of whether we can reconceptualize the core element of the analytic framework offered by the editors—the motivational drivers of anticorruption campaigns—in a more complex (if less elegant) manner. Each of the three parts of the volume is intended to highlight the centrality of a discrete type of motivation focused either on private interests, party/military loyalty, or political institutionalization. Yet, as the editors acknowledge at the outset, these distinct motivations inevitably overlap to some extent. If that is indeed the case, then the comparative study of anticorruption campaigns will do well to move away from a mono-causal understanding of the effects of each of the motivations and instead work on capturing the relative weights and complex interactions of these (and other) motivations. There is much to be gained by illumi-nating the various pathways through which these different motivations might interact with each other and with various contextual attributes to generate different outcomes within different institutional environments.

In fact, within each part of the volume, we can see at least one case where the author makes reference to two or more types of motivations, although the relationship among these is not treated as an object of analysis. In part 1, for example, while Raquiza's study of the Philippines seeks to isolate the relevance of private networks using anticorruption to position themselves against competing elites, the narrative Aspinall offers about Indonesia is as much a story about enduring formal institutions being developed as about private networks. The same goes for part 2, which is designed to illuminate motivations related to loyalty to a party or to the military. While it is easy to see the role of media bias in favoring one or the other of two political coalitions in Goebel's account of Taiwan, it is less clear how one should even conceptualize partisan loyalty in the context of the one-party system in Vietnam, where Malesky and Phan's story of anticorruption campaigns could just as easily be framed as one designed to boost the long-term institutional legitimacy of the communist party-state. And, in part 3, which is designed to foreground the push for political institutionalization, while Wedeman's treatment of China does indeed link anticorruption campaigns to institutionalization, Connors's study of Thailand is as much about partisan loyalty as about institution-alization, whereas Kim's story about South Korea's new anticorruption law (the Kim Young-ran Act) highlights a phenomenon of network-based collective corruption that may be driven as much by private interests as by commitment to institution building. In effect, for each of the three parts of the volume, at most one of the chapters focuses on the conse-quences of the singular motivation distinguishing that part, while in each of the other countries, it is easy to find a mix of motivational factors at play.

What this suggests is not that one or more of the studies is flawed, but that, in the process of comparing the political dynamics unfolding in each of the cases, perhaps the motivational bases for anticorruption campaigns are best understood as Weberian ideal types. That is, the comparative study of anticorruption campaigns stands to gain *not* by zeroing in on the impact of any one kind of motivation in a given polit-ical setting, but by seeing how different motivations might be ordered and analytically connected within each of the cases. In some cases, it is possible that one type of motivation will be subsumed within another, as is implied in the narratives about Thailand and South Korea. In others, it may be more useful to think about how the different motivations behind anticorruption campaigns affect one another, with the possible effect of reinforcing or diluting the long-term impact on the level of corruption. Put another way, it may behoove us to adopt a more "analytically eclectic" approach to motivations as they emerge within shifting political contexts and institutional environments. Analytic eclecticism is designed to turn attention away from theorizing on the basis of core analytic constructs and approaches embedded in specific research traditions; instead, it privileges efforts to connect concepts and analytic principles extricated from these frameworks and then redeployed in more complex analytic schemes designed to illuminate the interactive processes through which individual motivations and structural forces affect one another across both material and ideational domains (Sil and Katzenstein 2010). By adopting a more eclectic approach to the forces driving anticorruption campaigns, it becomes possible to move toward more pragmatic perspectives on the impact of different constellations of motivations on anticorruption campaigns designed within similar institutional settings. In the process, researchers may end up finding that relatively less institutionalized parties function in a manner that is not so different from a clustering of private interests, or that initiatives initially motivated by partisan loyalty at one point in time can devolve into ones aimed at more private individual / group interests, or that "partisan" loyalty to a single political party can in time morph into a push for deeper, more lasting institutionalization of state organs and agencies.

Second, there is the question of what exactly distinguishes the current spate of anticorruption campaigns in Asia from past efforts to combat corruption. Indeed, the discrete motivations employed to organize the chapters in this volume—the advancement of private interests and networks, the role of loyalty to specific parties or the military, and the push to deepen institutional legitimacy—are not really new. Throughout the post-colonial history of states of Asia and Africa, opponents of a leader (elected or not), senior officials in the army, or incumbents seeking to keep new challengers at bay have frequently lobbed charges of corruption as a pretext for some type of political or military action. Even in relatively stable democracies such as India, electoral competition between parties and politicians has been continually laced with charges of corruption—sometimes aimed at advancing the interests of specific groups, sometimes intended to consolidate the strength of a given party, and sometimes to promote better governance and public trust in previously dysfunctional institutions.

But, if the battle against corruption is neither new nor driven by entirely new motivations, then what is distinctive about the efforts to

combat corruption in the countries examined in this volume? I would suggest that the unfolding of anticorruption campaigns in recent years differs
from past efforts to battle corruption in at least two crucial respects. They
are more likely to tap into public frustrations and to encourage or enlist
citizen participation. And, they tend to be more conscious of international
audiences, be they international financial institutions or businesses in a
position to boost foreign investment. In past efforts to combat corruption,
including during the period of the Cold War, the international audience
did not matter nearly as much as the domestic audience, and the latter's
active participation was not a precondition for efforts to target particular
individuals for corrupt practices. Corruption was frequently the justification for a military coup or for undermining a civilian leader seeking to be
reelected; in such cases, the main focus was to mobilize an elite coalition
as part of an effort to set up a new leadership at the helm of a country.
Of course, these dynamics have not gone away and are indeed very much
in evidence in some countries at present. But, there is also much greater
awareness of a large and growing international audience as well as a more
proactive effort to engage social movements that cite corruption as a key
reason for the challenges they issue to the ruling elites.

Thus, in several of the preceding chapters, there is substantial evidence
that domestic audiences were either enlisted by officials launching anticorruption campaigns or mobilized on their own to form social movements
to put pressure on political actors. This is seen, for example, in Aspinall's
discussion of the increased activism of NGOs in the case of Indonesia
and in Connors's description of a constant antipolitics movement against
successive elected governments in Thailand. There are also at least passing
references in a few of the chapters to political elites' increased awareness
of—and even responsiveness to—international audiences, be they international financial institutions or global business elites (Rose-Ackerman
and Carrington 2013). This is most clearly evident in Malesky and Phan's
mention of the attention to the OECD Anti-Bribery Convention in the
adoption of rules governing business relations in Vietnam, but it is also
implicit in Connors's chapter on Thailand where the initial discourses
shaping Thailand's "antipolitics" took root on an international stage marked
by a growing global push for greater accountability and transparency. Of
course, it has not been the editors' intention to get the authors to systematically analyze and compare the roles played by domestic social movements
and transnational actors in recent anticorruption battles. But, the passing
nods in the preceding chapters to the mobilization of citizen activism

and social movements in the domestic arena, and to the pressures and influences brought to bear by various transnational actors and institutions, suggest that the comparative study of anticorruption movements may do well in the future to explicitly and systematically examine the relevance and influence of various domestic and international audiences in shaping the objectives, content, and effectiveness of anticorruption campaigns.

A third path forward for building on the present research on anticorruption programs might be to expand the scope for qualitative comparative analysis of methodically selected cases within and across geographic regions. As noted earlier, examining individual countries situated within a single geographic region works well as a starting point. It allows the analyst to control for a range of cultural and historical factors while providing a common regional setting within which dynamics of a series of countries can be better understood. But, there is much more scope for using an analytic framework such as the one Chen and Weiss have developed here for systematic cross-national small-N comparisons of cases both within a single region and across regions. *Within* a region, comparable cases can help us gain more leverage on the aforementioned issue of determining the relative weights of, and relations between, different individual/group motivations and various institutional features. For example, there are grounds here for directly comparing the cases of China and Vietnam where preexisting national communist parties retain a firm grip on political power while launching anticorruption campaigns. Directly juxtaposing these campaigns can help us gain some leverage when it comes to either measuring the relative effectiveness of certain moves or explaining the different strategies that party elites might adopt within comparable political contexts. At the same time, a comparison of Indonesia, Taiwan, and Thailand might be instructive when it comes to generating hypotheses about the role (or manipulation) of a mobilized citizenry demanding a "clean" government in a more pluralistic and competitive political setting. Individual country studies are essential for setting the stage for comparative work, but in the end the cross-case comparisons are critical to decisively establishing the role of causal mechanisms that are not bound to a given national or local context.

There is also the possibility for more ambitious small-N comparisons where cases are drawn from more than one geographic area in all cases. Certainly, as was noted earlier, examining countries within a single area may have certain advantages for analyzing certain problems, as is the case with the strategy adopted in this volume that implicitly treats regional history and political culture as controls so as to spotlight the impact of discrete sets of motivations on anticorruption campaigns. But, as suggested in a recent volume on "comparative area studies" (Ahram, Köllner, and Sil 2018), there are a host of questions where the appropriate set of comparable cases do not require regionally based controls and might even yield distorted inferences if confined to a single geographic region that does not encompass the full range of variation on a given outcome. Such questions, in fact, are better suited for cross-regional small-N comparisons—qualitative comparative analysis of cases from different regions—at least for the purpose of determining the impact of different regional or resource contexts on strengthening or diluting the effects of certain causal mechanisms. One obvious example is the comparative analysis of anti-corruption campaigns across "petro-states" in different areas that have in common a high degree of dependence on fossil fuel exports for government revenue (e.g., Kuwait, Nigeria, and Kazakhstan), or across rising powers that are investing significant resources to increase their regional clout and international influence (e.g., China, Russia, and Turkey). These options can point the way to other types of causal mechanisms that can account for many different features of anticorruption drives and that may uncover other sets of motivations and contextual factors not explicitly theorized in the studies compiled in this volume.

Finally, there is the need to accumulate more findings over a longer time horizon. This volume began from the presumption that an earlier generation of scholars was wrong to view corruption as a transient "substitute" in fulfilling key developmental tasks in modernizing regimes lacking adequate institutionalization. This latter view was laid out most explicitly in Samuel Huntington's (1968) classic treatise, *Political Order in Changing Societies*. The chapters in the volume do offer enough of a long view that we can see how, in the fifty years since the publication of Huntington's book, the countries discussed here have each had plenty of time to build political institutions and set up the infrastructure for economic development. And, with the passage of time, it has become possible to conclude that there is no guarantee that corruption will fulfill a set of critical developmental functions for a period and then disappear as new institutions take root in modernized societies. This also implies, however, that we would do well to stretch our own time horizons as we examine the historical roots and long-term consequences, intended or not, of the current spate of anticorruption campaigns worldwide, including in the Asian countries examined in this volume. These chapters tend to focus on a period that is limited to a decade, at most two. This is not exactly a short period of time, and it has certainly proven to be a plausible and fruitful course—especially when it comes to examining the aftermath of new laws and institutions (as in the cases of Indonesia and South Korea), the unfolding of electoral politics after regime change (as in the cases of Taiwan and Thailand), or the efforts initiated by a given leader at the helm of a single party (as in the cases of China and Vietnam). At the same time, as Paul Pierson reminds us, many long-term processes are so "slow-moving" or even "invisible" that the full measure of their effects (intended or not) is contingent on reaching a more temporally distant threshold (Pierson 2004). In other words, just as there are likely to be novel insights from engaging in cross-national comparisons of cases from different regions, there are also payoffs to be gained by engaging in dia-chronic comparisons to track the evolving cycles of anticorruption efforts in terms of their content and impact. In this regard, there may be one important component of Huntington's analysis of political and economic development that continues to be just as relevant today as in the past. The passage I have in mind is worth quoting at length:

> Modernization, particularly among the later modernizing coun-tries, involves the expansion of governmental authority and the multiplication of the activities subjected to governmental regulation. . . . The multiplication of laws thus multiplies the possibilities of corruption. The extent to which this possibility is realized in practice depends in large part upon the extent to which the laws have the general support of the population, the ease with which the law can be broken without detection, and the profit to be made by breaking it. . . . Hence in a soci-ety where corruption is widespread the passage of strict laws against corruption serves only to multiply the opportunities for corruption. (Huntington 1968, 61–62)

This argument implies that the expansion of regulatory efforts—including new laws and programs specifically designed to target corrupt practices at present—may have the unintended effect of spurring new, different forms of corruption even as progress is made in curtailing certain practices. Thus, over successive drives to combat corruption, if the number of laws and regulations continue to multiply, it may be worth shifting the focus of the question from the motivations giving rise to a campaign to the aggregate impact of that campaign on corruption writ large given the new opportunities being created for bypassing new laws and regulations.[1]

These suggestions for building on the research presented in this volume should not be taken as an indication that the volume itself should have aspired to do more. Far from it. The objective has been to lay out how the present studies, taken as a whole, have brought us to a point where we can systematically consider more expansive research projects along the lines envisioned here. Although social scientists invest a great deal of effort in assessing individual pieces of scholarship, in the end, the overall quality and impact of our research is most reflected in the collective efforts of scholars wishing to shed light on substantive problems of theoretical and practical import. The subject of corruption, as well as questions concerning the origins, content, and impact of anticorruption campaigns, have been around for a long time and will be with us for still longer. And for good reason. Thus, the real question is not how much this one volume has accomplished but how it has built on past findings and set the stage for further research by scholars studying other parts of the world—at present and well into the future.

Notes

1. Huntington discusses three drivers of corruption. Two of them—the survival of preexisting norms alongside new rules and standards as well as the impact of newly emergent centers of wealth and power—may be expected to gradually decline in terms of their impact as societies become more attuned to the norms and practices of a developed market economy. Huntington's third driver, however, is a function of the number of laws and regulations, which may well keep growing over various cycles of anticorruption campaigns. See Huntington (1968, 59–61).

Bibliography

Ahram, Ariel, Patrick Köllner, and Rudra Sil, eds. *Comparative Area Studies: Methodological Rationales and Cross-Regional Applications*. New York: Oxford University Press, 2018.

Huntington, Samuel P. *Political Order in Changing Societies*. New Haven: Yale University Press, 1968.

Kroeze, Ronald, Andre Vitoria, and G. Geltner, eds. *Anti-Corruption in History: From Antiquity to the Modern Era*. Oxford: Oxford University Press, 2018.

Merton, Ronald K. *Social Theory and Social Structure*, revised edition. New York: The Free Press, 1968.

Pierson, Paul. *Politics in Time: History, Institutions and Social Analysis.* Princeton: Princeton University Press, 2004.

Rose-Ackerman, Susan, and Paul D. Carrington, eds. *Anti-Corruption Policy: Can International Actors Play a Constructive Role?* Durham: Carolina Academic Press, 2013.

Sil, Rudra, and Peter J. Katzenstein. "Analytic Eclecticism in the Study of World Politics: Reconfiguring Problems and Mechanisms Across Research Traditions." *Perspectives on Politics* 8, no. 2 (2010): 411–431.

Contributors

Edward Aspinall is Professor in the Department of Political and Social Change, Coral Bell School of Asia Pacific Affairs, Australian National University. He researches politics in Southeast Asia, especially Indonesia, with interests in democratization, ethnicity, and clientelism, among other topics. He has authored three books, *Opposing Suharto: Compromise, Resistance and Regime Change in Indonesia* (2005), *Islam and Nation: Separatist Rebellion in Aceh, Indonesia* (2009), and *Democracy for Sale: Elections, Clientelism, and the State in Indonesia* (2019, with Ward Berenschot), and coedited ten others, the most recent being *Electoral Dynamics in Indonesia: Money Politics, Patronage and Clientelism at the Grassroots* (2016).

Cheng Chen is Professor of Political Science at the University at Albany, SUNY. Her research and teaching interests include post-communist politics; nationalism and nation building; Chinese politics; and comparative-historical methodology. She is the author of *The Return of Ideology: The Search for Regime Identities in Post-Communist Russia and China* (2016) and *The Prospects for Liberal Nationalism in Post-Leninist States* (2007). She is also coeditor of *Confronting the Challenges of Urbanization in China: Insights from Social Science Perspectives* (2016) and *The Emergence of a New Urban China: Insiders' Perspectives* (2012), which was selected by *Choice* as an "Outstanding Academic Title" in 2012.

Michael K. Connors is a lecturer in the Department of International Relations at Xi'an Jiaotong–Liverpool University and a visiting fellow at the Institute of Asian Studies, Chulalongkorn University. He was formerly Head, School of Politics, History and International Relations at the University of Nottingham Malaysia and founding director of the Institute of Asia Pacific

Studies (Malaysia). He has taught at La Trobe University, the University of Leeds, and Thammasat University. He works in the area of Southeast Asian politics and the international relations of the Asia Pacific. The third edition of his coauthored *The New Global Politics of the Asia Pacific: Conflict and Cooperation in the Asian Century* was published in 2018.

Christian Goebel is University Professor of Modern China Studies at the University of Vienna, Department of East Asian Studies. A political scientist and sinologist by training, he is interested in the relationship among technological innovation, policy innovation, and regime stability in East Asia, among other topics. He conducts firsthand research mainly on China and Taiwan. He is the author of *The Politics of Rural Reform in China: State Policy and Village Predicament in the Early 2000s* (2010) and coauthor of *The Politics of Community Building in Urban China* (2011).

Ray Dongryul Kim is Associate Professor in the Department of Political Science at Rochester Institute of Technology. He was a visiting research fellow at Academia Sinica in Taiwan during 2018. In 2013–2015, he worked for the Korean government to train junior diplomats at the Korea National Diplomatic Academy and analyze foreign policies at the Institute of Foreign Affairs and National Security. His primary research field is comparative political economy, focusing on the role of the bureaucracy in economic development in East Asia, and recently extending the scope to reforms and corruption in East Asia. He also writes about security issues related to the Korean Peninsula. His articles have been published in various journals, including *Korean Journal of Policy Studies*, *KEDI Journal of Educational Policy*, and *North Korean Review*.

Edmund Malesky is Professor of Political Economy and the Associate Chair of the Political Science Department at Duke University and is a noted specialist in economic development, authoritarian institutions, and comparative political economy in Vietnam. In 2012, Malesky received a state medal from the Government of Vietnam for his role in promoting economic development for USAID's Vietnam Provincial Competitiveness Index and, in 2013, he was appointed by President Obama to serve on the board of the Vietnam Education Foundation. He has published extensively in the leading political science and economic journals and has received various awards, including the Harvard Academy Fellowship and the Rockefeller Bellagio Residency Fellowship.

Ngoc Phan is a PhD candidate in political science at Duke University. His research interests include corruption, development, and authoritarian politics. Geographically, Phan focuses on studying the political economy of developing countries, especially his native land of Vietnam.

Antoinette R. Raquiza is Associate Professor at the Asian Center and convener of the Political Economy Program of the Center for Integrative and Development Studies at University of the Philippines, Diliman. Receiving her PhD in Political Science from the City University of New York, Graduate Center, she specializes in and has published on the political economy of emerging markets, international political economy, as well as comparative politics and governance. At the Asian Center, she recently headed a two-year research program that examined the changing development paradigms, processes, and practices of a rising Asia.

Rudra Sil is Professor of Political Science and the SAS Director of the Huntsman Program in International Relations and Business at the University of Pennsylvania. His research interests encompass Russian/post-communist studies, Asian studies, labor politics, international development, and comparative-historical methodology. He has authored, coauthored, or coedited seven books. Most recently, he is coeditor (with Ariel Ahram and Patrick Köllner) of *Comparative Area Studies: Methodological Rationales and Cross-Regional Applications* (2018). Rudra Sil's articles have appeared in a wide range of journals, including *Current History*, *Perspectives on Politics*, *Journal of Theoretical Politics*, *International Studies Quarterly*, *Post-Soviet Affairs*, and *Studies in Comparative International Development*.

Andrew Wedeman is Professor of Political Science at Georgia State University, where he heads the China Studies Initiative. He received his doctorate in political science from the University of California, Los Angeles, in 1994. Previously, he was Professor of Political Science at the University of Nebraska–Lincoln. He has held posts as Visiting Research Professor at Beijing University, Visiting Associate Professor of Political Science at the Johns Hopkins Nanjing University Center for Sino-American Studies, Fulbright Research Professor at Taiwan National University, and Research Fellow at the Woodrow Wilson Center for International Scholars. His publications include *Double Paradox: Rapid Growth and Rising Corruption in China* (2012) and *From Mao to Market: Rent Seeking, Local Protectionism, and Marketization in China* (2003).

Meredith L. Weiss is Professor and Chair of Political Science at the University at Albany, SUNY. Her research focuses on political mobilization and contention, the politics of identity and development, and electoral politics in Southeast Asia. Her books include *The Roots of Resilience: Authoritarian Acculturation in Malaysia and Singapore* (forthcoming), *Student Activism in Malaysia: Crucible, Mirror, Sideshow* (2011), and *Protest and Possibilities: Civil Society and Coalitions for Political Change in Malaysia* (2006), as well as a number of edited or coedited volumes. Her articles appear in *Asian Survey, Critical Asian Studies, Democratization, Journal of Contemporary Asia, Perspectives on Politics*, and elsewhere. She has been a visiting professor/fellow at universities and institutes in the United States, Malaysia, Singapore, the Philippines, Australia, and Japan.

Index

sovereignty wars, 165
Special Act on Confiscation of Illegal
  Wealth, 182
Special Committee on Punishment of
  Treason, 179
"speed/grease money," 105, 108, 122
sponsored-prosecutor scandal, 186
state behavior, remaking of, 50
state power, selling of, 105
statement bias, 82, 92–93, 98
Strauss, Julia, 204–205
Strike against Economic Crime, 211
Strike Hard anticrime campaigns,
  223n13
Stromseth, Jonathan, 129
structural-functionalist approach, 28,
  38
student protests, 49, 53, 54–55, 67, 69
Suharto
  children of, 52, 55
  end of rule of, 49
  feudal nature of regime of, 53
  "New Order" regime of, 52–54
  public opposition to corruption
    and, 50–51
  wife of, 53
Sungsidh, Piriyarangsan, 139
supply-side governance reforms, 58,
  59
Suppression of Counterrevolutionaries
  Campaign, 204
Susilo, Djoko, 63

Taiwan
  conclusions regarding, 98–99
  economy of, 4
  introduction to, 77–79
  partisan bias in media of, 86–97
  party loyalty and, 9, 11, 17
  political attitudes and media in,
    80–86
  regime of, 4

Taiwan's Agency against Corruption
  (AAC), 80
Tamexco, 115–116
Tanzi, Vito, 192n8, 194n20
Tao, Lung-Sheng, 205
television stations, in Taiwan, 81
Thai Rak Thai, 164
Thailand
  authoritarianism and, 147–151,
    152–155t
  conclusions regarding, 164–165
  economy of, 4
  interpreting anticorruption politics
    in, 143–147
  introduction to, 139–143
  party loyalty and, 9, 11
  political institutionalization and, 12,
    14, 17
  regime of, 4
  state of ambivalence in, 143, 151,
    156–157t, 158–164
Thaksin Shinawatra, 140–141, 144–
  145, 146, 159, 161, 162–164
Thanh Niên, 118–119
Thayer, Carlyle A., 110, 128, 130
Thitinan Pongsudhirak, 142, 147
"Three Antis Campaign," 203
Tipikor court, 58–59
topic-modeling algorithms, 79
Trần Đinh Triển, 127
transparency, in Vietnam, 106, 130
Transparency International Indonesia
  (TII), 56, 64, 80
Transparency International (TI), 8, 77,
  105–106, 146, 147t
Trịnh Xuan Thanh, 103, 126
Trương Tấn Sang, 117, 120
Truth Today, 163–164
Tuổi Trẻ, 118–119

United Daily, 79, 81, 83–84, 85, 88,
  90, 92, 96–97, 98

www.ingramcontent.com/pod-product-compliance
Lightning Source LLC
Chambersburg PA
CBHW020343270326
41926CB00007B/299